Burgess-Carpenter Library
406 Butler
Columbia University
New York, N. Y. 10027

W9-BCJ-472

DENNIS CLARK:

Crisis
o Game
d: Northern Ireland and the American Conscience
in Philadelphia
hia 1776–2076: A Three Hundred Year View (editor)
the Human Spirit

The Irish Relations

Also by

Cities in
The Ghett
Irish Bloo
The Irish
Philadelp
Work and

The Irish Relations

Trials of an Immigrant Tradition

Dennis Clark

WITHDRAWN

Rutherford ● Madison ● Teaneck
Fairleigh Dickinson University Press
London and Toronto: Associated University Presses

© 1982 by Associated University Presses, Inc.

Associated University Presses, Inc.
4 Cornwall Drive
East Brunswick, N.J. 08816

Associated University Presses Ltd
69 Fleet Street
London EC4Y 1EU, England

Associated University Presses
Toronto M5E 1A7, Canada

Library of Congress Cataloging in Publication Data

Clark, Dennis, 1927–
    The Irish relations.

    Bibliography: p.
    Includes index.
    1. Irish Americans—Pennsylvania—Philadelphia—
History.   2. Philadelphia (Pa.)—History.   3. Philadelphia
(Pa.)—Ethnic relations.   I. Title.
F158.9.I6C56   974.8'110049162   81-65293
ISBN 0-8386-3083-9   AACR2

Printed in the United States of America

Do mhuintuir mo mhuintuire
to the people of my people

850304 - 4R

Contents

My name is Paddy Leary
From a spot called Tipperary,
The hearts of all the girls I am a thorn in;
But before the break of morn
Sure, 'tis they'll all be forlorn
For I'm off to Philadelphia in the mornin'.

Nineteenth-century Irish ballad

Introduction

This is a book about one of the central issues of American history—how groups of people from foreign backgrounds were able to withstand the difficulties confronting them in a growing country and establish their own traditions within the framework of an increasingly democratic society. For the Irish, whose history of immigration began before the setting up of our republic, the adaptation to America has required repeated adjustments throughout the entire history of the nation and has been enacted in all the regions where our government held sway. We still know only part of the story of this very extensive social drama, and this book confines itself to the activities of Irish people in the vicinity of one city, Philadelphia. However, the city of Philadelphia is where the American nation was first proclaimed, and a study of how the Irish participated in its life can provide us with insights into the toll that was paid for its progress, the way that active subcultures affect a modern city and the way that ethnic traditions have been maintained amid the crosscurrents of urban community life. This knowledge could be valuable to us in a time when our cities still struggle to meet such problems as immigration, differences between groups, and the costs to be paid for our urban life-style. These problems have been part of our society for generations, but we have failed to address them humanely and effectively on a long-term basis.

The study of American history in the last two decades has included a whole new dimension of the study of the past that has been designated the "new social history.". David Brion Davis of Yale University has explained this reinvigoration of historical scholarship as a movement to "reconstruct the behavior, culture and quality of life of non-elite peoples."[1] This trend has emerged from new conditions surrounding the study of history. A more

mature America has overcome many of the prejudices that kept it
from studying blacks, the Spanish-speaking, and other groups.
The study of history has become more democratic at the university
level, and it is less preoccupied with father figures and narratives
of patriotic glory. The social sciences have added new perspectives
on the importance of the lives of ordinary citizens, who after all are
the true exponents of democracy. As a result labor history, the
history of women, the study of slavery, and the study of cities,
political movements, and many institutions have all benefited
enormously.

The difficulties of revealing the vast and dynamic substructure
of ethnic and cultural diversity that has been one of the driving
forces of American development are numerous. Our amazing and
attractive mainstream culture continues to override these smaller
traditions. The real history of each group has to be sorted out from
the prejudice, defensive mythology, and neglect of the past. The
distinctive features of each group must then be faithfully aligned
with the cycles and trends of the mainstream of American history
so that we can see just how each group has been part of the whole.

In 1974 I had published a previous book, *The Irish in Philadelphia: Ten Generations of Urban Experience*.[2] I was impressed then
and am still impressed that so little study has been devoted to an
Irish tradition that has been highly important for our industrial and
urban growth. The Irish in our major cities have numbered in the
millions through the course of the nation's history. In Philadelphia
for over half a century after 1860 the total of Irish-born people
never fell below 100,000. The group deeply affected the work life,
religious growth, political development, and ethnic vitality of the
city. There was so much to be discovered and interpreted about the
group even in one city that during my investigations I came to
understand that one book would hardly suffice.

Another issue made very clear by my studies of this Irish
community was its continuity. Despite all the changes and pressures to which it had been subjected, the Philadelphia Irish
community had an astonishing continuity and consciousness of
itself that stretched back to colonial times. Such organizations as
the Friendly Sons of Saint Patrick in the city have continuous
records of meetings and associations that reach back to the years

before the American Revolution. Hence, those who view ethnic studies as a mere appendix to the study of late-nineteenth-century immigration are far short of a full comprehension of the subject. The Irish—and others as well—have been engaged with the problems of American life from the beginning, and assessment of their role must take account of the fact that they have responded with flexibility and ingenuity to dozens of major shifts in American opinion, behavior, and enterprise.

The pursuit of the history of one group in one city might seem a limitation in terms of research, except that Philadelphia is and has long been a huge city, complex and rife with all the influences of modern urban experience. Maintaining a local focus has under-scored another fundamental characteristic of studying ethnic traditions. For most people life is local. This was especially true for immigrants in the past, wrapped in the protective ethnic group life of their own communities. It was true for working people and the poor in times before mass communications and travel. Most such people did not rise to eminence. They led lives of relative obscurity, yet their collective contribution to our society has been very great. Until just the last decade the study of local history has been one of our weakest fields of research. Consequently, we have left largely untold this portion of our past. To discover the role of the Irish in a city such as Philadelphia is to substantially modify the traditional portrayal of the city as a Quakerly community full of lawyers, dignified gentlemen of means, and Main Line socialite dowagers, a city sufficient to itself in its Anglo-Saxon propriety.

Local history only becomes intelligible, however, if we can see some of the broader implications, and Irish-American experience is grounded in such historic facts as the following:

1. The Irish came to America early enough and in large enough numbers to establish a strong minority position in American life that engaged them with all major periods of American expansion. As the fastest-growing white minority element in American society after 1820, the Irish by their religious and political pressures ratified and made real in social fact the pluralism that had been but a constitutional promise in the design of the founding fathers.

2. As a religious and educational force they constructed an institutional network of schools and human-service facilities that

served immigrants of many backgrounds and that constitutes one of the outstanding legacies of our urban culture.

3. As partisans of nationalism in behalf of the old country the Irish established a tradition of exile agitation by the year 1800, and this kind of agitation has continued as part of our political heritage throughout our history.

4. As a labor force the Irish were crucial to industrial growth, paving the way for other groups in the advancement of technical and economic development, but this contribution exacted a terrible toll from those employed in making it.

5. "The Irish seem to have experienced more overt economic and legal discrimination than any other European group, partly because they were the first large ethnic group entering the nation to present the triple threat of religious, class and ethnic differences."[3]

6. On the frontier and as soldiers and in urban slums the Irish were involved heavily in the tradition of American violence, and their clashes with blacks, Indians, and others confirmed the cruelty of life among that portion of the population forced to live in deprivation and instability.

7. As a demographic and political force the Irish did much to define our urban tradition and style of government and democratic behavior, and this contribution has continued into the last quarter of the twentieth century.

One of the rewards of historical research is the delight of running down clues and seeking evidence that re-creates the lives and interests of people, now dead, who were every bit as real as oneself. Finding sources of information is the occupational obsession of historians. Even the best books on the Irish in America have in the past been limited in their sources of information. For example, a fine book such as Carl Wittke's *The Irish in America* is based largely on newspapers, biographies, and secondary sources in various journals. William V. Shannon's *The American Irish: A Political and Social Portrait* is panoramic and makes good use of literary and cultural materials but also relies to a great extent on newspapers and accounts of prominent people. Thomas N. Brown's excellent study of *Irish-American Nationalism, 1870–1890* relies heavily on newspapers and biographies of Irish leaders in New York and Chicago.[4] The essays in this book are derived from what I believe is a wide array of sources, and this is intentional. I hope that this array of sources will encourage others to look more intently at the richness of local archives and materials that have too long been ignored. Research can be local, but it can be exciting and professionally satisfying in the diversity and extent of the resources available. Because of the interest that a discussion of sources may hold for other researchers and students, I have added a note on this subject at the end of the book. These rich local sources are the key to the recognition of what Dr. David Doyle of University College, Dublin has termed the "maturity," that is, the complexity, of Irish-American life in the second half of the nineteenth century and the dynamic interaction of the group with the broad range of American values and social issues.[5]

It is with undiminished delight that I can express my gratitude to those who have been helpful to me in writing this book. To such younger scholars as the prodigious Limerick man, Mick Moloney, and to Drs. Ted Hershberg and Dale Light I extend thanks. To the staffs of the remarkable treasure houses of historical materials in the Philadelphia area, I proffer a salute and extend my deepest thanks. Skillfully professional, helpful, and even cheerful, these staffs have tolerated obscure questions and many searches in the Archives of the City of Philadelphia, the Historical Society of Pennsylvania, the Library Company of Philadelphia, the Balch Institute for Ethnic Studies, the Temple University Urban Archives, the Éleutherian Mills–Hagley Foundation Library, and the archives of the American Catholic Historical Society of Philadelphia. To the late Owen B. Hunt, to John J. Reilly, Robert V. Clarke, Thomas Regan, James McGill, Jane Duffin, William Brennan, Norbert McGettigan, Isador Kranzel, and Milton Mustin I am indebted for their stories, insights, and patient assistance. Indeed, to great numbers of Irish Philadelphians and others I am grateful for conversations and recollections, interviews, and instructions in meetings, saloon sessions, classes, dinners, disputes, and orations. To the typists who made all the writing into an orderly manuscript, I pay grateful tribute: Lynda King Clark and Alexandra King Brown, Margie Lieb, Mrs. Margaret Brennan, and my son, Padraig. To these and all those unmentioned, the book itself is an expression of gratitude.

NOTES

1. *New York Times*, November 10, 1976.

2. (Philadelphia: Temple University Press, 1973).

3. Alice Kessler Harris and Virginia Yans McLaughlin, "European Immigrant Groups," in *American Ethnic Groups*, edited by Thomas Sowell (Washington, D.C.: The Urban Institute, 1978), p. 130.

4. (Baton Rouge, La.: Louisiana State University Press, 1956); (New York: The Macmillan Co., 1963); (Philadelphia: J. B. Lippincott Co., 1966).

5. David Doyle, *Irish-Americans, Native Rights and National Empires* (New York: Arno Press, 1976); R. A. Burchell, *The San Francisco Irish, 1848–1880* (Berkeley, Calif.: University of California Press, 1980).

The Irish Relations

PART I: Worked to the Bone

The social progress made by Irish-Americans should not obscure the fact that the record of exploitation suffered by this group from the 1830s to the 1930s constitutes what is probably the longest record of exploitation against any white immigrant group in America. The Irish were the chief victims of the industrialization process, and as workers they had to endure a century-long period of economic and social abuse in the mining, railroad, heavy-metal, textile, and port industries.

The slow pace of change frequently left child workers and women far behind males. These workers were often the worst paid and least protected. Examples of the persistence of adverse conditions among the Irish are given in the following three chapters: one dealing with the continuation of child indentures long after they were believed to have been abandoned; another dealing with the unenviable position of women workers who were moving to improvement in the 1880s; and a third describing the astonishing record of misfortune of Irish workers in the making of explosives and in steel mills and textile factories.

1   Babes in Bondage

The experiences of childhood—emotional experiences, enhanced by the innocence of youth, and profoundly affecting—are a challenge to the imagination of the social historian. Children, even more than adults submerged in the mass of illiterate and inarticulate people in the past, are largely without historical chroniclers.[1] A study of the influence of social customs, home life, education, and work life requires insight into the conditions of childhood. Not only were attitudes toward childhood different in the past from those of our own time, but there were types of juvenile experience quite different from contemporary forms of childhood participation. This difference is readily illustrated by an examination of the institution of child indentures in the nineteenth century, and Philadelphia, one of the nation's oldest cities, is a good place to study this institution.

In Philadelphia the practice of legally binding children extended back to colonial times, when it was derived from England. Part of William Penn's original scheme for populating his vast holdings was a plan by which emigrants would first be indentured to captains of ships in England and upon their landing in Pennsylvania would then be sold to an American buyer.[2] The institution of indenture was ancient, rooted in law and custom, and accepted as part of the economic and social life of the colonies. This was so much the case that the liberating influences of the American Revolution had little or no practical effect upon its functioning. Indentured labor was an inheritance from the medieval guild practices of work training and social control.[3] It was carried into the age of mercantile economics and artisan indepen-

This article is reprinted with the permission of the *Pennsylvania Magazine of History and Biography*, in which it originally appeared in 101, no. 1 (October 1977).

dence by the contract system of English common law. In America it served its time-honored functions of training the young in skills and giving some stability to diffuse and petty work relationships.[4] In addition, it was an instrument for imparting social discipline to the young and the alien, as well as providing for rudimentary education. As problems of destitution and child abandonment increased in America, they were frequently dealt with by indenturing the unfortunates involved. The indenture system of labor was used as a consciously humanitarian device to assign responsibility and to facilitate charity for the victims of poverty and for orphans. Indenture was also an alternative to slavery in a society in which there were various forms of servitude and influence curtailing mobility. In some cases indentured service was barely distinguishable from the involuntary servitude of slavery; in others it was a refuge for the young from fates much worse. In the British Isles and America, too, there was added the widespread practice of creating "redemptioners," that is, emigrants who paid for their passage to the New World by signing contracts for terms of servitude in their new country, usually terms of seven or fourteen years.

Although indentured servants and apprentices had the right in law to appeal to the courts for relief from unjust contracts, or from mistreatment, or to correct abuses, the indentured person was rarely in a position to obtain real redress.[5] The courts tended to side with those possessed of those two paramount legal resources, property and education. Hence, the system was both open to abuse by harsh and heedless masters and difficult to supervise and correct because of its ubiquity and the irregularities that creep into any widespread social institution.

The economic advantage of having indentured workers instead of workers receiving regular wages was not disregarded by artisans, merchants, and householders. Wages in America tended to be high because of a chronic labor shortage. In addition, indentured workers were not free to move away in search of better pay or living conditions. They were bound by law to their master. The Irish exile Archibald Hamilton Rowan, who was living near Philadelphia in 1791, observed tartly that his Quaker neighbors were not above a "brisk trade for 'Irish slaves'." He wrote:

The members of the society for the abolition of slavery have not the least objection to buying an Irishman or Dutchman, and will chaffer with himself or the captain to get him indented at about the eighth part of the wages they would have to pay a "country born."[6]

Lists of indentured persons from the eighteenth century in Philadelphia show that beggars, those unable to pay jail fees, convicted criminals, orphans, and runaways were signed into contracts for years of service by public authorities. Debtors were still another class of persons available to authorities for indenture. The Guardians of the Poor in Philadelphia had the power to indenture those in their charge.[7] Thus, in addition to redemptioners paying for their passage through their labor and the contracts of private individuals and families, there was a brisk trade in indentures by public officials. Considering the fact that indentures probably were signed most frequently for juveniles rather than adults, the perils of the system for the poor and undefended were manifold.

The traffic in bound servants from overseas was mostly Irish in the eighteenth century. Most of the servants coming from British ports were Irish, and agents, called appropriately "soul drivers," toured Ireland itself seeking indenture subjects.[8] The Irish had poor reputations as servants. They were likely to run away. The most common reasons for running away were that the work to which they were bound was too hard, the hours too long, the punishments meted out by masters too disagreeable, and the living conditions too unsatisfactory.[9] The fact that servants or apprentices lived with the families of their masters could produce considerable friction in itself. The Irish usually could speak English, and this also made it easier for them to abscond.

In one study of runaways in Pennsylvania in the years 1771–76 more than half the runaways were Irish.[10] This disposition to break free of the indenture developed because the Irish had little reason to respect English legal documents, or simply because the disciplines of such agreements did not accord with the psychology of those who came from a more pastoral and fluid society. It was not only youths who made the break for freedom. Advertisements, such as the following offering forty shillings reward for a runaway, were common all through the eighteenth century:

> Last Wednesday noon at break of day,
> From Philadelphia ran away
> An Irishman named John McKeown,
> To fraud and imposition prone;
> About five feet, five inches high
> Can curse and swear as well as lie;
> How old he is I can't engage
> But forty-five is near his age.
> He came (as all reports agree)
> From Belfast town in sixty-three.[11]

During the nineteenth century the Irish immigrants were very likely to be included in great numbers among the ranks of the debtors, orphans, criminals, and the servant class. Coming from a rural background, they frequently lacked the skills needed in the emerging industrial order. Even if they had been in a city such as Philadelphia for some time, they were still more likely to be considered social problems. They were to be found in disproportionate numbers among the inmates of almshouses and prisons, and their group was stigmatized in the public mind as feckless, untrustworthy, and prone to violence.[12]

The actual agreements by which the children of this group were bound to artisans and tradesmen were traditional documents rarely varying in form. One signed April 26, 1802, reads:

Biddy Dougherty, with the advise [sic] and consent of her mother Catherine of the City of Philadelphia, was bound apprentice to Arthur Howell of the City of Philadelphia, Tanner and Currier, to him, his heirs and assigns for and during the term of seven years, to be taught domestic work, to be provided with meat and drink, clothing, lodging, working, fitting for an apprentice during the said term of seven years, to have four quarters half days schooling and when free to have two suits apparel, one whereof to be new.[13]

In an agreement signed February 9, 1801, for John Lahy, age

twelve, whose father had died, his mother bound him for "eight years, two months, and twenty-one days" to John Wright, an oak cooper, with provision for four quarters evening schooling.[14] On August 11, 1801, an agreement was signed for John McCoy, "whose parents reside in Ireland," by John McConaughey of the District of Southwark, "his next friend," to bind the boy to Robert Christy for two years and four months "to learn the art, trade, and mistery [sic] of a cordwainer."[15]

It was, at this time, that one of the earliest craft unions in the nation, the Philadelphia Typographical Society, drew up its charter and rules that made apprenticeship a formal requirement of the craft. The system was very hard to control, however, and in 1828 the *Mechanics Free Press* in the city complained that lower-paid apprentices were being used instead of journeymen in the shops of some artisans. For children like Biddy Dougherty, bound in 1802 to learn domestic service, working conditions as a kitchen slavey could be very repugnant, with interminable hours. The dangers to maidenly virtue were proverbial. The drinking habits and rowdy temptations of hardy workmen sent many an indentured lad into early dissipation.[16] The gambling, sports, and drinking of craftsmen, who could, after all, often make their own work schedules, led to some of our earliest temperance efforts.

It is notable that the precocious working men's movement in Philadelphia in the late 1820s barely mentioned the plight of the indentured. Master mechanics and journeymen were too worried about their own problems to fret over the indentured subclass. The *Mechanics Free Press*, the organ of the movement, carried accounts in 1830 of charges against the House of Refuge managers that they were using inmate boys improperly to compete with local labor and that boys were plucked off the streets for forced labor. The charges were denied, and the managers of the House of Refuge assured the workingmen's committee that they indentured boys to rural masters to "obviate the evil of competition."[17] One plea signed simply by "Paul" did protest apprenticeship conditions, saying that the country's liberty was a mockery "as long as our youth are robbed of the just reward of their extreme toil and labour, or rather so long as they are required to labour incessantly from the morning's dawn to the going down of the sun, for almost nothing."[18] Another kind of complaint derived from disgruntled parents, who paid to have their children taught a trade and then found that the indenture had been in vain. One such parent wrote to the *Mechanics Free Press* in 1828:

> When we bind our sons for five, six or seven years, to learn a trade, it is with an idea that when he has faithfully served out the term of his apprenticeship, he will be enabled at least to find employment as a journeyman. This reasonable expectation very often ends in disappoingment; for the very moment he assumes his independence his troubles begin: he is thrown out of employment by his parsimonious and ungenerous master, with whom no consideration of past services has any weight, and whose heart can melt at the sight of nothing but money.[19]

However, the concern of the worker committees for political representation, for abolition of debtors prison, and for free public education stopped short of addressing the problems of bound children. The *Mechanics Free Press* continued to carry advertisements like the one placed by Edward Short:

> Five Dollars Reward—Ran away from the Subscriber on or about the 1st inst. an indented apprentice to the shoemaking business, named James Maher. He is lame in one of his feet. Whoever returns the said apprentice to me at 148 South Front Street shall receive the above reward, but no charges.[20]

Although conditions of indentured youths were hard, the alternative of remaining, for instance, in custody of an almshouse was even less attractive. The physician for the Philadelphia Almshouse, writing in the 1830s, stated:

> A hundred or more children were sheltered on their way to an early grave to which most of them were destined. Illegitimate and other outcasts formed the majority, and opthalmia, that curse of children's asylums, made them a sore-eyed, puny group most pitiable to see. . . . I pointed out to the committee of the board how the disease was disseminated by the children washing

in the same basins and using the same towels . . . and also by
the insufficient food permitted them. . . . But, of course, the
committee . . . knew better than I, and . . . nothing was done to
correct the wrong.[21]

From 1830 onward the District of Moyamensing in South
Philadelphia was an area of heavy Irish concentration. The
Indenture Book of the Moyamensing Board of Commissioners for
1836–45 has survived, and the contract receipts for children with
names like Mary Ann Callaghan, James Kearney, and Patrick
Duffy fill its pages. Most were indentured before their eleventh
birthday, but Josephine Develin was bound out at the tender age of
one year and Mary Roach at the age of five for a term of thirteen
years. Mary Ann Callaghan was bound to "housewifery" for ten
years at the age of seven, and Timothy Donovan was bound for
eleven years to a bootmaker at the age of nine. John Donnelly,
eight years old, had the good fortune to be indentured to a skilled
cabinetmaker for thirteen years, but most of the indentures were
for menial servant work. One-third of the indentures in the book
were for children with distinctively Irish names.[22]

Oscar and Mary Handlin, in their book on youth in America,
point out that apprenticeship and indenture meant, for children,
life in a "family of contract" rather than the family of birth. The
master took the place of the blood father. Where the master took
his responsibility seriously, the child was subject both to family
discipline and to the obedience required of a shop worker.[23]
Subduing the willfulness of children was the first and foremost duty
of religious parents. Bernard Wishy has emphasized how seriously
this duty was regarded in an age of evangelical zeal, such as the
1840s. It was in the 1840s, too, that the Irish Catholic immigrants
arrived in vast numbers. The Children's Aid Society of New York
warned of the immigrant slum children, "This dangerous class has
not yet begun to show itself as it will in eight or ten years, when
these boys and girls are matured. . . . They will poison society."
Protestant masters were expected to work for the religious discipline of their charges.[24]

It would be misleading to interpret the situation of indentured children according to our contemporary notions of child status and welfare. Doubtless, many were fortunate to be bound to a responsible masters. However, to be removed from the family of one's nativity at an early age, to be bound to a family of different ethnic and religious background, and in a condition of all but total subordination, could not but produce troubled psychological reactions in many cases. If there was not an "identity crisis" for the child, there was at least a condition in which the child was highly vulnerable psychologically.[25] The riotous behavior of apprentices, which became a fixture of urban life in the first half of the nineteenth century, might be in part attributable to this circumstance.

It should be recalled that conditions in the new factories of the 1840s were no escape from the rigors of indenture for children. A report on factory problems in Philadelphia in 1838 records that the workday extended from five o'clock in the morning until seven in the evening for children who carried boxes up four stories on their heads. An Irishman testified that children worked longer hours in the United States than in Irish and Scottish mills where he had worked. A seventy-hour week was the norm, and one John Mulligan testified that a sixty-nine-hour week would not be economically damaging and urged it. The views of employers were sought, and "the reason alleged by them for the employment of children is that they are forced on them by poor, and in many instances, worthless parents."[26]

The use of indenture for philanthropic reasons is illustrated by the surviving indenture records of Girard College. Stephen Girard in his will endowed this school for "poor, white, male orphans," and this was construed to mean boys whose father had died but whose mother might be living. Girard expressly forbade the presence of any clergyman on the premises of the college. In 1847, of the 102 indentures for entering boys, 23 had recognizably Irish names. Robert Emmet O'Brien was entered by "his next friend, Adelia Rodgers," whose signature was by mark. Indeed, 11 of those relatives or friends entering children of Irish names signed the indenture by mark for names including Kelly, McClay, Collins, Devine, Dougherty, Donahue, Miles, McIlhenny, McFadden, and Kane. Such signers probably saw Girard College as a boon compared to regular indentures or factory employment, whatever their personal or religious misgivings might have been.[27]

Herrick, in his book on white servitude in Pennsylvania, says, "The indentured system continued much later than is generally supposed. Indeed, it did not disappear until near the close of the first third of the nineteenth century."[28] I have already cited indentures extending beyond the end of the first third of the nineteenth century. There was, obviously, a continued use of indentures by both public and philanthropic officials. The Committee on the Children's Asylum of the Guardians of the Poor of Philadelphia was indenturing children as late as 1866. The minutes of the committee reveal an indenture on July 2, 1857, for Anna Donnally, bound out at three years of age. Mary Rowan, bound out to William Kelly, had her indenture canceled because she pilfered and was a bad example to Kelly's own children. Margaret Boyle was returned to the committee's charge in 1860 when her indenture expired. Bridget Larkin's indenture was canceled by consent of both parties that year. Although it was a city agency, the committee did provide indentures to farmers in the city and elsewhere. In 1866 John Dailey was bound to D. Cadwalader, farmer, of Montgomery County.[29]

It is difficult to believe that the Guardians of the Poor would be free of political and economic pressures for the assignment of children practically as chattel. Edward Everett Hale, in 1855, found in a survey that in most cases in Massachusetts and New York the education of bound children was not provided for, and there is no reason to assume that Pennsylvania would have been different.[30] The contracting into bondage of children of a lower-class and stigmatized group probably was fraught with much greater abuses than the omission of education, and perhaps these abuses were the very reason the indenture system continued under public auspices in Philadelphia, a city seldom esteemed for the purity of its politics.

The growth of population itself helped cause the decline of the indenture system. Mass populations required mass production, and the old individual entrepreneur and artisan declined as the factory order flourished. In 1848 a Pennsylvania act made it illegal for minors to work more than twelve hours a day in textile mills,

but the struggle over child labor had hardly begun.[31] The spread of
the wage system and the abandonment of traditional methods of
craft training did, however, hasten the demise of indentures.[32]

Although some of those who experienced life as indentured
youths became successful as adults, the fate of most is obscure.
Boys such as Hugh Craig, born in Coleraine, Ireland, and Horatio
Fitzgerald, the sons of poor parents, were able to rise to prominence as flour and grocery merchants. John Welsh, indentured
until the age of twenty-two, took this route and became a noted
leader in the city in the second half of the nineteenth century.[33]

The hazards of childhood in the growing city changed but did not
diminish for thousands of poor Irish children. The Philadelphia
Society to Protect Children was investigating cases in the 1870s,
including vicious instances of child abuse and exploitation. Thirty
years later, when young Scott Nearing was an investigator for the
Child Labor Association, the grim record of child brutalization was
still continuing.[34]

As late as 1899 an act of the General Assembly of Pennsylvania
empowered "benevolent and charitable" institutions, asylums, and
corporations to bind children by indentures under certain conditions.[35] Whereas most child-placement societies abandoned the
use of indentures by the end of the nineteenth century in favor of
agreements with foster parents, a study by the U.S. Children's
Bureau showed that the indenture form was actually used by
juvenile courts in selected cases up until the 1920s.[36]

As the immigrants made social and economic progress, they
became less subject to victimization through indenture. Laurence
Glasco found that as early as 1855 the number of Irish girls
working in live-in domestic services in Buffalo, N.Y., declined
after three years of residence in the United States.[37] In Philadelphia the U.S. Census records of occupations of Irish males in
1850, 1860, and 1870 show a steady expansion of skilled
occupations.[38] In the last third of the nineteenth century the
problem of child labor would draw the increasing interest of
reformers, and campaigns to assert the dignity of working people
would increasingly be waged in the face of the massive industrialism that would dominate the economic life of the nation.

NOTES

1. The beginnings of a broader-based study of family and childhood have emerged in such studies as Shirley Glubock, ed., *Home Life and Child Care in Colonial Days* (New York: Macmillan Co., 1969); Harvey Graff, "Patterns of Dependency and Child Development in the Mid-Nineteenth Century City: A Sample from Boston," *History of Education Quarterly* 17, no. 21 (Summer 1973): 129–43; Joseph F. Kett, "Adolescence and Youth in Nineteenth Century America," *Journal of Interdisciplinary History* 2, no. 2 (Autumn 1971): 283–98.

2. Karl Frederick Geiser, *Redemptioners and Indentured Servants in the Colony and Commonwealth of Pennsylvania* (New Haven, Conn.: The Tuttle, Morehouse and Taylor Co., 1901), p. 6; Merrill Jensen, ed., *English Historical Documents* (London: Eyre and Spottiswoode, 1955), pp. 488–90.

3. Ian M. G. Quimby, "Apprenticeship in Colonial Philadelphia," M.A. diss., University of Delaware, 1963. See also the materials in John R. Commons et al., *Documentary History of American Industrial Society*, 11 vols. (Cleveland, Ohio: Arthur H. Clark Co., 1910), and Robert F. S. Seybolt, *Apprenticeship and Apprenticeship Education in Colonial New York* (New York: Columbia Teachers College, 1917); James D. Motley, *Apprenticeship in American Trade Unions* (Baltimore, Md.: Johns Hopkins University Press, 1907), pp. 9–40.

4. Richard B. Morris, *Government and Labor in Early America* (New York: Harper and Row, 1965), pp. 340, 376, 382.

5. Oscar and Mary Handlin, *Facing Life: Youth and the Family in American History* (Boston: Little, Brown and Co., 1971), pp. 30–31, note the problems involved in indentures. Morris, in ibid., p. 336, provides an example of a case in which an Irish servant girl did obtain redress from Philadelphia courts. For a legal opinion on the strong enforcement of indentures in the early nineteenth century see Grace Abbott, *The Child and the State* (Chicago: University of Chicago Press, 1938), pp. 216–18.

6. Drummond, William H., ed., *The Autobiography of Archibald Hamilton Rowan* (Shannon, Ireland: Irish University Press, 1972), p. 318.

7. Lewis R. Harley, "The Redemptioners: An Address to the Montgomery County Historical Society" (Norristown, Pa.: Montgomery County Historical Society, 1893), pp. 1–2.

8. Ibid., pp. 3–5.

9. Handlin, *Facing Life*, p. 30.

10. Geiser, *Redemptioners and Indentured Servants*, p. 6; Gibson Bell Smith, "Footloose and Fancy Free: The Demography and Sociology of the Runaway Class in Colonial Pennsylvania, 1771–1776," Master of Arts paper, Bryn Mawr College (April 29, 1971), pp. 6–17. This research based on census materials and colonial advertisements for runaways shows over half of the runaways to be Irish. In Philadelphia in 1773–74 approximately 10 percent of the indentured ran away, and of these almost half were Irish. Another authority states that most indentured servants were Irish in the eighteenth century, and the Irish were most likely to break their indentures and run away. See Cheesman A. Herrick, *White Servitude in Pennsylvania* (Philadelphia: John J. McVey, 1926), pp. 159, 167. Lewis Harley, in "The Redemptioners," p. 3, agrees with this assessment.

11. Geiser, *Redemptioners and Indentured Servants*, p. 80.

12. Dennis Clark, *The Irish in Philadelphia: Ten Generations of Urban Experience* (Philadelphia: Temple University Press, 1973), pp. 44–49.

13. Records of Indentures and Marriages (October 27, 1800–October 18, 1806), R.G. 60.14, April 26, 1802, Archives of the City of Philadelphia.

14. Ibid., February 9, 1801.

15. Ibid., August 11, 1801.

16. David R. Johnson, "Crime Patterns in Philadelphia, 1840–70," in *The Peoples of Philadelphia: A History of Ethnic Groups and Lower-Class Life 1790–1940*, ed. by Allen Davis and Mark Haller (Philadelphia: Temple University Press, 1973), pp. 97–98; Bruce Laurie, "Nothing on Impulse: Lifestyles of Philadelphia Artisans 1820–1850," *Labor History* 15, no. 3 (Summer 1974): 345; Michael Feldberg, *The Philadelphia Riots of 1844* (Westport, Conn.: Greenwood Press, 1975).

17. *Mechanics Free Press* (Philadelphia), January 30, 1830.

18. Ibid., July 3, 1830.

19. Ibid., November 29, 1828.

20. Ibid., March 27, 1830.

21. Homer Folks, *Destitute, Neglected and Delinquent Children* (New York: The Macmillan Co., 1902), pp. 9–10.

22. Indenture Book (1836–1845), Moyamensing Board of Commissioners, R.G. 214.2, Archives of the City of Philadelphia.

23. Handlin, *Facing Life*, p. 30.

24. Bernard Wishy, *The Child and the Republic* (Philadelphia: University of Pennsylvania Press, 1968), p. 16; William G. McLoughlin, "Evangelical Child-Rearing in the Age of Jackson," *Journal of Social History* 9, no. 1 (Fall 1975): 20.

25. John Trisediotis, *In Search of Origins: The Experience of Adopted People* (Boston: Beacon Press, 1973), pp. 9–10.

26. Report of the Select Committee Appointed to Visit the Manufacturing Districts of the Commonwealth for the Purpose of Investigating the Employment of Children in Manufacturies—Mr. Petty, Chairman, Senate of the Commonwealth of Pennsylvania (Harrisburg, Pa.: Thompson and Clark, Printers, 1838), pp. 6–42. Much information on this period is also provided by William A. Sullivan, *The Industrial Worker in Pennsylvania: 1800–1840* (Harrisburg, Pa.: Pennsylvania Historical and Museum Commission, 1955).

27. Indentures Made to Girard College, 1847–1853, R.G. 35.134, Archives of the City of Philadelphia.

28. Herrick, *White Servitude in Pennsylvania*, p. 265.

29. Guardians of the Poor, Minutes of the Committee on the Children's Asylum (July 1857–November 1856), R.G. 35.23, Archives of the City of Philadelphia.

30. Robert H. Bremner, ed., *Children and Youth in America*, (Cambridge, Mass.: Harvard University Press, 1970), vol. 1, p. 575. One investigation into Boston conditions found only sixteen of 353 Boston family sons apprenticed in 1860, but half of the fifteen-year-olds counted enrolled in school. See Harvey L. Graff, "Patterns of Dependency and Child Development in the Mid-Nineteenth Century City: A Sample from Boston," *History of Education Quarterly* 17, no. 21 (Summer 1973): 142.

31. Miriam E. Loughran, *The Historical Development of Child Labor Legislation in the United States*, Ph.D. diss. Catholic University of America, Washington, D.C., June 1921, pp. 69–70.

32. Abbott, *The Child and the State*, p. 230.

33. Biographies of Philadelphians, Clippings collected by Thompson Westcott, vol. A, pp. 49 and 53, Collection of the Historical Society of Pennsylvania; *Biographies of Philadelphia Merchants* (Philadelphia: James K. Simon, 1864), pp. 167–68.

34. Records of the Philadelphia Society to Protect Children, and Records of the Child

Labor Association of Philadelphia (1904) in the Urban Archives, Temple University, Philadelphia, Pa.

35. Abbott, *The Child and the State*, p. 230.

36. Ibid., pp. 232–33.

37. Laurence Glasco, "The Life Cycles and Household Structure of American Ethnic Groups," *Journal of Urban History* 1, no. 3 (May 1975): 356.

38. Clark, *The Irish in Philadelphia*, pp. 73–85.

2 Woman of the House

The female center of the household and family is called *Ban a Tighe* in Gaelic, that is, "woman of the house." The idea of wife and mother separable from the household and its domestic responsibilities did not exist in the traditional rural culture of Ireland in the nineteenth century. That is why it is of interest to examine what became of women and their roles when the Irish became urbanized in American cities. The transition from rural traditional cultures to urban, change-oriented cultures is still progressing all over the globe. The changes that have affected women, who were especially bound by traditional strictures on their behavior, are of special significance to us today as the roles of women are being further altered by continued migration to cities.

Little serious study has been devoted to Irish immigrant women and the daughters of Irish immigrants. Carol Groneman has shown that in the 1850s in New York City the Irish family was not torn apart and made pathological as a result of the Great Famine, emigration, and the struggle to survive that the Irish experienced following 1846. On the contrary, the family remained a source of strength and mutual aid through it all, and the role of women in this response was primary.[1]

The part that individual women played in this process is largely lost to us, however. Irish-born women and the daughters of Irish immigrants emerge as individuals later and appear as isolated personalities that are rarely seen as part of the Irish-American tradition. Even Irish-Americans aware of their own history are generally conscious of the fact that the following women are part of their heritage: Mary Elizabeth Lease, populist farm agitator; Carry Moore Nation, fiery prohibitionist; Margaret Higgins Sanger, birth-control pioneer; labor evangelists Elizabeth Gurley Flynn, Leonora O'Reilly, Kate Mullaney, and the magnificent "Mother

the subject of remark and eulogy by every stranger. . . . The
instances of connubial defection are fewer in Ireland, for its
size, than any other country of equal civilization. . . . The
instances of ladies "living and dying in single blessedness" are
rare indeed. . . . The upper classes of Irish women are very
handsome and finely formed.

Carr also wrote:

The lower Irish countrywomen are so disfigured by the smoke of
their cabins and their feet are so enlarged by being exposed
without either shoes or stockings, that I think them inferior in
complexion and form to the female peasantry of England. The
commonest women of Dublin are, however, in general remarkable for the delicateness of their hands and arms and the
whiteness of the bosom. They are also in general powerfully
made and able to protect themselves. . . . In England, the low
Irishwomen by their valour alone have established the right of
carrying baskets in Covent Garden, that is, of conveying the
vegetables and fruit purchased there to the house of the buyer on
their own body.[2]

These oblique views are typical of the disparate and ill-assorted
information that Philadelphians might have encountered about
females of a group that was to be the city's largest foreign-born
population element for several generations. Nevertheless, these
observations do note some attributes frequently referred to by
commentators on Irish women in the nineteenth century: their
family loyalty, their physical vigor in the midst of hard work, and
their vivacity and attractiveness when not disfigured by poverty
and grim living conditions.

Philadelphia was to know firsthand the virtues and vices of
Irishwomen as the immigrant population increased in the 1830s
and then soared in the 1840s and 1850s so that by 1860 there were
94,989 Irish-born people in the city. The strengths of the rural
families who had escaped the hard subsistence life in Ireland may
have been the key to sustaining the Irish in Philadelphia, but
detailed study of this subject has not been pursued. However,
although the Philadelphia Almshouse contained a disproportionate

Jones," who was Mary Harris from County Cork. Mary O'Reill
secretary of the Women's Department of the Knights of Labor, wa
reviled by priests as a "vulgar lady tramp" for her efforts t
improve the working conditions of her laboring sisters. He
treatment indicates that the role of female activist was likely to rur
directly counter to the passive role assigned to females in church
thinking in the Victorian era, and this is one reason why we know
so little of female life among immigrants. It should remind us,
however, that even within the church there were broad areas for
female disposal of energy and resources, for religious congregations of sisters played a crucial role in education, health, and
social service. The social contributions of such women's organizations were usually cloaked by a consciously cultivated anonymity.
The work was for the "glory of God" and not individual celebrity.
Victorian suppression of women, and religious sanctions of it, the
conservative role assigned women in traditional rural cultures, and
the masking influence of simple poverty and the lack of the means
of documentation cloak women's history. Millions of women were
deprived of the literacy, habits, and cultural skills necessary for
leaving records of their own lives. In studying immigrant women
and their daughters we are inquiring into an area of virtual
mystery.

Concentrating on one locality such as Philadelphia does provide
a reasonable context into which the scarce materials about immigrant women can be placed. The development of the city as a major
industrial center meant that women coming into it from Ireland had
to make sharp adjustments to a new social milieu. They were
received into a city that reflected Anglo-Saxon attitudes about
them. In the early nineteenth century, English commentators on
Ireland provided observations on Irish "ladies" and "the lower
Irish country-women" that would have been readily absorbed by
the educated Philadelphia leaders of the time. A book published in
Philadelphia in 1806 by John Carr, a London lawyer, stated:

> The ladies of Ireland possess a peculiarly pleasing frankness,
> and a vivacity in conversation, which render highly arresting all
> they do and all they say. In this open sweetness of deportment,
> the libertine finds no encouragement; for their modesty must be

number of Irish in 1865, the docket kept by the courts listing families deserted by husbands contains very few Irish names.[3]

By the 1870s, evidence of the distress of immigrant women becomes more abundant as newspapers expand their coverage of local conditions. In 1877 the Philadelphia Society to Protect Children was recording cases of severe child beating. A child named Mary Agnes Murphy asked to be removed from the house of her mother, Nora Murphy, who operated an "odious house of ill-fame." Children of habitually drunken mothers were aided, as were children forced by their parents into petty crime or to work as runners for houses of prostitution.[4]

In 1878 the *Philadelphia Public Ledger* reported on meetings of an organization "devising plans to suppress pauperism." One goal of the meetings was to see how idleness and beggary might be suppressed. Perhaps in response to some of the charges that the poor neglected their children, a working woman had an amanuensis state her case about child care and daily work for publication in the newspaper:

> It is very true that the woman who makes seersucker coats for six cents apiece or does other sewing at the same rate, and has to work eighteen hours out of the twenty-four cannot spare a minute to take care of her child, and all the time she takes to wash, dress and feed it is so much time stolen from the effort to keep a roof over its head or get it bread.
>
> Her "X" Mark[5]

Her complaint attests to the fact that it was the Irish who were the first group to be exploited in the chronically troubled garment industry that was to have such an unsavory history of labor strife with Jews and Italians in the 1890s and with blacks and the Spanish-speaking at a later period. By 1860 Philadelphia already had 352 ready-made—clothing establishments, with 8,078 women outnumbering men in their work force.[6] As seamstresses, tailors, pattern makers and finishers, immigrant women working in their homes often had to compete with factories that were increasingly equipped with sewing machines.

For many women the struggle was simply too much. Their

families dispersed or they themselves fell outside of organized
family life. The Female Vagrant Register in 1874, for instance,
lists for two days the following Irish-born women as homeless:
Josephine Wright, age thirty-five; Bridget Quinn, age forty; Rose
Callahan, age twenty-nine; Sarah Thompson, age twenty-eight; and
Anne Mathews, age seventy-three. Tabulation of the ages of
women born in Ireland who were listed as vagrants in a two-week
period shows them to have been on the average about forty-three
years old. Fifty-three of seventy women listed in this period were
Irish-born, certainly a high proportion of the total female vagrant
population. This vagrancy is one example of the toll taken by
emigration and the harsh life of the city's conditions. At age
forty-three these women of the working class were probably used
up, often widowed, prematurely old, tired, and defeated in the
effort to deal with jobs, family cares, and the battle to maintain
some dignity in a hostile world. Very few would live to be
seventy-eight like old Julia McGinniss, the oldest woman listed,
for the conditions of the time just did not permit it. Although these
women had lived beyond the dangerous age of childbearing, their
lives were all but over.[7]

The jobs open to immigrant Irish women were limited enough in
the period when Irish immigration was heaviest. Even before 1850
these women had become the standard household-servant class. In
this capacity they were the subject of continuous complaint and
criticism by Victorian matrons who set high standards for servants.
In thousands of kitchens, laundry rooms, and belowstairs servant
halls they labored to sustain the elaborate artifices with which the
well-to-do households of the day were equipped. In the parlors and
drawing rooms abovestairs their mistresses worried about the
cleanliness, the lack of punctilious grace, and the Catholic
influence of Irish servant girls. To train candidates for service
correctly a "Lodging House" under the supervision of a matron was
established by worthy Protestant women in 1862. The house for
girls under eighteen was to improve the "moral and religious
condition" of poor girls and to train them "in habits of neatness and
industry, bring them under moral influences, and then, as soon as
possible, pass them through to a place." It was intended to "teach
them to work, to be clean, and to understand the virtues of order

and punctuality; to lay the foundation of a housekeeper or servant. . . ." There is evidence that going into domestic service was a course more likely for girls recently arrived in American than for those who already had several years residence in the country. One study by Laurence Glasco shows, too, that one fourth of the girls who were live-in domestics in a given city were ten to fourteen years old, surely at a tender age to be hard at work in a new land.[8]

The predicament of Irish country girls entering the world of gewgaws and claptrap in Victorian households stemmed in part from the contrast between the plain, and at times stark, simplicity of rural cottage life and the overstuffed elaboration of the fashionable urban household. The traditionalism of the rural household placed implements in an almost ritual arrangement in the house. When this pattern was broken and a multitude of new objects and procedures were introduced, daily chores became much more difficult, to the amusement, but also to the chagrin, of those in charge of servants.[9]

Although huge numbers of immigrant girls "went into service" and managed somebody else's household, others found a more congenial setting for household skills in conducting boardinghouses. Such lodgings were an important part of a society where immigrants without families and people holding temporary jobs needed shelter. Working people could not afford hotels, and settled families needing extra income frequently obtained it by letting out rooms. Widows, female inheritors of houses, and more enterprising women conducted full-fledged lodging houses and boardinghouses that served as living facilities for the large unattached male population that had come to America "to dig gold in the streets." *Boyd's Philadelphia City Business Directory* for 1877 lists 164 boardinghouses, with about one-fourth, or 43, operated by women. Of these boardinghouses run by women, about half were listed with distinctly Irish names. The foreign-born were three times as likely to keep boardinghouses as the native-born, and in the 1890s 14.8 percent of all households of Irish-born people had lodgers.[10] Doubtless a good many other lodging houses listed under male names were actually operated by women. Add to this the great number of informal and unlisted boardinghouses, and a rather extensive network of such houses is evident.

The Irish boardinghouse in some cases may have been a primly conducted facility of fastidious order. More often it was a way station for hardy lads trying their luck in America, a "put-your-rent-on-the-table" domicile for cousins and neighbors from the old country, and a safe haven under watchful eyes for working girls on six-day-a-week schedules. Irish landladies served an important social function in the immigrant communities. They provided some focus for quasi-domestic stability for otherwise footloose working-men. They organized groups of lodgers from similar backgrounds, wrote letters for those not "handy with a pen," and served as watchdogs of virtue according to Irish Catholic views. They were also, often enough, informal marriage brokers who cannily matched girls and boys whose families were not present to guide their romantic impulses. As key contacts for job referrals and social orientation, the boardinghouse matron was in a position somewhat analogous to that of the priest and the saloon keeper in the Irish community. She aided lodgers by trusting them for rent payments until they got their start, lending them money to get to Scranton or Pittsburgh where relatives were, for example, or holding messages about their whereabouts when they migrated into the hinterlands for work. The boardinghouse manager was a font of information about how to send money back to Ireland, where to find a doctor, or who to see about one's legal status as an immigrant. Joan Younger Dickinson has speculated that the landlady provided a surrogate home and family not only for the immigrant lodgers but also, in the cases of single women, for themselves, and she relates this to the tragic conditions in Ireland that prevented marriage, forced emigration, and dispersed natural families. However this might have been, in the immigrant community the landlady became an archetypal figure. She mothered greenhorns and gave them their first instructions about America.

Domestic service and the management of households at least had some relation to the domestic roles familiar to women from rural Ireland. Factory work was a much more radical change from previous experience for such women. By the 1880s Philadelphia was in its full development as a textile manufacturing center. In South Philadelphia and in the mill districts of Kensington, huge textile factories employed thousands of women to tend machines.

In the thirty years from 1880 to 1910 the city's textile industry was heavily dependent on immigrant females. In 1900 about 8,000 of the foreign-born cotton-mill workers, that is, about 10 percent, were Irish.[11] Thousands of other Irish women worked in woolen, lace, linen, and carpet mills. The Irish population was the only foreign-born group with a sharp female majority at the end of the nineteenth century. Fifty-three percent of all the Irish immigrants were females. The group also had a lower marriage rate and a higher rate of female labor-force participation at that time. Two-thirds of the Irish girls were unmarried under the age of 21, and 28 percent of all Irish females were in the labor force in 1900.[12] Add to these facts the continued laboring status of thousands of second- and third-generation Irish females, and the role of the group as a central resource for the industrial system in the city can be seen.

A closer look at the Irish neighborhoods that were textile areas shows the degree to which families depended upon textile work for income. In the Twenty-first Ward of the city was the Manayunk section, a district where mills had originally been built to take advantage of waterpower in the 1830s and 1840s. The compilations of census data by the Philadelphia Social History Project provide a close view of some of the neighborhood's streets. On four blocks of four separate streets in 1880, a sample of females above the age of twelve who were children of Irish-born parents showed that of forty-two such females thirty-five were employed in textile mills. On Mechanic Street lived John Gallagher, age twenty-five, and his four sisters and two brothers. All four girls, ages fifteen to twenty-two, worked in cotton mills. On the same street Mary O'Donnell kept house for her four sons, three of whom worked in cotton mills as did her daughter, Mary, and one of her Irish-born boarders. On nearby Cresson Street Mary Kern ran a boardinghouse for ten boarders, all of whom were in mills. Mary Harley, her neighbor, worked in a cotton mill, as did her daughter Alice, fifteen, and her two sons, aged twelve and thirteen. Not far away on Hermitage Street Mrs. James McElvain kept house while James worked in a dye house. Their daughters, Ellen, sixteen, and Catherine, thirteen, worked in cotton mills as did their sons, James, fourteen, and Edward, eleven. The same kind of employment pattern held true for the Garveys, Carrs, Kellys, Donleys, and Doughertys on Hermitage Street. Children apparently stayed in school until about age ten, then went to the mills. Mothers kept house for big families. In Manayunk it would be hard to find an Irish girl above the age of ten who was not working in a mill, so long as she was unmarried.

In another heavily Irish neighborhood in Kensington's Twenty-fifth Ward along Columbia Avenue and Diamond Street, cotton-mill work for women was common, but silk weavers, shirtmakers, and servants also lived there. A sample of fifty Irish females on Somerset Street showed that thirty-five kept house, while there were dressmakers and tailoresses as well as mill workers. The families in this area were apparently less dependent on female labor than those in Manayunk.

On Bainbridge Street in the Thirtieth Ward in South Philadelphia some of the female occupations on a sample block for Irish-born women were:

Eliza Smith—Milliner
Eliza Niece—Saleslady
Sarah Miller—Dressmaker
Melinda Miller (Sarah's daughter)—Dressmaker
Bridget Lynch—Grocery store
Nancy McFadden—"On her means"
Lititia McCullough—Grocery store
Margaret Simpson—Servant of L. McCullough
Eliza Erskine—Teacher
Martha McCue—Laundress
Jennie McCue (Martha's daughter)—Laundress

In this area dressmakers were common, but teachers, milliners, and salesladies also appeared in the census. Thus, in contrast to Manayunk, the Kensington and South Philadelphia areas show more diversity in women's occupations.[13]

The environment in the textile mills of the 1880s was both unlovely and unhealthy. In the long rooms where the spinning, knitting, and weaving machines clattered away on every side, the temperature was oppressively hot and in the summer almost insufferable. The air was filled with lint, dust, and the smell of hot oil. If there were toilets they were generally inferior, and some employers provided only buckets for toilets.

The hazards of this environment had grim effects on the health of the women and men in the mills. "Weaver's deafness," with partial or total hearing loss, was common. Respiratory problems, often leading to tuberculosis and chronic breathing difficulties, were the penalty paid for poor ventilation and workrooms filled with fiber particles. Accidents due to poor machine design, fatigue, or poor supervision occurred with depressing frequency. Fires, too, were a constant peril, for factory air became combustible because of the clouds of lint and dust. In 1882 there were eleven major textile-factory fires in the city, and the William Wood Company mill caught fire twice, causing a total of more than $300,000 damage. The owner of Randolph Mills, Joseph Harvey, was indicted for manslaughter in April 1882 because of a fire that killed nine mill workers unable to get out because of inadequate fire escapes for the building. A labor force in such conditions naturally sought improvements. The women at Leedom's Mills in 1885 went on strike to obtain the rate of six cents a yard for their weaving. Weavers from Lowell, Mass., were imported by Leedom to break the strike. Other strikes occurred the same year in Dobson's Mills and the Thornton Mill.

Women who worked in textile mills in this period as bobbin girls or loom tenders toiled from 7 A.M. to 6 P.M. with a half day on Saturday for four dollars a week. They knew that older women in the mills were frequently deaf from the noise of the machines and that tuberculosis from the effects of airborne lint on the lungs was a hazard of the work. If a fourteen-year-old girl was good at tending one loom, she would be asked to tend two at once. Women interviewed remembered the deadening boredom of the work and their strong desire to escape it.[14]

In the 1880s it did become possible for some of the Irish girls to escape the life of the mills. Their families had made sufficient progress to be able to send them to such institutions as the Girls Normal School to prepare for teaching careers. In 1880 eight girls who received teacher certificates were named McIntire, McGrotty, MacAulay, Quinn (2), Dugan, McQuade, and Kenny. These eight girls were part of a class of ninety-five.[15] Not only were careers in

retail sales, office work, and teaching expanding at the end of the
nineteenth century, but Irish girls could enter the Training School
for Nurses at the Philadelphia Hospital. In 1897 Mary Ann Moran,
Teresa McElwee, and Ann McParland did so. In 1898 and 1899
five other girls of Irish background enrolled. They were still a
distinct minority, but their pioneering ambition seems to have
brought twelve others into the school in 1901: girls with names
including Alice O'Hallovan, twenty-three years old, Catherine
McMenamin, twenty-five, and Martha O'Connor, twenty-two. It is
notable that the home addresses for most of the girls were in
neighborhoods that were new and better residential areas.[16] A
decade earlier the bulk of the Irish female names in the list of
employees of the Philadelphia Department of Charities at the
Philadelphia Hospital were "attendants." Even in 1888, however,
there were a few "pupil nurses" with Irish names studying and
working for a nine-dollar-a-month salary.[17] Thus, as the nineteenth
century closed there were real changes in opportunities for women.
As Finley Peter Dunne's "Mister Dooley" put it in 1899, "Molly
Donahue have up and become a 'new woman'!"[18]

In her study of immigrant women in the two decades from 1890
to 1910, Joan Younger Dickinson found a pronounced shift out of
domestic and needle-trades work in the 1890s by Irish females and
others representing the "old immigration." These women were
being replaced by Italians, Jews, and East Europeans. At this time
there was a national growth in the number of nurses and teachers.[19]
In household service, though, the Irish had been involved since
the 1830s, and they had the advantage of speaking English, so
that their displacement was more gradual.

In 1900, for every girl advancing to a better job or a real career
there were still others coming into the city from Ireland with most
of the same disabilities as their forerunners a generation before.
Information gathered through a questionnaire circulated to the
grandchildren of Irish women who came to Philadelphia in the late
nineteenth or early twentieth century shows that these women led
sharply circumscribed lives. Of twenty-five such women, twenty
were maids for well-to-do families, one was a cook, one was a
waitress, one was a teacher, and one held no occupation except
housewife. Twenty-four women left jobs to marry and keep house.

Eight had one or two children, while six had nine or more, with the median family size being six. Although some had interests in Irish and American politics, most concentrated upon their families almost exclusively. One woman put nine children through college on a policeman's earnings. Most had a strong interest in their religious duties and Catholic parish affairs. What the *Catholic Standard and Times* said of Rose O'Brien in 1900 would have been true of most of these women: she "was noted for her sterling faith and open charity and for her generous labors freely offered to pastors and congregations throughout the city."[20]

The almost total immersion of these women in domestic life after their having been servants in the houses of others was not at that time a socially regrettable condition. For girls born in poverty in County Mayo or County Leitrim to preside over a populous and clean American household was a respected accomplishment. They may have envied as life moved on those women who were breaking new ground in the career world, but the rituals and absorptions of family life were sufficient for most, for their horizons were delimited by custom and perception. Their pride was more in their households and the advancement of their children than in themselves. This self-effacement would be unbearable to the current generation of feminists, but it was normal and acceptable to these immigrant women, who had more modest aspirations and expectations. The most important fact about their roles, however, is that even in a time when other Irish women—some no doubt the daughters of granddaughters of immigrants—were entering new realms of occupation and status, this sample of immigrants from 1890 to 1910 were still bound to domestic service.

This brief examination of the positions and labors of Irish women reveals the protracted depths of their distress in the city of the nineteenth century. Their utility as a laboring group made them vulnerable to all the exactions of a crude industrialism and a society that had but little regard for them. Disease, large families, overwork, and social disabilities did not take from them, however, their own sense of worth as moderators of households and inspirers of their offspring. It was this sense of worth that animated the first female "break out" generation that reached for white-collar and career jobs in the 1890s. Even while they did so, however, there were still immigrant women locked into the old subservient roles. The slow pace of change for such women contains a message for the feminists of today whose own campaigns proceed with vexatious slowness. The message is: these women bore a brutal burden; you owe them fidelity in the advancement of women's rights.

NOTES

1. Carol Groneman, "She Earns as a Child—She Pays as a Man: Women Workers in a Mid-Nineteenth Century New York City Community," in *Immigrants in Industrial America, 1850–1920*, ed. by Richard L. Ehrlich (Charlottesville, Va.: University Press of Virginia, 1977), pp. 33–46.

2. John Carr, *A Stranger in Ireland in the Year 1805* (Philadelphia: T. and G. Palmer, 1806), pp. 148–49.

3. Desertion Docket (1865), Archives of the City of Philadelphia, City Hall, Philadelphia, R.G. 21.7.

4. Case Records, vol. I, Philadelphia Society to Protect Children (1877–78), Urban Archives, Temple University, Philadelphia.

5. *Philadelphia Public Ledger*, June 13, 1878, and October 13, 1878.

6. Charles E. Zaretz, *The Amalgamated Clothing Workers of America* (New York: Ancon Publishing Co., 1934), p. 19.

7. Female Vagrant Register (1874–76), Archives of the City of Philadelphia.

8. Laurence Glasco, "The Life Cycles and Household Structure of American Ethnic Groups: Irish, Germans and Native-born Whites in Buffalo, New York, 1955," *Journal of Urban History* 1, no. 3 (May 1975): 339–64; Blaine Edward McKinley, "The Stranger at the Gates: Employer Reactions towards Servants in America, 1825–1875," Ph.D. diss., Michigan State University, 1969, p. 129.

9. Page Smith, *Daughters of the Promised Land: Women in American History* (Boston: Little, Brown and Co., 1970), p. 205.

10. *Boyd's Philadelphia City Business Directory* (Philadelphia: Central News Co., 1877), pp. 100–101. Groneman found in her sample up to 25 percent of New York Irish women who were married in the lodging-house business. See Groneman, "She Earns as a Child," p. 39. Data on boardinghouse significance in other cities is in John Modell and Tamara Haraven, "Urbanization and the Malleable Household: An Examination of Boarding and Lodging Houses in American Families," in *Family and Kin in Urban Communities, 1700–1930*, ed. by Tamara Haraven (New York: New Viewpoints, 1977), pp. 164–86. See also Joan Younger Dickinson, "The Role of the Immigrant Women in the U.S. Labor Force, 1890–1910," Ph.D. diss., University of Pennsylvania, 1975, p. 114.

11. Dickinson, "The Role of Immigrant Women," p. 185.

12. Ibid., p. 132.

13. These samples and family occupational patterns were drawn from the compilations of 1880 Census material made by the Philadelphia Social History Project directed by Dr. Theodore Hershberg at the University of Pennsylvania.

14. Daniel Nelson, *Origins of the New Factory System in the United States, 1880–1920* (Madison, Wis.: University of Wisconsin Press, 1975), pp. 11–13. References to fires are in the *Report of Mayor Samuel G. King, 1882* (Philadelphia: City of Philadelphia, 1883), and

Philadelphia: City of Firsts (Philadelphia: Historical Publication Society, 1926), pp. 370–72. Strikes are noted in *The Irish World* (New York), March 7, 1885, and June 27, 1885. Conditions in factories were described to the author in interviews by Mrs. Patricia Lynch, age eighty-three, January 6, 1977 (Philadelphia), and Mrs. May Quinlan, age eighty-two, March 9, 1978 (Philadelphia).

15. *Sixty-Second Annual Report of the Board of Education of Philadelphia* (Philadelphia: E. C. Merkley, 1881), pp. 79–82.

16. Register, Training School for Nurses, 1897–1901, Philadelphia Hospital. Archives of the City of Philadelphia.

17. Register of Nurses, Attendants and Petty Office, Department of Charities, 1888–91. Archives of the City of Philadelphia.

18. Finley Peter Dunne, *Mister Dooley in Peace and War* (Boston: Small and Maynard, 1899), pp. 136–40.

19. Dickinson, "The Role of the Immigrant Women," pp. 84–85; Louise A. Tilly and Joan W. Scott, *Women, Work and Family* (New York: Holt, Rinehart and Winston, 1978), pp. 156–57.

20. These questionnaires were collected by the writer with the aid of Dr. Paula Benkart of St. Joseph's College, Philadelphia; Dr. Kay Gavigan of Cabrini College, Radnor, Pa.; James McGill of the Donegal Society of Philadelphia; and James Lee of the Emerald Society of Philadelphia. For Rose O'Brien see the *Catholic Standard and Times* (Philadelphia), March 3, 1900.

3 Hazardous Pay

In a study entitled *Work without Salvation,* James B. Gilbert gives
the opinion concerning America's industrial growth that "The
greatest factor in this urban industrial phenomenon was foreign
immigration."[1] Whether this judgment is fully accepted or not, it
underscores the tremendous role that immigrants and their children played in the struggle to build a complex, unprecedented,
and mighty technical economy. In the century-long evolution of
industry from its beginnings amid rickety steam engines and
jerry-built plants to fully developed systems of the twentieth
century with new forms of energy and sophisticated machinery, the
Irish had a special role to play in the process of growth. During this
period from 1830 to 1930 they constituted a massive labor supply.
It is estimated that almost six million of them came to America in
these decades.[2] They were the first major immigrant group to be
concentrated in industry. As unskilled and disadvantaged workers
they were retained in its toils for a longer period than any other
group, and they and their children were the group most exploited
by industrialization when the process was in its crudest and
cruelest stage.

The Irish influx into the industrial process in the decades of the
mid-nineteenth century took place when the production machinery
was novel and only half understood. Working conditions for those
serving machines were little more than an afterthought as the
nation beguiled itself with the romance of technology and the
wonders of growing production. Within the networks of manufacture and transport that made up the new system, there were
countless jobs that were too dirty, too onerous, or too dangerous to
be popular among skilled workers or those who could avoid them.
In the first century of the country's industrial activity, it was most

frequently the Irish who wound up with these jobs. They were an underclass concentrated in the industrial regions and were marked by a minority status that consigned them to industry's most hazardous pits and perils.

There were other considerations that consigned Irish immigrants to hazardous occupations besides the fact that as an out-group in American society they were easily regarded as expendable. Immigrants tended to be young, and the young are often reckless and heedless of danger. Immigrants at the bottom of a larger society are also vulnerable because of their ignorance of the processes in which they are involved, as the Irish from rural backgrounds were likely to be ignorant of the industrial perils around them. Newcomers to America from rural backgrounds were also grateful to get whatever employment they could and were willing to gamble with the dangers entailed in the work. The Irish self-image, too, played a role, for this ethnic group conceived of itself as given to daring and especially endowed with adventurous qualities. It is notable that, as this chapter is intended to show, the Irish were still especially prominent in dangerous occupations as late as the 1890s.

An example of the continuity of Irish involvement with hazardous occupations may be seen in the employment of generations of Irish men by the Du Pont explosives and gunpowder works at the Hagley Yard and related facilities south of Philadelphia in nearby Delaware along the Brandywine Creek. The earliest records of accidental explosions at the powder mills reach back to 1802, but the records continue right through the nineteenth century, surely one of the longest documentations of industrial misfortune in American history. The process of making gunpowder and explosives was, of course, known to be perilous when the Du Pont mills began production with the encouragement of President Thomas Jefferson, but all the causes and relationships of the explosive problem would not be understood for generations. In 1805 and 1809 serious explosions occurred, but in 1815 nine died with a roar of combustion on the Brandywine. Among those killed were John, Hugh, and Patrick Brady, all of one family. In 1818 an even greater detonation took thirty-three lives. These included victims

with the following Irish names, all of whom were single: Daniel
Dougherty, William Dougherty, John Terry, Peter Cooney, David
Flinn, Thomas Kennedy, Patrick McCarney, John Mulloy, John
Strain, Patrick Follan, John Ferry, Phillip Dugin, Peter Cooney,
John Donovan, John O'Brien, Patrick Boyle, and John Donahue.
Also killed were Mrs. Michael Tanner and her infant, who
happened to be in the yard at the time. It was said that a worker
named McCullough had inadvertently carried hot coals into a
powder building on his shovel, causing the calamity. Thus, from
the outset it appears that Du Pont's employees paid a high price for
this dangerous work.

One of the most hazardous tasks involved with explosives
manufacture was the pounding procedure. The explosive elements
were placed in mixing vats and pounded or reduced to powder
form. The pounding mill where this was done was a place of special
jeopardy. In 1822 it blew up twice. In 1824 Charles Dunnion was
the only man to blow up a "full charge" in the powder rolling mill
and survive after a swift aerial transit from the structure. The story
was told of one William Green's being dug out of blast ruins in
1825 and saying to the mill's superintendent, "I'm sorry for your
great loss, sir." More explosions happened almost annually in the
1830s, but Green was killed in 1847 when another monstrous
detonation occurred, this one in the packing house. With him were
killed William Connor, Daniel Doughry, Michael O'Brien, Bernard Shields, James McDevitt, Matthew McGarvey, John McGin-
nis, and others of Irish birth or family. The persistence of the Irish
in the toll is manifest. They were predominant among the victims
because Du Pont had especially recruited them through George
McHenry's Packet Line in Philadelphia.

In 1848 a man named Dougherty was killed at the mill in a
cave-in, and it is recorded that there was consternation among
some Du Pont family members when Dougherty's family was
awarded a one-hundred-dollar pension as if he had been killed in
an explosion. At this time the Du Ponts themselves still shared the
dangers by being on site at the mill. In 1849 and 1850 blowups
occurred; in 1853 John Devine and James McCaffrey died in a
conflagration; and in 1855 Edward Cassidy died of burns after an
explosion. In 1859 men named Gibbons, Walsh, Dougherty,

O'Donnell, and Moran were part of the toll. In addition to explosion fatalities, other deaths were caused by men being caught in machinery, and what the human cost was of being in contact with the chemicals used we can only speculate.

The Civil War provided more demand than ever for Du Pont's deadly products, so the company prospered even further. When James Mulloy was blown up in 1869, sixteen powder workers quit. F. G. du Pont was incredulous. "Why?" he asked when he had given them a half day off for the funeral. By the 1880s the Irish had long been a fixture in the works. Many lived in the nearby community of Squirrel Run, where they had built their little Saint Joseph's Church. The company had built houses there with a pump. The local tavern owned by Tim McCarthy was called, with keen Irish irony, "The Blazing Rag"—all that would be left of a worker after one of the Hagley blowups. Workers told stories of having to bury logs in the coffins of fellow workers so that the families would have something after an explosion with which to hold obsequies.

The explosion rate did not slacken appreciably as time went on. In 1882 ten incidents occurred, and three or four a year were considered normal. In 1890 a blowup killed thirteen people, including a woman and her daughter walking nearby. In 1898 James Mulherin was unloading a wagon when a spark was struck from a wheel and four died. The Spanish-American War brought feverish new production. On April 29, 1899, a building called the "Doghouse" blew up, killing a man named McGill. The record is clear that for the entire course of the nineteenth century casualties at Du Pont included a heavily disproportionate number of Irish, almost all of whom were either immigrants or sons of immigrants. More than Irish luck was needed to work at Du Pont on the Brandywine and stay alive.[3]

In 1895 a writer for *McClure's Magazine* in an article entitled "Life and Work in the Powder Mills" took a bucolic view of such employment. "They are perfectly happy, these stolid Irishmen, who go on risking their lives year after year, for about the same wages as are paid in less dangerous employment."[4] How stolid and happy the workers were is problematical at least. When other immigrants became available, the Irish at last moved out of the explosion zone at Du Pont. In an explosion in 1904 the first Italian names appear on the casualty lists.

The iron and steel mills of Philadelphia were another arena in which workers suffered high casualties. Rebecca Harding Davis, writing in the *Atlantic Monthly* in April 1861, caught the sombre spectacle of men trooping from the mills: "Masses of men, with dull, besotted faces bent to the ground, sharpened here or there by pain or cunning; skin and muscle and flesh begrimed with smoke and ashes; stooping all night over boiling cauldrons of metal, laired by day in dens of drunkenness and infamy, breathing from infancy an air saturated with fog and grease and soot. . . ."[5] This was the atmosphere of the workers who came home through the little streets of Nicetown in Northwest Philadelphia where the coal and ore brought by the Pennsylvania Railroad was fired and forged into iron and steel.

In 1867 the Butcher Steel Works was set up above Nicetown not far from the Germantown wagon road. This firm was the predecessor of the mighty Midvale Steel Company that would forge the steel used to construct the technological wonder of the Brooklyn Bridge and tens of thousands of miles of rails, pipes, girders, and trusses. The first records of the mills were kept by Mickey Kelley, and among the earliest employees were Peter McAnally and John Slattery. McAnally would be in the mills a full fifty years, and how he stood it only the tough old-timers could understand.[6]

For generations the heavy-metals industry would have a harrowing record of injuries that placed it just below coal mining in the casualties it exacted. Midvale Steel's own history of its growth characterized its early operations as "reckless and wanting in system."[7] Daniel Kane O'Donnell, a Philadelphia writer, in 1863 penned a poem called "The Song of the Iron and the Song of the Slave" that portrays the open-hearth and blooming mills:

> "O'er flaming, roaring forges
> The dingy rafters are
> Black with a sooty midnight
> And red with sun nor star,
> Where toil the iron workers
> In leathern guise and grim

As bounds the heavy hammer,
Resounds their sturdy hymn."[8]

By 1877 such accidents as the extensive oil fire that shut down the Midvale Works that year were thought to be ordinary hazards of the business. In 1880 the company set up a special bed in Germantown Hospital with a special ambulance to serve the mill. The conditions that produced accidents were studied by Frederick W. Taylor, the apostle of scientific management, who came to work at Midvale in 1879. The work day was from 6:30 A.M. to 5:10 P.M. The handling of raging furnaces, molten metal, flaming ingots, and white-hot forgings was carried out on superheated, slippery work floors where showers of seething sparks, constant clouds of smoke, and infernal noise created a bedlam of distraction and danger. Under this system, Taylor found, the speeding up of work required bargaining with or coercing the workers involved. More often than not these men tried to slow down the work in self-defense.[9] Working under such conditions led the men at times to drink heavily, and in 1881 superintendents were instructed to bar from jobs those who were absent for drunkenness. They were also ordered to report all accidents "at once," since there had been delays and cover-ups after accidents.[10]

In the 1870s and 1880s the Irish were the largest ethnic group in employ at Midvale. As the largest immigrant group in the city they especially supplied the unskilled labor for its heavy industries. This custom continued up until the turn of the century, when Eastern Europeans were employed in greater numbers. Company records of long-term employees retiring in the 1920s show the work force to be at least half Irish in earlier decades.[11] These men were oven tenders, chippers, grinders, firemen, and laborers.

The confrontation of Frederick Taylor with this work force in the 1880s was precipitated when he introduced his famous "speedup" tactics and tried to rationalize production. His tactics, such as redesign of shovels to permit heavier amounts to be lifted and mechanical prescriptions for human motion, earned him the hatred of his worker guinea pigs. His methods were arbitrary and authoritarian in the extreme, and at one point workers threatened to shoot him.[12]

Just how dangerous steel and iron manufacture was is high-
lighted by the investigations of the U.S. Immigration Commission.
Although the Commission studies of immigrants in the industry
took place for several years prior to 1910, the working conditions
they portray for Eastern and Southern European workers were
actually somewhat better than those which obtained during the
years when the Irish were more numerous in the labor force of the
mills. Conditions were so dangerous that it mattered little at what
level of skill the men were employed in the steel mills. "It seems to
be true," the Commission reported, "that the skilled occupations
are more dangerous than the unskilled." In one year the several
mills studied produced an average casualty list of 295 a month.
Wounds, burns, sprains, eye injuries, fractures, and amputations
were part of the toll taken to forge the iron and steel produced.[13]

For workers who spent most of their lives at Midvale the sights
and sounds of mill accidents must have left a grim imprint upon
their minds. The records list Hugh Dougherty retiring on total
disability after being an over tender for twenty-nine years; Michael
Gallagher, a fireman for thirty years; Hugh Cummings, a chipper
for thirty-seven years; and Michael Melloy, a laborer at the plant
for fifty years.[14] These men were the lucky ones. They had outlived
the brutal regime of Frederick Taylor, and they had not been
blinded, crippled, maimed, or debilitated and thus forced to quit
work early in their lives.

It is important that consideration of dangerous working conditions among immigrants not omit allusion to the perils surrounding
the largely female work forces in textile mills. The atmosphere in
these mills was usually filled with particles of lint that frequently
led to respiratory ailments. In some mills the air also had to be
kept humid so that the fiber would not dry out and break in the
spinning and weaving process. The noise of the machines, which
even to this day produces "weaver's deafness," was even greater in
the last century, and partial or total hearing loss was quite common
among workers. Long hours, poor sanitation facilities, bad ventilation, and inadequate lighting added to the dangers of textile-mill
employment.[15]

In 1880 there were more than 120,000 women in the city who
were either Irish-born or the daughters of Irish-born parents. Of

the 18,000 women engaged in textile work at that time, it can be estimated that about half were drawn from this large Irish female labor pool. Census schedules show that whole neighborhoods in the city sent their able-bodied Irish girls into the mills. Many of these girls, of course, were children when they entered the dangers of the cloth factories.[16]

One of the most serious hazards of the textile industry for generations was fire. The storing of bales and bins of fiber was akin to storing tinder, especially in old, overcrowded, and badly ventilated mill lofts. Sparks or flames from various sources were hazardous enough, but the capacity of lint to explode in the air due to its own combustible nature added to the danger. In 1882 the Annual Report of the Mayor of Philadelphia listed twelve major textile-mill fires. The heavy cost of fires like the William Wood Company factory fire that year causing a total of more than $300,000 in damage is indicative of the scale of this peril. A single fire at the Campbell and Company Mill in South Philadelphia caused $240,500 damage. Randolph Mills burned, and nine deaths resulted due to inadequate fire escapes. The owner, Joseph Harvey, was indicted for manslaughter, but this was unusual.

Such huge employment systems as the railroads also had shocking records of accidents and injuries among workers. In 1879 the records of the Coroner of Philadelphia showed that of 1,390 violent deaths of all kinds 72 were caused by railroad mishaps. The casualties occurring throughout the city in all kinds of rough and dangerous work, however, are equally impressive. The work-related deaths read like battle-casualty reports from the great industrial war front where moving materials and tending machines placed the Irish in the forefront of the fray. Here is a partial listing of the death toll in 1878 and the causes:

James Coyle—railroad accident
Michael McKeown—crushed by cotton bale
Patrick Waters and John Gallagher—blast furnace burns
John McCready—cave-in
Patrick McGarvey—run over by train
Daniel Reardon—run over by train
John McDermott—crushed at Brill Car Works

John Sherry—caught in wheel at Crowley's Mill
Francis Callahan—explosion at Elkins Oil Works
George Moore—derrick fell
James Cruise—cave-in
Charles Meenan—caught in machine
Owen McCullough—fall from scaffold
John Farrell—drowned off wharf
James Farrell—coal fall
Charles Cassidy—stone fall
Dan Crowley—rail accident

One scholar says that the railroads were "the leading violent killer in Philadelphia."[18]

The records of accident patients of the Pennsylvania Hospital as far back as 1854 show that approximately half the patients in the "Fracture Book" had Irish names and many suffered work-related bone breaks. The patient records from 1886 show Irish-named workers being injured by being run over by trains or by falls in construction work, losing limbs to machinery, having eye damage due to flying shuttles, being caught in balers, and being crushed by iron in foundries. The Pennsylvania Hospital cared for these same kinds of worker casualties year after year and had a heavily Irish clientele up through the 1890s, at which time Eastern and Southern European names become more frequent. The same was even more true of Saint Mary's Hospital, near the docks of the Delaware and the mill districts of North Philadelphia.[19] The Saint Mary's records of frostbite and *coup de soleil* (sunstroke) also remind us that in the 1800s workers were exposed much more severely to extremes of weather than in contemporary work life.

The persistence of an Irish group of highly vulnerable workers had, of course, a residential dimension as well. The 1910 reports of the U.S. Immigration Commission investigated several pockets of Irish concentration in North Philadelphia and the old community of Schuylkill. What investigators found was the worst kind of slum housing, with outside water faucets, outside toilets, open drains, and some of the houses built in excavations below the street level and in courts. Forty-four percent of the Irish males were laborers, and 24 percent of the employed females were domestics. One-fifth of the Irish could not read or write English, perhaps because they were Gaelic speakers. With such housing conditions added to bad working conditions, life for many surely seemed to be a trap, as some observers perceived. Dr. Charles K. Mills of Philadelphia Polytechnic and College for Graduates in Medicine had stated that neurasthenia, which he defined as a breakdown of personality in the environment of industrialism, was widespread.[20]

To those Irish removed from their stricken native culture and exposed to the hardships and perils of the industrial system, it would not matter greatly that one of their number, James F. Sullivan of County Cork, would become a vice-president of Midvale Steel. The distance between his success and their condition was too obvious. Daniel Kane O'Donnell in a bit of sentimental poetry caught something of the pathos of their condition. Writing of a slum street in Philadelphia absurdly called Paradise Alley, he pictured its working-class children:

> So, upward and downward they run and they dally,
> Dishevelled and ragged, in Paradise Alley!
> Poor children, I wonder what fate will be yours
> When, like father and mother, you go from the doors?
> Here Biddy played truant, but now for her bread
> She frets and she wrinkles with thimble and thread;
> And Michael the laborer worn with his load,
> With a sunstroke at noon-day fell down in the road.
> So we laugh, so we weep—thus I think as I sally—
> 'Tis the way of the world, and of Paradise Alley.[21]

These sentimental lines are, of course, an inadequate reflection of the grim reality. However, we Americans with our ideas of "progress" generally sentimentalize the past and the achievements of technology and industry. We emphasize our great positive growth and expansion, but we have too long been unable or unwilling to count its human costs, costs such as those borne by the workers recalled in this chapter.

NOTES

1. James B. Gilbert, *Work without Salvation: America's Intellectuals and Industrial Alienation, 1880–1910* (Baltimore, Md.: Johns Hopkins University Press, 1977), p. xiii.

2. This calculation is based on an adaptation of statistics from tables in W. E. Vaugh and A. J. Fitzpatrick, eds., *Irish Historical Statistics* (Dublin: Royal Irish Academy, 1978), pp. 259–67.

3. Data on these explosions is drawn from the collection at the Eleutherian–Hagley Mills Historical Library, Greenville, Del., of the Lammot Du Pont Papers, Box 27, Series B, and Box 52, Explosion Records (1882–1902), and Boxes 59–G-69 and 42-1 (1805–26); Glen Howard Prior, "Workers' Lives at the DuPont Powder Mills, 1887–1912," Bachelors thesis, University of Delaware, 1977, pp. 3–61. A celebratory volume, *Du Pont: The Autobiography of an American Enterprise* (New York: Charles Scribner's Sons, 1952), p. 19, states that, although neither laws nor customs of the times required it, the company did award pensions to the survivors' families after the explosion of 1818. The book gives the toll killed as forty. It also notes that the workers were largely without outside contact even in the 1880s.

4. Prior, "Workers Lives at the Du Pont Powder Mills," p. 27.

5. Rebecca Harding, "Life in the Mills," *Atlantic Monthly*, vol. 7, no. 42 (April 1861).

6. *The Midvale Steel Company Fiftieth Anniversary 1867–1917* (Philadelphia: The Midvale Steel Company, 1917), p. 10.

7. Ibid., p. 12.

8. Daniel Kane O'Donnell, *The Song of the Iron and the Song of the Slaves and Other Poems* (Philadelphia: King and Baird, 1863).

9. Frederick W. Taylor, *Shop Management* (New York: Harper and Brothers, 1912), p. 44.

10. Midvale Steel Company Papers, Journal of Activities (1876–1887), The Franklin Institute, Philadelphia, Pa. Entries for December 28, 1881, and February 1, 1884.

11. Midvale Steel Company Papers, Box 1, List of retirees.

12. Daniel Nelson, "Taylorism and the Workers at Bethlehem Steel," *Pennsylvania Magazine of History and Briography* 101, no. 4 (October 1977): 488; Sudhir Kahar, *Frederick Taylor: A Study in Personality and Innovation* (Cambridge, Mass.: MIT Press, 1970), p. 59.

13. Report of the U.S. Immigration Commission, Sixty-First Congress, Second Session (1910), Committee on Immigration (Washington, D.C.: U.S. Government Printing Office, 1911), vol. 70, pp. 383–84.

14. Midvale Steel Company Papers, Box 1, List of retirees.

15. Daniel Nelson, *Managers and Workers: Origins of the New Factory System in the United States, 1880–1920* (Madison, Wis.: University of Wisconsin Press, 1975), pp. 11–33.

16. The U.S. Census of Population (1880) and the U.S. Census of Manufacturing (1870–1880) as analyzed by the Philadelphia Social History Project are the source of the total female estimate, and the numbers of Irish females in textiles are the author's estimate. The Census of Manufacturing for 1880 is not broken down ethnically. Anthony F. C. Wallace in his study of early textile employment discusses uncleanliness, long hours, and moral hazards but not dangers from machinery or unhealthful conditions. See Anthony F. C. Wallace, *Rockdale* (New York: Alfred A. Knopf, 1978), pp. 330–31, 365–69, 388–94.

17. Report of Mayor Samuel G. King for 1882, City of Philadelphia, Archives of the City of Philadelphia, and *City of Firsts* (Philadelphia: Historical Publication Society, 1926), pp. 370–72.

18. *Records of Coroner of the City of Philadelphia 1878–80*, Archives of the City of Philadelphia, and Roger Lane, *Violent Death in the City* (Cambridge, Mass.: Harvard University Press, 1979), pp. 38–39.

19. Fractures Book, vol. I (1854–56); Patients Records of Accidents, vol. I (1886–70); Casualty Book, vol. II (1885–87); Casualty Book (1899–1900); Archives of the Pennsylvania Hospital, Philadelphia; *Third Annual Report, St. Mary's Hospital, 1870* (Philadelphia: Hardy and Mahony, 1871).

20. Reports of the U.S. Immigration Commission, Immigration in Cities, Sixty-First Congress, Second Session Committee on Immigration (1920; Washington, D.C.: Government Printing Office, 1911), vol. 66, pp. 352–399, 420.

21. O'Donnell, *The Song of the Iron*, pp. 70–71.

PART II: **Putting Coin on Coin**

The enterprise of immigrants in the "Age of Enterprise" in the second half of the nineteenth century in some cases produced great fortunes. For others, however, business remained limited, part of the small business tradition of America. The way in which immigrants specialized and worked their way into the fabric of urban economics has not received much attention because most study has been focused on large businesses and the most successful undertakings. However, the small business experience of urban entrepreneurs was much more typical of immigrant activity, and it is in such enterprises that immigrants excelled because of their tutelage in village economies in the old country and their preoccupation with ethnic ties in their local communities.

The three chapters that follow deal with Irish-American business traditions that became identified with the Irish as a group and that became part of the institutional pattern of the city's life. The saloon keeper, the travel agent, and the building contractor were each intimately involved with the needs of their ethnic community, and their functions fitted into the growing elaboration of American urban economics.

4 The Shebeen as an Institution

The word *shebeen*, meaning "a drinking place," has come into English from the Gaelic *seibin*, a word for a little mug or jug that was a measure of ale in Ireland in the eighteenth century. Through usage the word came to mean small beer or cheap ale and a place where such fermentations are available. The term *shebeen* has been used wherever the Irish have found themselves. An acquaintance once related that when he wished a drink on the docks of Shanghai, having no facility in Chinese, he made a gesture mimicking the process of taking a glass of spirits, and a Chinese sailor immediately said, "Ah, Shebeen!" and pointed to a nearby establishment. The blacks in South Africa, a people as exploited in the twentieth century as the Irish were in the nineteenth, refer to their local drinking places as shebeens.

The social roots of the Irish tradition of keeping shebeens and purveying potables go deep into Ireland's history.[1] If the Irish did not invent whiskey, or *uisge baugh* ("water of life"), their language gave the drink its most expressive name. Part of the explanation of the beverage tradition of the Irish is due to their distinctive heritage of hospitality. Gaelic literature is full of the theme of hospitality and its obligations, and several Gaelic epics revolve around the theme. Over the centuries all the ingenious fermentations and distillations from grains and fruits made their way into Ireland, and a brisk wine trade with Spain and Holland was part of the seaport life of Ireland's coastal cities. When the potato was introduced from the New World, whiskey was made from that tuber as well. Whether in the family, at a feast, or at a fair, pledges and bargains were sealed with a toast, and a full life meant a full glass for all.

When English administration finally penetrated Ireland in the eighteenth century, officials did what they always do with respect to distillation: they proceeded to regulate and tax it. This regulation was resented by the Irish, and they carried on illicit whiskey making with a relish. The devastation of Gaelic culture under English rule removed the context and constraints governing drink among the Gaels, and this removal may have contributed toward excessive drinking, or at least toward a cultural distress that encouraged excessive intake.

Not much real information about the abuse of alcohol has been compiled for earlier times, but the national misfortunes of the seventeenth and eighteenth centuries and the increased availability of various beverages seem to have combined to promote alcoholic excess in the same way as is depicted by Hogarth and Mayhew among the English poor. Foreign rule consigned the Irish to poverty and exploitation. The psychological depression induced by low status and frustrated hopes joined with poverty to produce a cult of alcoholic indulgence.[2]

The Irish climate, dark, full of chill and damp in winter, and rainy even in the summer, is often cited as a contributing factor to the cult of drink. The diet of rural and urban Irish working people, never very elaborate, may also have played a role in encouraging reliance on beverages. The structure of Irish villages and towns, with their crowded and inadequate housing and scarcity of recreational facilities, provided conditions in which the shebeen or drinking place could become the central socializing influence for adults.

The increasing emigration in the nineteenth century resulted in the separation of families, estrangements, and often a melancholy loneliness. In some areas a depopulation occurred that left only the very young and the very old at home. This occurrence surely added to the reliance on drink as a sedative and palliative for loneliness. The rural poverty that compelled delayed and late marriages was another part of the loneliness quotient that could not be offset by the traditional sociability of the people.[3]

The bulk of the Irish Catholics were excluded from most small businesses by the active religious discrimination enforced by both English officials and their Protestant allies in Ireland. Small businesses and skilled trades were difficult for Catholics to penetrate, and they tended to cluster in marginal enterprises.

Operating illegal stills or drinking establishments was one of the few small-business options open to Catholics in many towns and villages. Successful pub keepers became the models of affluence and leadership in a land where only the priest had stood out among Catholics as a leadership figure. Thus, saloon keepers also became community fixtures in the American settings where the Irish found themselves in the great period of emigration of the nineteenth century.[4]

After the onset of the great tide of Irish emigration in the early nineteenth century, the Irish drinking places, already a common sight on the American scene, gathered new attributes. The saloons and taverns of the American-Irish became crucial centers for referral of immigrants to employment. In an age when employment agencies and labor exchanges did not exist, the saloons filled their roles. The immigrants were predominantly single males during long periods of the extensive Irish immigration process: the "boys" needed some social facility to form their group ties and give them word of work, and the saloon served these purposes well.[5] During the later Victorian period, when segregation of the sexes was the rule in much of daily life, the drinking place became a bastion of male dominance and exclusivity.

The organization of immigrants to exercise the franchise and assert their grievances in political action took place with the saloon providing a focus for political leadership and communication. It was a shy saloon keeper indeed who did not give some form of political shoulder to local party politics. The saloon served also as a rallying point for Irish nationalist sentiment and stimulation. The broader American society was largely oblivious to this function, but it was central to Irish-American ethnic identity. Just as underground Irish nationalist groups sought refuge in selected local pubs, so the labor-union enthusiasts, regarded by law and society as conspirators and radical anarchists, found safe haven among the workers at the bar.[6]

The saloon was a locus for sporting talk and sport teams as well. Ambitious saloon keepers frequently organized teams to further their prestige and trade. It is notable that many sports were illegal in the nineteenth century, including horse racing, cockfighting and prize fighting, and practitioners and followers of such sports did find sympathetic allies where males congregated to drink. The association with illegal sports prompted association with other illegal activities, and saloons gained their reputations in a Protestant society as dens of iniquity. Not only was the "devil's brew" served in them, but all manner of illicit pleasure was thought to be purveyed in them as well.

Add to all this the simple need of the Irish to indulge their renowned facility for table talk, storytelling, oratory, and gossip, and their irrepressible convivial disposition, and it is obvious that the saloon served them as an important, familiar, and attractive institution. In the immigrant areas where work was hard, housing inadequate to outrageous, and accessible entertainment limited, the saloon was a powerful resort for men torn from their native environments and cast into American cities.

For the enterprising Irish man, one of the advantages of going into the tavern business was that it required only a modest capital investment. Indeed the stories of tavernkeepers who began operation solely with what bottles they had on the shelf behind the bar are legion. In the early and more rustic days of the nineteenth century, two barrels with a board across their tops often constituted a bar. Nor did the business require any great formal education, although some education about human nature was of paramount importance. If a man had the ability to count money and stand up before customers and had an even disposition and a sense of humor, he could make a go of a shebeen. It must be remembered that women, too, were not uncommon in the business, usually as widows or daughters who inherited family enterprises. There were, of course, madams whose ancient profession involved them with saloons, and in cities like Philadelphia the business of prostitution was for two generations a largely Irish activity.[7]

Early records of tavern and liquor businesses give evidence of Irish enterprise in the field. On the frontier where Ulster Irish Protestants were creating a legend of their own ferocious prowess, distillation of whiskey was an avid occupation from the earliest days right through the Whiskey Rebellion in 1794 and well beyond. The Appalachian tradition of whiskey making has been long and venerable and owes much to the Ulster emigrants and run-away Irish indentured servants of the eighteenth century.[8]

In the cities, according to Carl Bridenbaugh, "The tavern was the most flourishing of all urban institutions." It is interesting to note the extent to which the caucuses and drafting sessions of much of our Revolutionary period took place in taverns, "The tavern was probably the most important social institution in the little seaports" of America, Bridenbaugh asserts.[9] In Philadelphia where the Revolution had its climax, the local taverns as early as 1758 included Isabella Barry's "The Faithful Irishman" in Strawberry Alley; "The Lamb," owned by Francis O'Skullion, at Second and Lombard Street; and the "Three Jolly Irishmen" at Water and Race Streets.[10]

By 1820 the Irish immigration to the city had increased, and the Southwark district was a heavily Irish community. That district had a total of eighty-three liquor licenses granted in 1820 by the Quarter Sessions Court of Philadelphia in its March term alone. Thirty-one licenses went to people with clearly recognizable Irish names, such as Michael Cavanaugh at South and Queen Street, Patrick Duffy at Second and Plumb Street, and Susannah Ennis at Front and Almond Street. Of all the liquor licenses granted in 1820 by the court—which numbered 527—82, or about one-fifth, went to Irish-named people.[11] This is a conservative estimate because a number of English- or Scandinavian-sounding names would also be borne by Irish. It is apparent that the Irish were predominant in the shebeen business early in the city's history. Their business did not proceed without criticism, for even before 1820 foes of liquor were pamphleteering against it. John Watson in 1813 penned a tract entitled *An Alarming Portraiture of the Pernicious Effects of the Customary Use of Distilled Spirituous Liquors.*[12] Such works were only the leading edge of a long and vigorous prohibition tradition.

As American society became more conscious of itself, antiliquor sentiment and the refinement of public policy resulted in an increasing amount of legislation designed to control the tavern business. In Kensington, which was a separate local jurisdiction within Philadelphia County until 1854, the legislation to control taverns was adopted in 1819, then revised in 1834 and again in 1841. The ordinances applying to "Taverns and Tippling Houses" provided for penalties against tavern keepers who promoted "games of hazard, cock-fighting . . . or horse racing" or served any spirits to persons assembled for such amusements. Also forbidden were bowling and shuffleboard. Tavern keepers were forbidden to "receive, harbor, entertain or trust any person under the age of twenty-one years or any apprentice or servant" under penalty of stiff fines. Constables in charge of enforcing this law were themselves subject to fine for disregarding it.[13] The Kensington district was heavily Irish by the late 1840s and was the scene of the original anti-Catholic and largely anti-Irish riots in 1844. One of the important stimulants to Protestant hostility toward the Irish Catholics was the identification of the latter with the whiskey business. Protestant clergy preached against this threat to what they saw as the pure morality of the Protestant republic founded by their forefathers.[14]

The terrible conditions of the immigrant ghettos of the mid-nineteenth century swelled the ranks of those whose opinion identified immigrants with grog shops and drunken dissipation and who traced the misfortunes of the immigrants to the booze business. Saloon keepers had to deal not only with Protestant crusades but with Catholic Total Abstinence Brotherhoods and temperance societies that received strong backing from the Catholic clergy.[15] These antiliquor crusades often drew on the energies of stern female supporters, and the custom of solemnly visiting the parish rectory to "take the pledge" in the presence of the priest was endorsed by several generations of matrons worried by their husband's drinking.

The Catholic temperance movement of the 1870s was a particularly vigorous movement. The *Philadelphia Times* editorialized in 1875 after a huge temperance parade, "Intemperance has been the Irishman's greatest enemy for many generations, and it is most inspiriting to see these thousands of young men united in a manly fight against it."[16] *Our Union*, publication of the Women's Christian Temperance Union, in 1876 saw a convergence of social forces acting to subvert the liquor trade: "Thus, religion, the spirit of the age and material interests of society all point to the repression of intoxicants."[17] The *Philadelphia Press*, a paper more tolerant of saloon culture, however, carried advertisements that stated, "If a man wants a bottle of whiskey, let him buy it and take it home, and not sneak home with a bottle of 'bitters' or 'cordial.'"[18]

The tavern business was often blended with the hotel business, and in Boyd's *Philadelphia City Directory* for 1877 the two kinds of businesses were listed together in natural affinity. Of the 327 enterprises listed, one-eighth had Irish-named proprietors or operators. Irish men and women on the move or recently arrived in the country could find shelter and refreshment at these premises, which were located from one end of the city to the other.[19]

Saloon keepers in the vice districts and waterfront areas of the city were frequently the toughest of the tough, and they were the subject of scathing propaganda by prohibitionists and anti-immigrant and anti-Irish zealots. In 1881 a political satire was published in Philadelphia by Henry C. Lea under a pseudonym as part of a campaign against municipal corruption. The prejudicial and anti-Irish character of the book, called *Solid for Mulhooly*, is manifest throughout. It purports to be the history of a crooked Irish politician. It was republished in 1889 with cartoons by Thomas Nast that skillfully express its ethnic venom. One cartoon entitled "His First School" shows Mulhooly as a child seated in a bar inhabited by several unlovely types. Another cartoon captioned "His Paddy-gree" shows an infant Mulhooly in a pigsty brandishing a whiskey bottle. Andrew Sinclair in his study of prohibitionism, *The Era of Excess*, details how distorted much of the antiliquor propaganda was.[20]

Richard Stivers, who has analyzed Irish drinking habits, attributes much of the faithful saloon clientele to the retarded family formation that kept young males footloose. All-male groups formed for mutual consolation and used the shebeen for their celibate emotional retreat. The extended adolescence of these single males led to demonstrative drinking competitions at worst and steady habitual drinking as the norm. Large numbers of unattached males in the Irish immigrant population all too easily fit into this pattern.[21] The ravages of liquor were evident, but the biases of its foes were often less evident because they were cloaked in religious or medical garb. There were plenty of rascals in the saloon trade, but the saloon was such a widespread institution and so familiar to so many that it could hardly have had such a broad and persistent patronage among men of high and low degree if it were not on the whole run by decent men deserving of common approbation.

A fairly common family saloon career is represented by the enterprise of Edward J. Trainer. The son of immigrants from Omagh, County Tyrone, Trainer was raised in the dockside area of Port Richmond on the Delaware. He married Ann Mulgrew, whose family was from Pomeroy in County Tyrone. In 1863, with $200 capital, the couple opened a saloon in the front room to their row house at 804 South Front Street in the old Southwark section of the city. The first day's receipts were thirty-six cents. Whiskey sold at three cents a glass. Protestant neighbors boycotted the saloon and shunned the Trainers, so Edward had to work as a house painter to make ends meet.

Trainer informed Hugh O'Donnell, the largest liquor dealer in the area, of the boycott, and O'Donnell arranged to have the members of the Saint Philip's Parish Literary Institute meet at the fledgling saloon keeper's place. Next came Fenian Mike Donahue, a roaring character, who—on his own whim—obligingly wrecked a competing neighboring saloon at 809 South Front Street in a brawl.

In 1864 Trainer branched out into the wholesale liquor business and purchased various properties and liquor dealer O'Donnell's estate. He prospered and the family grew to include nine children. Edward's brother James had gone to sea out of Port Richmond, but with Edward's aid James decided to open a saloon at Twelfth and Federal streets and another in Port Richmond. Another brother, John, was in the business at Sixteenth and Stiles streets. Through these family connections Edward's wholesale business spread. Frank Trainer, still another brother of the family, returned from a sailor's life and opened a saloon with a "summer garden" at 909 Sansom Street, which became a favorite haunt of sportsmen, ballplayers, and the pugilist John L. Sullivan.

In 1888 high license fees were imposed on the city's 5,500 saloons. In addition, wholesale and retail liquor businesses were forbidden by law to operate together. Edward Trainer stuck with the wholesale trade and gave his retail interests into the care of his son, Henry, who at twenty-one became the youngest saloon keeper in Philadelphia. Henry and others in the family suffered with the high license fees. James and Frank Trainer left the city for Camden and New York, where they entered business. Edward Trainer, however, was in a position to aid saloon keepers who were starting out, and although the Trainers were Democrats, he led them in tavern keepers' political fights as Republicans in the Third Ward to defend the saloon business. Through his business and political ties Edward Trainer finally went into the distilling business in the 1890s.

The careers of the Trainers indicate the way in which family ties linked the Irish in the widely separated areas of the city in which they lived and had their saloons. The pressure of prohibitionists for such measures as high license fees for saloons strongly influenced saloon keepers in their participation in politics.[22]

In the 1880s Philadelphia had a number of downtown saloons that had become the resorts of political leaders, journalists, and professional men. Near the financial and hotel district were Martin Burn's at Seventh and Chestnut and Dooner's at Eighth and Chestnut. Across from the State House (Independence Hall) on Chestnut was Charlie McShain's. Joe Madden's at Eighth and Sansom was a newspaperman's hangout, as was Alex McCuen's at Eleventh and Chestnut.[23] Such saloons represented an evolution beyond the immigrant bars and neighborhood workingman's tap-rooms that the Irish had so assiduously established. These down-town oases featured good food, magnificent mahogany bars, elaborate Victorian decor, and singing waiters, as well as quiet meeting rooms where politics and high policy could be discussed. Paintings over the bar might portray the Lakes of Killarney, the Vale of Avoca, and scantily clad maidens with the buxom proportions beloved at the time, as well as pugilist heroes, famous horses, and racing dogs. Some saloons painted favorite stanzas on the bar mirror, such as:

> Romantic Ireland never dies,
> She lives beyond all time.
> The bread of angels gives her strength,
> The blood of martyrs is her wine.

Election posters, Irish Land League meeting notices, framed stories from the sporting pages, and honors bestowed by the Ancient Order of Hibernians were all placed so that they became the objects of the gazes of reflective imbibers.

In the Gay Nineties, Irish saloon culture was probably at its highest peak. A sample of the hundreds of liquor licenses issued in 1888 shows that more than one-third went to Irish-named individuals.[24] A whole almanac of Irish meetings, observances, and organizational campaigns generated caucuses, committee sessions, and lobbying activities in saloons. A perusal of the *Philadelphia Hibernian* newspaper in the 1890s shows dozens of saloon advertisements of places where members of the Irish Catholic Benevolent Union chapters could meet or where enthusiasts of the twenty-four Irish Land League branches could gather before and after official meetings.[25]

The Shebeen keeper learned, through hard experience, a catechism of admonitions, such as:

Never hire relatives, and don't trust the ones your wife makes you hire.

When you're closed, you're closed. *Everybody* out.

When women ask, say, "He's not here."

Always treat a priest.

Don't let women stand at the bar. [prior to the 1920s]

Cash checks quietly, and don't trust a drinker.

Don't fight with cops. Pay them.

Tavern-keepers associations came and went through much of the nineteenth century, largely in response to prohibitionist campaigns. In 1907, however, there arose an organization concerning itself with the problems of regulation that were routine features of the liquor business by then and which were becoming enforced with increasing vigor. The Philadelphia Retail Liquor Dealers Association founded in 1907 originally had sixty-five members, all but fourteen of them Irish.[26] Under its president, Thomas P. Watson, it grew, for by 1918 there were more than 1700 liquor dealers listed in Boyd's *Philadelphia Business Directory* and almost one-third of them had Irish names. However, prohibition sentiment was growing also, and it portended disaster for hundreds of saloon keepers.[27]

Prohibition hit the saloon industry in 1920 like an avalanche. Men who had been prosperous businessmen one day were tradeless bankrupts the next. The Protestant and fundamentalist sentiment behind the banning of spirits was like a whirlwind, and the Irish reacted to it with a tempest of their own. Not only were saloons as retail liquor outlets affected, but political and nationalist meetings had to be relocated. Irish musicians and singers whose chief loci for performance were drinking places had their circuit interrupted. The social lives of both bachelors and married men were interdicted. The resulting rage was momentous. The antagonism toward the Protestant apostles of the dry crusade was long frustrated and did not really find an outlet until the candidacy of Alfred E. Smith for the presidency in 1928, when Irish Catholics found a wet leader.

Not every Irish saloon keeper was willing to wither into dry desiccation under the reign of prohibitionist virtue, however. Many simply went underground and opened speakeasies. The true effect of Prohibition, though, was to democratize the making and purveying of liquor. The trade was taken out of the hands of businesspersons and put up for grabs in a welter of illegal and spontaneous operations. The Irish remained part of the underground flow of booze, but thousands of people joined in the bootlegging craze, and bootleggers large and small brought a great new miscellany to the beer and liquor field.

In Philadelphia the Irish bootleggers ranged from gangster chieftains, such as Eddie Regan, to a wide variety of home-brew specialists and energetic amateurs. The Liquor Seizure Docket of the Common Pleas Courts for 1924 and 1925 reveals a mad collection of portable potable schemes. Patrick J. Mulligan was forced to give up five cases of illicit whiskey on February 21, 1924. The next week Harry Flanagan was caught with nine boxes of beer, and John Dougherty surrendered sixty-four pints. On April 25 James Murphy was caught next to his thirty-gallon copper still, and on the same day Harry Burke gave up to the law forty-five barrels of beer. The truck of James Doyle with ten beer barrels was seized in

June, as was the Dodge sedan of Bernard Maguire, which held
three five-gallon casks. Several Irish taxi drivers lost their cabs
because they had turned them into mobile bars.[28] The ingenuity of
it all was endless. Some of the wiser heads knew that such an
unpopular law as Prohibition would be doomed eventually, and
they carefully amassed their resources, looking toward the day
when once again they could open business at a shiny mahogany bar
behind those happily swinging doors.

Deliverance was to be a long time coming, however, and it was
not until 1933 that the baneful Eighteenth Amendment outlawing
alcohol was repealed by the Twenty-first Amendment. Even then,
the spell cast by the righteous prohibitionists made people wary of
advertising drink. By the mid-1930s the telephone directory had
replaced the old city directories as a listing of businesses. The
Philadelphia Telephone Directory in 1937 had no listings for
saloons or bars or retail liquor dealers. Drinking places were listed
discreetly under "restaurant" or "café." If the listings are any
guide, the Irish lost a good bit of ground in the Prohibition years
and had not recovered by the Depression period. Only about 100 of
the more than 1,000 "restaurants" listed have recognizable Irish
names, and only about one-sixth of the 300 "cafés."[29]

The Irish, forced into a minority position in the field they had
dominated before Prohibition, had difficulty adjusting to the new
situation after 1933. Two tavern-keepers' associations were the
result. The Philadelphia Tavern Association was formed in 1935
by Leo Sullivan, Patrick Dillon, James Haggerty, Patrick O'Connor, and James Lavin. The strength of the organization was in
heavily Irish West Philadelphia. The older Retail Liquor Dealers
Association became the rival group, but it also had some Irish
members. The split lasted until 1950 when Patrick Cavanaugh,
owner of the Railroad Bar at Thirtieth and Market streets, a
revered haunt of newspapermen, post-office employees, and railroad workers, took the situation in hand. The United Tavern
Owners Association brought the two factions together.[30]

The Irish saloons of Philadelphia added something special to the
social constitution of the city. Much of the population of the city
lived in stable row-house neighborhoods until the great suburbanization after World War II. At the ends of these row-house blocks

were corner locations where, in addition to grocery stores and tailors, saloons flourished. From them generations of Catholics carried home the "fish on Friday" fare of old-style Catholicism. This fried seafood, oyster chowder, and snapper soup was the delicious folk food that came with end-of-the-week paydays and weekend celebrations with beer before, during, and after. A Pennsylvania peculiarity also led to a whole range of "drinking clubs" that were variants on the saloon. Up until the 1960s saloons had to shut tight on Sundays, an injunction imposed on the entire state by rural fundamentalists who dominated the legislature. The clubs were conceived to be "private" and not businesses under the law, hence they could function on Sundays. In Philadelphia "Sunday drinking clubs" abounded. Because Irish Catholics went to Mass on Sunday morning, many of these clubs were close to churches. After all, men with only one or two days off from work a week were not disposed to waste half of a Sunday in isolation. These clubs were ethnic, political, social, and in some cases, religious.

Many formed the network for the city's magnificent New Year's Day Mummers Parade, for their members spent months annually planning and making the needed costumes and practicing parade music. The neighborhood "drinking clubs" were the headquarters of mutual-aid societies, civic groups, ward politics, immigrant networks, and fraternal organizations. They were part of the institutional fabric that held the city together.

The advent of such phenomena as the singles bar and the disco bar in the 1970s was viewed with some disdain by the Irish tavern owners. The habitats of male fraternity and serious sipping were threatened by such noisy innovations. Yet Philadelphia's working-class neighborhoods had bars that retained their old character. Many were the resorts of the still-active Irish immigrant communities, although some were touched up to be as nostalgic as old movie sets. When the *Philadelphia Inquirer* columnist John Corr did a Saint Patrick's Day story on the city's Irish bars in 1978, he found that McGillin's founded in the 1860s, was still going strong on Drury Lane in center city. McGlinchey's, Kelly's (under non-Irish owners), and the fashionable new Downey's in Society Hill, Gavin's bar in Schuylkill, O'Hara's in West Philadelphia, "Kelly's

Happy Tap" in Fishtown, and the "Mollie Maguire" in Kensington were all hot as boiler rooms with thirsty celebrants. Even in the outer reaches of the city and into the suburbs the Irish bars were local landmarks.[31] The shebeen tradition, after two centuries of purveying potables to travelers, laboring men, political stalwarts, and just plain thirsty citizens, was alive and well in Philadelphia.

NOTES

1. K. H. Connell, *Irish Peasant Society* (London: Oxford University Press, 1968), pp. 1–50.

2. For examples see L. M. Cullen, *Life in Ireland* (London: B. T. Batsford, 1968), p. 108; R. B. McDowell, "Ireland on the Eve of the Famine," in R. Dudley Edwards and T. Desmond Williams, *The Great Famine* (Dublin: Browne and Nolan, 1956) pp. 38–39.

3. Illegal distillation is portrayed in William Carleton's novel *The Emigrants of Ahadarra*, in *The Works of William Carleton*, 3 vols. (New York: P. F. Collier 1881), 2: 508. Hugh Brody's *Irishkillane: Change and Decline in the West of Ireland* (London: Penguin Press, 1973) gives a fine description of the social and economic conditions and the drinking habits that accompany them.

4. Carl Wittke, *The Irish in America* (Baton Rouge, La.: Louisiana State University Press, 1956), pp. 182–83.

5. William V. Shannon, *The American Irish* (New York: The Macmillan Company, 1963), pp. 40 and 80; Andrew Sinclair, *The Era of Excess* (New York: Harper and Row, 1962), pp. 74–76.

6. For many years the Irish-American Club on Arch Street in Philadelphia was the focus of nationalist activities where the secret Clan na Gael met in the 1880s and 1890s. The Federation of Irish Societies met for a generation in the same building as the Tavern Owners Association on North Broad Street. Joseph McGarrity, powerful Clan na Gael leader in the early twentieth century, owned several saloons.

7. Sinclair, *The Era of Excess*, p. 78; Dennis Clark, *The Irish in Philadelphia* (Philadelphia: Temple University Press, 1974), pp. 130–31.

8. Joseph Earl Dabney, *Mountain Spirits: A Chronicle of Corn Whiskey from King James Ulster Plantation to America's Appalacians* (New York: Charles Scribner's Sons, 1974), pp. 34–41.

9. Carl Bridenbaugh, *Cities in the Wilderness* (New York: Capricorn Books, 1968), pp. 107 and 15a.

10. John F. Watson, *Annals of Philadelphia and Pennsylvania*, 3 vols. (Philadelphia: Edwin S. Stuart, 1884), 3: 345.

11. Records of the Quarter Sessions Court of Philadelphia, 1820, Archives of the City of Philadelphia, City Hall Annex, Philadelphia.

12. (Philadelphia: Kimber and Conrad, 1813), in the Historical Society of Pennsylvania collection.

13. Elihu D. Tarr, *Digest of the Acts of Assembly Relating to the Kensington District of Northern Liberties* (Philadelphia: Isaac Ashmead, 1847), pp. 259–61.

14. Ray Allen Billington, *The Protestant Crusade: A Study of the Origins of American Nativism* (Chicago: Quadrangle Books, 1964), p. 195.

15. Ibid., p. 212, n.9. See also William J. McMullen, *An Appeal to the Taxpayers* (Philadelphia: Jared Craig, 1852).

16. *Philadelphia Times*, March 18, 1875.

17. *Our Union* (Philadelphia), October 1876.

18. *Philadelphia Press*, January 4, 1875.

19. William Boyd, *Philadelphia City Business Directory* (Philadelphia: Central News Company, 1877), pp. 299–303.

20. Rufus E. Shapley, *Solid For Mulhooly* (Philadelphia: Gebbie and Co., 1889).

21. Andrew Sinclair, *The Era of Excess*, pp. 36–62. Richard Stivers, *A Hair of the Dog: Irish Drinking and American Stereotypes* (University Park, Pa.: Pennsylvania State University Press, 1976), pp. 1–14.

22. Francis Trainer, "History of the Trainer Family," mimeographed (Philadelphia).

23. George Morgan, *City of Firsts: A Complete History of the City of Philadelphia* (Philadelphia: Historical Society of Philadelphia, 1926), p. 282; and Gerald Carson, Society of Philadelphia, 1926), p. 282; and Gerald Carson, "The Saloon," *American Heritage* 14, no. 3 April 1963: 25–31, 103.

24. Records of Liquor Licenses (1888), Archives of the City of Philadelphia, City Hall Annex, Philadelphia.

25. *Philadelphia Hibernian* (1893), Archives of the American Catholic Historical Society, Saint Charles Seminary, Overbrook, Pa.

26. Interview with John McMonagle, secretary of the United Tavern Owners Association of Philadelphia, March 6, 1978, Philadelphia.

27. William H. Boyd, *Philadelphia City Business Directory* (Philadelphia: C. E. Howe Co., 1918), pp. 2034–45.

28. Liquor Seizure Dockett 19 (1924–25), Common Pleas Court of the County of Philadelphia, Archives of the City of Philadelphia.

29. Pennsylvania Historical Society collection.

30. Interview with John McMonagle, March 6, 1978, Philadelphia.

31. John Corr, "Where to Go to Celebrate," *Philadelphia Inquirer*, March 17, 1978.

5   I'll Take You Home Again, Kathleen

In his songs and stories of exile Joe Heaney tells of the "American wakes" that he attended as a child. Heaney, a fine-looking man in his seventies, was born in County Galway to an Irish-speaking family, and he presents the ballads and tales of his early life in the *sean nos*, or old style, of grave and wonderfully entertaining monologue and song. To American audiences this traditional storyteller recounts the setting and circumstances of the highly emotional gatherings preceding the emigration to America of Irish family members through the early part of this century. He tells of how friends and relatives would gather and share nightlong hospitality in the home of the prospective emigrant. Such homes often enough would be impoverished thatched cottages set amid the rocky fields of Ireland's western counties. The merriment and dancing would gradually fade toward morning, and at last the young boy or girl emigrant would begin to move through the gathering saying farewell. As dawn would be breaking the person departing would have at last to take leave of parents and brothers and sisters amid tears and expressions of affection. Then the would-be emigrant would go off down the road, perhaps accompanied for a distance by those who wished in their hearts to postpone the final parting.[1]

This ritual leave-taking was a customary feature of Irish life for generations. Emigration was such a pervasive experience in Irish life that this folk ritual became a method for confronting it socially and emotionally. The wrenching emotional effect of the "American wake," however, was something that few emigrants would forget. Through the nineteenth and early twentieth century the stark impossibility of most of these emigrants' ever returning home gave the departure ritual a profoundly melancholy significance. Most Irish immigrants in America remained so poor in the nineteenth century that it was never possible for them to see their parents and birthplaces again. Efforts to save enough money for a passage home were constantly frustrated by other needs, such as expenses of marriage and setting up households, medical bills, and the strongly felt obligation to send remittances back to Ireland to help support the old people or to bring relatives out to America. Thus, for most of the Irish who came to the United States, emigration was final and permanent, and the prospect of returning to the old country was an unrealistic hope, a tantalizing dream.

Because humans are the complex creatures that they are, however, there was more than love and familial yearning mingled in the emigrants' fantasies about returning to Ireland. Some youngsters, and some husbands, ran away from their homes. No "American wake" for them, but a quick and stealthy departure. Boys fed up with the struggling labor in the fields or disappointed in love, girls sick of the rural loneliness, husbands bitter at the poverty or the wife's domineering relatives, all had real reasons for leaving. Emigrants such as these may not have been able to face the prospect of going back. Fear kept them away. Political exiles as well would not have been welcome returnees. For others, life in America was successful, so successful and beguiling that they never seriously considered going back to visit the scenes of their former poverty and dejection.

Caroline Golab in *Immigrant Destinations* says that the "Irish of the Old Immigration and Eastern European Jews of the New" are classic examples of emigrants . . . they had no intention of returning to Ireland or Russia." For Jews this is accurate, but for the Irish not so. The sentimental lure of childhood scenes and memories, the romanticism of selective recollection, and the elemental ties of family were potent psychological factors. While the sheer scale of the mid-nineteenth–century Irish emigration did sweep tens of thousands of whole families overseas, these years and earlier decades also saw an emigration of the young separating from their families. True, the harrowing memories of the Great Hunger of the 1840s may have convinced multitudes of the Irish that they should never return to a doomed land. Others in the thousands, however, longed for return. Golab points out that only slightly more than ten percent of the Irish emigrants repatriated.[2]

Repatriation was different from going back for reunions and visits. A large proportion probably did aspire to repatriation, but many, many more yearned to return for family reasons, to share their American adventures and advancements. There was a flattering egotism to much of the dreaming of return. Their songs told of the yearning—songs of exile by the score, remembered and sung for generations:

> Oh! Erin, my country, tho' sad and forsaken,
> In dreams I revisit thy sea-beaten shore;
> But, alas! in a far foreign land I awaken,
> And sigh for the friends who can meet me no more.

Philip Taylor's fine book *The Distant Magnet* describes the trans-Atlantic passenger trade during the decades of heavy immigration to the United States and notes the role of the passenger broker or agent. Until the 1850s it was largely the captains and shipowners themselves who arranged passages. As the scale of traffic increased, agents became more common. In the late 1860s the change to steam-powered vessels shortened the journey, enlarged shipping companies, and created a more manageable market for passenger booking. The steamship agent not only arranged passage. He provided vital information, stored baggage, transmitted funds, and handled prepaid passages for relatives. These kinds of services came to be provided even for major shipping lines by a whole range of individual entrepreneurs in Ireland and America, and also by Irish benevolent and mutual-aid organizations.[3]

During the 1850s immigrants who could afford to return to Ireland would have recourse to "Intelligence Offices." These offices were fixtures in the immigrant communities. They combined the business of making travel arrangements with employment referral, sending remittances, and holding mail and packages as a sort of "will call" facility. Newspapers from home, death notices, wedding presents, and passage tickets were all picked up at the "Intelligence Offices," which were located where the immigrants were concentrated. In Philadelphia in 1859 the largest Irish concentration in the city in the Schuylkill district was served by

Margaret McGinley's office at 256 South 20th Street, while Sarah Regan ran the office serving the Irish in Kensington at 214 Girard Avenue. Laurens Nugent's office on South Front Street drew people from the Southwark area, and William MacSorley on Callowhill Street served the Irish in Saint Augustine's parish. There were also agents for such shipping companies as the New York and Galway Line, whereas the American Emigration, Land and Employment Office on North Seventh Street made arrangements for passage with various lines.[4]

By the 1880s Intelligence Offices had become rare and had been replaced by steamship agents. Some of these had their offices in the Irish neighborhoods, such as that of John O'Callahan in the heavily Irish Port Richmond area. A center-city office was operated under the name O'Donovan-Rossa, and this was indeed a name to conjure with.[5] Rossa was renowned. He had been a member of the revolutionary underground Fenian Brotherhood in Ireland in 1865 and had been imprisoned by the British. His career in prison had involved exceptional suffering, including having his hands chained behind him and being forced to eat from a bowl on the floor like an animal. Released in 1871 and exiled to the United States, Rossa became a symbol of the bitter resistance to English domination of Ireland. As a newspaper editor and travel agent, Rossa kept the Irish underground stimulated with a fierce activism. A steamship office operated by such a man was a very important focus—for communication among the revolutionaries who conducted a steady traffic in arms smuggling, espionage missions, and the hiding of men hunted by English authorities.

Most travel to Ireland, however, was not of a clandestine nature. It involved successful Irish-Americans returning to visit relatives or to recruit workers for their enterprises, such as textile factories, construction businesses, or food services. A man such as the well-to-do Philadelphia contractor James Ryan, for instance, might return to his birthplace in Kilkenny to recruit stonemasons to work on the Reading Railroad Terminal Building that he was building as partner in the firm of Ryan and Costigan.[6] When Ryan booked first-class accommodations on the Cunard Line, he could do so through that line's agent James Hogan on Chestnut Street. The trip to Cobh in County Cork could include a stay at the Killarney

Railway Hotel, an imposing facility near the scenic Lakes of Killarney. Apartments in the hotel included sitting rooms and bedrooms from five shillings a day up, with rooms for servants extra.[7] Trips to Ireland to recruit workers were common among Irish-American businessmen. Even if the recruiter paid workers' steamship passage, these workers could initially be paid less than regular American employees. Often enough, they would also be relatives or friends from the locale from which the visiting recruiter came in Ireland.

As more Irish-Americans became economically secure, the regular steamship traffic of the Hamburg American Line and Cunard Line included increasing numbers of Irish returnees. Men who had left to work in the American mines in the Far West or who had been pensioned by the railroads returned to their home places, sometimes to stay. Men and women came to the United States, worked for some years to build up a nest egg, then returned to buy a farm or a business.[8] The old status of the travel agent who was part of the Irish community in a city such as Philadelphia was enhanced by the improvement in communications and ocean travel. Whole families pooled funds to send immigrant parents back for a visit in style, and tours of Ireland became an organized feature of trans-Atlantic travel.

An example of the kind of travel agency specializing in Irish clientele is that of John McGettigan. Born in Glenree, County Donegal, McGettigan was the youngest of thirteen children. As a youth he was selected to enter the seminary and eventually studied in Rome, but he was not ordained as a priest. In 1907 he came to America and took posts teaching foreign languages in several colleges. After settling in Philadelphia, McGettigan, who was an unusually talented musician, formed the Four Provinces Irish Orchestra that became a popular group at dances and festivities in the area. He pioneered with his own radio program for the orchestra in the 1930s and had energy enough to conduct a music store, a furniture business, and a hotel as well. In 1930 he began a travel agency with the aid of his wife, and, because he was widely known, the agency built a steady business in bookings on such liners as the *Mauretania, Washington,* and *Georgia* to Cobh in Ireland.

The services provided by the McGettigan agency included making bookings on the installment plan for immigrants who wished to return to Ireland. Over a period of several years Irish working people would slowly accumulate the cost of the fare in weekly payments. For some people emergencies would intervene. If a family member was close to death in Ireland, McGettigan would extend credit for the passage. He boasted that he never lost a penny in doing so, for the credit was always repaid. Another service was to help prospective immigrants by obtaining affidavits for them that would assure the U.S. Immigration and Naturalization Service that they would not become destitute public charges after arrival. The provision of affidavits was a standard part of the agency business prior to the 1960s when the United States severely restricted Irish immigration.[9]

In 1947 American Airlines and Pan-American Airways began flying to Ireland, and a revolution in travel was launched. Flying passengers to the new Irish airport at Shannon became a big business. The McGettigan agency and others competed with the airlines in booking tours and religious pilgrimages. Aer Lingus, the Irish government's airline, opened offices in major U.S. cities. Irish societies, church groups, alumni associations, three-generation family parties, and throngs of vacationers booked through local agents for the booming Irish tourist circuit. A whole national industry was built in Ireland under *Bord Failte*, the national tourist organization, to cater to an American travel clientele that flooded in annually to visit everything from ruined family farms in the bogs of Mayo to the splendidly restored castles and ancient sites across the countryside.

By 1955 there was an Irish agitation in Philadelphia for a direct airline link from the city to Shannon. Irish organizations promoted the idea but were never able to convince airline officials that regular scheduled flights could be made to pay.[10] Still the booking of flights increased. McGettigan, O'Keefe, Durkin, Concannon, and other Irish-oriented travel agencies were busy with the new and flexible system that made charter flights widely available after 1955. These charter arrangements brought even more Irish society trips together. It became the usual thing for some Irish-born people to return home for visits twice a year, once at Christmas and once in the summer for a holiday. Fares as low as $180 made this possible.

Ceremonial occasions in Ireland helped to stimulate the traffic. Widely publicized religious events, such as pilgrimages to the Shrine of Our Lady of Knock in County Mayo or visits to Saint Patrick's Purgatory at Croagh Patrick, were patronized by Irish Catholics, with local churches acting as tour organizers. Old-timers would return for the dedication of monuments to Irish Republican Army veterans. James Joyce readers would fly to Dublin for annual meetings of the James Joyce Society. It was all unprecedented, a mass popular affirmation of a cultural tie that was part real and part fanciful travel promotion. The traffic became such a regular feature of Irish-American life that the dance programs of Irish societies carried advertisements of bars, hotels, and shops in tiny towns in the remotest reaches of Ireland. It was indeed a far cry from the days of the "American wake" and the enforced absence from the old country of the immigrants of the nineteenth century.

A survey of those flying to Shannon on one of the summer charter flights organized by local Irish organizations, and inquiries among other visitors to Ireland, in 1979 revealed the following reasons for taking the journey:

Among Irish-born travelers the reasons were:

Visit to a sister who had just had a baby.

Visit to a property in South Armagh to settle legal matters of an estate.

Visit to Northern Ireland to confer with nationalist organizers there.

Visit to a terminally ill uncle.

Visit to an elderly parent.

Holiday for family.

Return to parent's homeland to do plumbing and roofing work.

Holiday in Mayo to avoid the heat of the Philadelphia summer.

Return to hunt for employment so that a permanent repatriation would be possible.

Visit to celebrate brother's ordination to priesthood.

Return to purchase woolen products for a small Irish shop.

Return to obtain educational records needed for further education in Philadelphia.

Among American-born Irish the reasons were:

Visit to a daughter working in Ireland.
Visit to further a research project for graduate school.
Journeys to seek family and family records.
Visit to father's sister, last living member of the older generation.
Visit to arrange enrollment in Trinity College, Galway.
Tour of archaeological sites.
Return to purchase a house for summer use on the West coast of Ireland.[11]

For both the Irish-born and the American-born of Irish descent the 1970s were to expand horizons in every direction. The Irish-born were aware of a new assurance and new national social economy in Ireland that brought strong influences of modernization. Those of Irish background in America were animated by a greatly expanded interest in folk music, literature, and history that gave ties to the old country a much broader dimension. They were affected, too, by the renewed popular interest in "roots." Ireland was seen with a more instructed eye now.

This expansion of horizons put Ireland in a new perspective. It remained potent emotionally, but it was no longer the dominating feature in the mental landscape of the Irish-Americans. Ireland in the Common Market meant new relationships for Irish friends and relatives in the old country. The Irish in Ireland were also traveling in new directions. Reasonably priced tour packages were luring them to Torremolinos, Ibiza, the Canary Islands, and elsewhere. Boys from County Monaghan were going out to work in the Persian Gulf. In Philadelphia's Irish community this trend sent couples off to join their parents from Ireland on holiday in the Caribbean or France. Trips to Ireland were combined with trips to Spain or Norway because that was where some of the Irish relatives were working or vacationing. The travel routes had changed tremendously, and the old ritual of immigrant return and emigrant aspiration had been altered by prosperity and the options of the jet age.[12]

Perhaps the ultimate in Irish and American trans-Atlantic journeying was reached when it became possible to live on both sides of the ocean in alternation so swift that the dual residence seemed almost simultaneous. Dr. Lester Connors of Chestnut Hill College, advisor of the Yeats Summer School amid the mountain magnificence of County Sligo, seemed to fly back and forth frequently with perfect aplomb. Henry McIlhenny, art collector and owner of a large estate in County Donegal, made frequent crossings. Thomas Kinsella, poet and university teacher, maintained both Dublin and Philadelphia addresses for years. Jane Meehan, who became enthralled with County Clare and enjoyed collecting folk music, moved closer to habitual trans-Atlantic travel each year. A number of others, Philadelphians such as newspapermen Jack McKinney, music scholar Mick Moloney, and archaeological devotee Irene Mullen, all aspired to live in both Ireland and America at once. Because of the complexity of professional commitments, the terrors of the Irish winter, and the need of most people for a single focus for life and domestic tranquillity, this aspiration remained a reverie, but it was a dream that the old immigrants of yesteryear in a wild and passionate leap of lonely Celtic imagination would have been thrilled to entertain. Ireland, haunting Ireland, was only a day's journey away, and yet the riches and sweep of America were only the same distance back again. What a beguiling dream!

NOTES

1. Interview with Joe Heaney, Irish Center, Philadelphia, January 26, 1980, following a rendition of his songs and stories.

2. Caroline Golab, *Immigrant Destinations* (Philadelphia: Temple University Press, 1977), p. 48.

3. Philip Taylor, *The Distant Magnet* (New York: Harper and Row, 1971), pp. 109 and 117.

4. *Boyds Co-Partnership and Residence Directory of Philadelphia City, 1859–60* (Philadelphia: Joseph Monier, 1859), p. 205.

5. *Boyd's Directory*, 1880, p. 574.

6. Biographical entry for James Ryan in Daniel Dougherty, *History of the Friendly Sons*

of St. Patrick and the Hibernian Society, vol. 2 (Philadelphia: The Friendly Sons of St. Patrick, 1952), p. 360.

7. Advertisement card for the Killarney Railway Hotel, in the collection of the Balch Institute, Philadelphia.

8. Playwright Brian Friel has depicted such a return in his work "The Loves of Cass Maguire." The return of the emigrant to America is a frequently treated theme in Irish writing. See such accounts as Michael MacGowan, *The Hard Road to the Klondike,* translated from the Irish by Valentin Iremonger (London: Routledge and Kegan Paul, 1962), and Thomás Ó'Crohan, *The Islandman,* translated from the Irish by Robin Flower (New York: Charles Scribner's Sons, 1935), pp. 213–14.

9. Interview with Norbert McGettigan, president, McGettigan Travel, February 13, 1980. A recording of John McGettigan's renditions of immigrant songs is available with a historical note by Mick Moloney on "John McGettigan and his Irish minstrels," 12T367, London, Topic Records, 1978.

10. *Donegal Bulletin* (July 1955), in the collection of the Balch Institute, Philadelphia.

11. These reasons for travel were recorded among passengers on a Capitol International Airways charter flight organized by the Irish Center in Philadelphia leaving July 26, 1979.

12. Interview with Mary O'Keefe, O'Keefe Travel, Philadelphia, February 26, 1980.

6 The Contractor Bosses

In a period when Americans are seeking more intently than ever before to understand their cities, exploration of the complexities of our urban traditions may provide us with some further insights into how our cities have grown. What we know about the social development of our cities is embarrassing in contrast to what we do not know.[1] This is nowhere better illustrated than in the area of urban development where ethnic traditions and business activity intermingle. Knowledge of the specific development roles of the Irish, Jews, Italians, and Germans, as well as the economically emergent blacks and Puerto Ricans, might provide us with a better comprehension of the dynamics that have had a strong impact on our urban expansion. Yet, the extent to which our cities have been structured socially and institutionally by the interplay of ethnic traditions within them has only been broadly sketched in the past. One of our most able historians of business has noted "Many important social areas have never been examined by historians."[2] This is still true, in spite of the fact that the history of each of our major cities represents a densely interwoven process of urban growth that blends ethnic, business, and political themes.

The purpose of this chapter is to present information about a key tradition of urban enterprise strongly influenced by the ethnic affiliation and identity of men engaged in it. The information deals largely with businesses in Philadelphia, a city that provides a rich context for business and ethnic interaction. The enterprises chosen for examination are in the field of general construction contracting. This field tends to be dispersed, flexible, and economically eccentric. The enterprises in the field are not, of course, distinctly

This article was originally published under the title "Ethnic Enterprise and Urban Development," in *Ethnicity*, vol. 5 (1978), and is reproduced here with permission of the original publishers.

ethnic in themselves. General contracting shares the large scale and concentration of activity common to many urban pursuits. The field did, however, become the vehicle for ethnic business aspirations and development as successive ethnic groups sought livelihoods and fulfillment within it, and the Irish paved the way for this tradition in the nineteenth century in such cities as Philadelphia.

As ethnic representatives invested their labor and talents in specific areas of activity, they drew with them, in a natural fashion, familymembers, associates, and clients. Eventually, they became identified with certain enterprises, reenforcing this identification with an ethnic prominence that served to augment their business and community status.

The contractor-boss is one of the central figures in the history of the American city. The builder-developer with strong political ties and influence is a familiar figure. There is a considerable literature delineating the political features of the boss, whose influence is variously interpreted as nefarious or socially beneficial, depending on which historian or political scientist one reads.[3] The ethnic identification of these figures has begun to be reconsidered without the prejudice of filiopietism that previously attached to view of them.[4] The contractor as a builder and as an agent of urban expansion and development, as distinguished from the contractor as political boss, has rarely been examined in his role as a businessman, particularly as an ethnic business type.

An examination of the occupational statistics concerning immigrants compiled by Edward P. Hutchinson shows a notable concentration of Irish as builders and contractors. According to the 1870 and 1880 United States Census figures summarized by Hutchinson, the Irish led all other immigrants in this occupational category. By 1890 the Irish had twice the proportion of builders and contractors that other immigrant groups had.[5] This concentration was not accidental. Rather, it was a function of the social position of the Irish in nineteenth-century America. Among the immigrant groups in the last century, the Irish were the most urban in their demographic distribution.[6] The vast influx of refugees from the catastrophe of the Irish potato famine in the 1840s coincided with a period of rapid industrialization and urban expansion in the Eastern cities.[7] Because the Irish, coming from a society that was singularly rural, initially entered the United States largely without skills relevant to the new industrial technology, they entered the work force as unskilled labor, and such labor was in great demand for the construction of canals, railroads, and cities.[8]

For many men anxious to improve themselves, an opportune route out of the unskilled labor pool was to become a small-scale building contractor. It was not too far from the truth to say that any man with his own shovel and wheelbarrow could style himself a "contractor." Such a pursuit required little initial capital, but aggressiveness and strong backs were important, and these the Irish had. They also had easy access to fellow countrymen who, after a preliminary adjustment to city life, had developed skills in stonecutting, bricklaying, ironwork, and most of the trades associated with building. Because of ethnic and religious discrimination in public schools, the overwhelmingly Catholic Irish felt impelled to construct a whole network of churches, schools, and welfare institutions in the major cities. This they did with alacrity, and the building work for these institutions provided a continuing source of construction operations for the Irish contractors. An illustration of this evolution of the Irish construction magnate can be found in the city of Philadelphia, a city whose rich Colonial past has overshadowed its interesting history during the period of industrialization and urban expansion.[9]

When the Irish first arrived in Philadelphia in great numbers in the wave of immigration following the potato famine of 1846–47, the city was in a period of extensive growth.[10] In 1854 the consolidation of the outlying areas into the County of Philadelphia expanded the legally defined city greatly.[11] The development of street railways opened up the newly annexed hinterlands to workers and middle class alike. As early as 1852 Irish contractors were monopolizing most of the public construction work in the Port Richmond district.[12] In 1853 builder Thomas Dugan was selling three-story houses in the Kensington area for $1200 each.[13] In 1856 James Tagert advertised in the *Philadelphia Evening Bulletin*, "There is not a man in the consolidated City of Philadelphia but can avail himself of a home if he desires."[14] Tagert, born in County Tyrone, was president of the Farmers and Mechanics Bank and a promoter of various building activities.

Financing for home-building operations did not come easily. In the mid-nineteenth century most banks were wary of lending mortgage money to ordinary working people. This reluctance produced in Philadelphia an extraordinary proliferation of a local business invention, the Building and Loan Association. These popular societies grew up rapidly in the 1840s and 1850s. They were nonprofit savings organizations specifically designed to make capital available for the construction and purchase of homes.[15] In a city where brick row housing could be constructed economically, their utility was patent. The Irish immigrants organized dozens of these societies. One man, Bernard Rafferty, was secretary of thirty-five such societies in the 1970s and 1880s.[16] With this mechanism of capitalization behind them, the home-building contractors of the city worked to extend the row-house residential pattern that became the most prominent physical feature of the Philadelphia landscape.

Home building, however, had its limitations. Its market uncertainties were proverbial. Railroad and public-works construction offered a large-scale area for more lucrative operation. Tipperary-born Thomas Costigan did much local railroad work, as did William J. Nead and Francis McManus.[17] The large pool of Irish pick-and-shovel laborers in the city provided almost the only resource needed for a smart contractor to organize an excavating crew to perform the enormously arduous work of digging cuts, grades, and tunnels for the railroads.

The business of Patrick McManus indicates the kinds of jobs in which the contractor could become involved. McManus was born in Pottsville, Pa., of Irish parents in 1847. His first major job was the building of stockyards for the city of Philadelphia. He laid special tracks to serve the grounds of the great Centennial Exposition in 1876 in Fairmount Park. Later, he and his partner, James B. Reilly, built stone bridges over the Schuylkill River and constructed track beds and stations for the railroads, including the Reading Company's line to Atlantic City. N.J.[18]

In a city noted for the ubiquity of its brick construction, some contractors specialized exclusively in this work. Michael Magee and Company built huge brick structures in the closing decades of the nineteenth century. These buildings, often covering a whole

city block and ranging up to eight stories in height, included the
Disston Saw factories, the Bromley textile mills, the J. A.
Dougherty distilleries, and the elegant Lorraine Hotel. Magee
varied such work with the steady construction of Catholic hospitals
and institutions.[19]

In a period when business and politics were closely allied, the
contractors were engaged frequently in public works. Edward J.
Lafferty from South Philadelphia helped to build the city's famous
waterworks. Martin Maloney, who started as a simple mechanic,
invented a gas burner for street lamps. He went into business laying
gas utility lines and helped organize the United Gas Improvement
Company in the city.[20] The continuing expansion, renovation, and
rebuilding or urban facilities offered such men repeated opportunities. Corruption, fraud, and shady practices were common enough.
Seymour Mandelbaum has maintained that the only way that the
burgeoning cities could be controlled politically and ordered
physically was by resorting to massive payoff schemes.[21] Philadelphia's politics became a national byword for corruption, and the
contractors were in the middle of it. Although the dollar costs of
gouging the public can be estimated in some instances, the social
costs of not having expanded and built the city in a time of great
population growth and immigration can only be conjectured.
Whatever the malpractices involved, many of the contractors did
produce. They built, and the city is still full of their works, aging
but utilitarian, a century after their erection.

By 1900, 63 percent of the building firms in the nation were
located in 200 cities, and urban construction was 90 percent of the
national total.[22] What had transpired since the 1840s was an
unprecedented urban development, and the Irish contractors had
ridden the wave of this growth. Asa Briggs in his *Victorian Cities*
has pointed out the primary role that the provision of sanitation,
utilities, and public-works construction played in such growth.[23] It
was in these areas of construction that the Irish contractors made a
heavy contribution. They were one of the "new categories of talent
and connection" that city expansion called forth.[24] Starting in the
ditches as excavators, they had gained command of a business
medium that was flexible enough to meet the needs of the

fast-breaking urban building segment of the economy. Construction activity has historically been a speculative and economically eccentric field, more sensitive to cycles of boom and bust than most areas of the economy. This propensity has led to a saying in the field that a construction man must of necessity be a gambler. A sudden contraction of credit, a hard rock strata struck in excavation, or a laborers' strike could jeopardize not only a single project but a whole business. Competition in a field where heavy capitalization was not required for entry was always keen. The contractor could attempt to stabilize his work by obtaining jobs through political preference, but the high risk element remained.

The interaction of general contracting and politics suited the Irish admirably. Their early prominence in politics was consolidated until by the late nineteenth century they held strategic positions in both the Democratic and Republican parties in Philadelphia. As the new immigration from Southern And Eastern Europe developed, they took up the role of political intermediaries, and this role has been one of the distinctive features of the political history of the Irish in the cities.[25] In contracting, also, they were intermediaries as well as principals. In hiring labor or presiding over subcontractors, architects, engineers, union bosses, and clients, they demonstrated the same facility for maneuver and mobilization that they displayed in politics.

An example of the interaction of business and politics can be seen in the career of James P. "Sunny Jim" McNichol, the first Irish Catholic to become a top Republican potentate in the Philadelphia firmament. McNichol, born in the tough Tenth Ward, formed a building firm with his brother when he was a young man. Between 1893 and 1895 his business forged ahead, doing six million dollars' worth of work in those years.[26] From 1898 to 1902 McNichol served on the Select Council of the city, then in the State Senate. In 1907 he said, after a controversy involving municipal contract work, "Never again under any circumstances will I go after municipal contracts." Business sense, however, overcame political irritation. In 1908 McNichol was completing the subway excavation from City Hall into South Philadelphia, building the million-dollar Torresdale water-filtration plant, performing extensive sewer and utility pipe-laying work, handling asphalt and granite-block paving contracts, and conducting a half-million-dollar garbage-disposal business through his Penn Reduction Company.[27] A total of more than two and a half million dollars in contracts was thus handled by McNichol in one year. During his career McNichol built the subway tunnel for the Market Street line, the imposing Benjamin Franklin Parkway, which is still one of the most appealing features of the city, and the eight-mile Roosevelt Boulevard, which opened the broad fields of the Northeast section of the city to the automobile traffic and residential development of the twentieth century.[28] In terms of urban construction, few men in the last hundred years have changed Philadelphia's physical aspect and orientation more extensively than "Sunny Jim" McNichol.

Not all of the contractors, of course, ascended to such power. Many were content to make a good living and try to keep ahead in the rough contest of competitive bidding and control of costs. Such a man was David J. Duffin, who arrived in the city from County Antrim in the North of Ireland with the strong arms of a stonecutter. He began as an excavator with a horse and wagon, then with his sons went into home building and road work. After almost going broke excavating the foundations for Philadelphia's Convention Hall because of a hidden rock formation, the firm of Duffin and Sons prospered in building Catholic churches. The desire of the Irish Catholics for huge churches, schools, and institutions stimulated a huge network of parish building. With his own quarry supplying stone, Duffin worked on thirty separate parish complexes, raising walls and steeples for the "lace curtain" Irish in various parts of the city.[29]

Perhaps the most attractive of all the city's contractors was John B. Kelly, one of a family with talent to spare. One of Kelly's brothers was a Pulitzer Prize playwright, one was a noted entertainer, and Kelly's daughter, Grace, was a movie star. In the case of John B. Kelly's rise from bricklayer's apprentice to owner of the largest brickwork company in America, a somewhat more glamorous tinge is added to the contractor image. One of ten children of an immigrant from County Mayo, Kelly was raised in the Falls of the Schuylkill area of the city. After service in World War I, he made a spectacular record as an oarsman, winning 125 races and endearing himself to Irish everywhere by beating the British sculling champion in the Olympic Games of 1920.[30] John B. worked as a bricklayer, foreman, and superintendent for his contractor brother, Patrick, then set up his own company. The business grew until "Kelly for Brickwork" became a byword in Philadelphia. In 1933 he entered politics as a Democrat supporting the New Deal of Franklin D. Roosevelt. "Until I saw a bread line for the first time, I stayed out of politics," Kelly said. In 1935 he ran for mayor of Philadelphia, losing a close election that his adherents and many others considered stolen by the fraudulent vote tallies of his embattled Republican opponents.[31] Kelly remained a prominent figure in the city's business and political life. His rise in politics symbolized a change in the political life of the city. James Reichley, analyst of reform politics in Philadelphia, credits Kelly with bringing about the first true opposition party in the city since the Civil War.[32]

A keen competitor of Kelly's for contracting work was Matthew H. McCloskey, whose activities took the contractor-politico evolution one step further onto the national stage. McCloskey, one of eight children of a father from Dungiven, County Derry, went into business for himself when he was only eighteen. His first large job was construction of a wartime building at the Philadelphia Navy Yard in 1917. It was a job that typified the hard-driving McCloskey style. His men built 160,000 square feet of construction in sixty days. Reverses hit the young builder hard in 1923, however, and he barely escaped bankruptcy. He had lost money trying to complete a barracks at the U.S. Military Academy at West Point, N.Y. Recovering, McCloskey built more schools in the city than any other single contractor, a fact not without significance with respect to political considerations. He built the Philadelphia Convention Hall and government buildings in the state capitol of Harrisburg. For six decades McCloskey pursued his business, compounding his reputation as an intense competitor and a shrewd calculator of contract costs.[33] One of his most notable successes was a twenty-five-million-dollar project with the Pennsylvania

Railroad for the Penn Center transportation facilities, the keystone
of the downtown renovation that transformed the center-city
business district of Philadelphia in the 1960s.

In 1932 McCloskey went into politics after discussions with
James Farley, Franklin D. Roosevelt's able party chieftain. From
1955 to 1962 he was national finance chairman of the Democratic
party, a position that he handled with mastery. McCloskey's
association with President John F. Kennedy was especially warm.
In June 1962 he was appointed U.S. ambassador to Ireland, a post
that accorded with his interest and affections.[34]

Perhaps the largest contractor of all in this tradition is John
McShain. Son of a County Derry carpenter, McShain built an
immense construction business. His ability to figure huge contracts
tightly became legendary. Beginning in Philadelphia, he built the
Board of Education Building in 1930, then the Municipal Court
Building, as well as many schools and churches. He served on the
city's Board of Zoning Adjustments from 1936 until 1952, a
significant position for business and governmental ties. In Philadelphia he constructed the Veterans Hospital and the Naval
Hospital and worked on the Philadelphia International Airport and
various college and university building programs. He also became
a director of several banks and a transportation company. The
scope of McShain's work extended far beyond the city, however.
His contracts included work on the forty-million-dollar Clinical
Research Building of the National Institute of Health, the General
Accounting Office, the National Airport, the Jefferson Memorial,
the State Department Building, and restoration of the White
House, all in the nation's capital. It is calculated that his firm has
completed more than one billion dollars in government contract
work. The largest of all his projects was just outside the Pentagon
Building Washington, an eighty-million-dollar construction.[35]

McShain's political allegiances are not as clear as those of Kelly
or McCloskey. He has worked with administrations of both
political parties. As a contractor with a national enterprise, he has
apparently avoided close identification with either party. The scale
of the McShain work on government contracts is manifest testimony
to his business and political acumen. His Irish ties have remained.

A keen horse fancier, he acquired an 8500-acre estate in Killarney where his racing Thoroughbreds are stabled.[36]

There are numerous other examples of the Irish contractor tradition in Philadelphia, including Austin Meehan, long a power in the Republican machine that fought the reform movement of the Democrats in the post–World War II period.[37] Other examples would not add substantially to the characteristics displayed by Kelly, McCloskey, and McShain. Their careers represent the penetration of an American business medium by the sons of immigrants and a latter-day enactment of the Horatio Alger cycle. These men were gifted with strong initiative. They were men of practical education. Kelly stated, "Most of my education was in night schools, at the YMCA classes and at Spring Garden Institute."[38] McCloskey attended Banks Business College in 1908 and studied at Drexel Institute of Technology for three years before entering business at eighteen.[39] McShain attended La Salle High School, Saint Joseph's Prep School, and Georgetown University for one year. None of the three married into old-line Philadelphia families, and, despite their wealth, they do not appear in the Social Register.[40] Their common business attributes are a powerful drive for success and a ruggedness of character that withstands well the rigors of economic and political competition.

Upon analysis, the contracting enterprises described above reveal a pattern that is in accord with the general business history of urban building activities. The ethnic origins and connections of the contractors did not exempt their firms from the broad trends at work in their field. The early Irish contractors, such as Thomas Costigan, Edward Lafferty, and Patrick McManus, were part of what Mark Twain called "the Gilded Age" in the period from 1877 to 1897. Their enterprises were individually led businesses depending upon strong personal contacts and leadership. Their familiarity with the Irish laboring gangs and the reliability of their word went far toward drawing together the skills and resources they needed.[41]

The businesses of "Sunny Jim" McNichol and Michael Magee represent a more formalized institutional stage of contracting. Technological changes in building practices, such as the use of steel frames and elevators, and the advent of electrical equipment, made construction much more technical and complex. Building regulations by municipalities raised new legal and technical problems. These trends of the late nineteenth century led to new practices in planning and managing work that, while not so rigorous as the human engineering schemes of George Frederick Taylor, were still a step toward regularizing large-scale construction activity. The great factories built by Magee and the subway work of McNichol had to be governed according to a new rationale. Both contractors developed horizontal business ties that assured them of supplies and services. Magee had his own brickyards, and McNichol aligned a wide diversity of productive holdings. These businesses represented a stage of contracting that was fully incorporated, technologically adaptive, and moving toward further diversification.[42]

The businesses of John B. Kelly, Matthew McCloskey, and John McShain exemplify a third stage of contracting development. These men built enterprises that became enormous in scope, ranging far beyond the local area. They became fully diversified, with holdings in real estate and a great diversity of production and service fields. The complexity of contracting and these other business operations had become so great by the mid-twentieth century that systems-management skills became mandatory. What resulted were great contracting systems backed by consolidations of capital and resources that enhanced their power tremendously.

If the timing of the Irish influx coincided with a wave of city building, the character of the immigrants themselves contributed to their business rise as contractors. Their group ties and competitive spirit served them well as they worked to make a reality the pompous prophecy of that nineteenth-century Philadelphia rhetorician Russell Conwell, who declaimed that "never in the history of the world did a poor man without capital have such an opportunity to get rich quickly and honestly as he has now in our city."[43]

The history of American city growth has been mostly studied in terms of technological growth and architectural innovations.[44] Only recently have we added social and political dimensions to urban study relatively free of past prejudices and historiographical limitations. The connection between the physical growth of the cities and the ethnic needs, career drives, and business tendencies of various minorities still needs much exploration if we are to understand the complex forces behind our extraordinary city settlement and development patterns.

NOTES

1. Oscar Handlin and John Burchard, eds., *The Historian and the City* (Cambridge, Mass.: MIT Press, 1963), p. 26.

2. Thomas C. Cochran, *The Inner Revolution* (New York: Harper and Row, 1964), p. 33.

3. The dour view of American city government held by Lord James Bryce is now seen to have been heavily biased. See Robert C. Brooke, ed., *Bryce's American Commonwealth* (New York: Macmillan Company, 1939), pp. 56 and 95. Zen Miller sees the political machine and its boss performing crucial urban functions. See his *Boss Cox's Cincinnati* (New York: Oxford University Press, 1968). For a discussion of the differing interpretations of boss rule see Lyle Dorsett, *The Pendergast Machine* (New York: Oxford University Press, 1968), Introduction, and Lawrence Fuchs, *American Ethnic Politics* (New York: Harper and Row, 1968).

4. Edward Levine, *The Irish and Irish Politicians* (Notre Dame, Ind.: University of Notre Dame Press, 1966).

5. Edward P. Hutchinson, *Immigrants and Their Children* (New York: John Wiley and Sons, 1956), pp. 83, 103, 126.

6. Ibid., p. 95, and Maldwyn Allen Jones, *American Immigration* (Chicago: University of Chicago Press, 1960), p. 21.

7. Geoffrey G. Williamson, "Ante-Bellum Urbanization in the American Northeast," *Journal of Economic History* 24, no. 4 (October 1965):589.

8. Handlin shows that 48 percent of the Irish were laborers in Boston in the 1840s. See his *Boston's Immigrants* (New York: Atheneum, 1968), p. 57.

9. For a critique of the Colonial preoccupation of historians of the city, see R. H. Shryock, "Historical Traditions in Philadelphia and in the Middle Atlantic Area," *Pennsylvania Magazine of History and Biography* 68, no. 2 (April 1943):115–41.

10. Sam Bass Warner, "Innovation and Industrialization in Philadephia, 1800–1850," in *The Historian and the City*, ed. by Handlin and Burchard pp. 65–68; Edwin T. Freedley, *Philadelphia and Its Manufactures* (Philadelphia: Edward Young, 1859), pp. 15–43.

11. Sam Bass Warner, *The Private City: Philadelphia* (Philadelphia: University of Pennsylvania Press, 1968), pp. 152–57.

12. Board of Commissioners Minutes, Richmond District, 1852–54, R. G. 219.1, Archives of the City of Philadelphia, City Hall, Philadelphia.

13. *Deed Book Th 100* (1853), p. 549, Archives of the City of Philadelphia, City Hall, Philadelphia.

14. Carl Wittke, *The Irish in America* (Baton Rouge, La.: Louisiana State University Press, 1956), p. 231; *The Philadelphia Evening Bulletin*, September 14, 1856.

15. H. Morton Bodfish, ed., *History of Building and Loan in the United States* (Chicago: U.S. Building and Loan League, 1931), pp. 32–79.

16. A biographical note on Bernard Rafferty with titles of some of the Irish Building and Loan Associations is cntained in John H. Campbell, *History of the Friendly Sons of St. Patrick* (Philadelphia: The Hibernian Society, 1892), p. 57.

17. For Thomas Costigan see Wittke, *The Irish in America*, p. 228. For Francis McManus and William Nead see Campbell, Ibid., pp. 486 and 489.

18. J. St. George Joyce, ed., *The Story of Philadelphia* (Philadelphia: City of Philadelphia, 1919), pp. 436–37.

19. See advertisement in Daniel H. Mahony, *Historical Sketches of Catholic Churches and Institutions in Philadelphia* (Philadelphia: D. H. Mahony, 1895), xxxviii.

20. Campbell, *History of the Friendly Sons of St. Patrick*, p. 449, and Wittke, *The Irish in America*, p. 231.

21. Seymour Mandelbaum, *Boss Tweed's New York* (New York: John Wiley and Sons, 1965), p. 58.

22. Edward C. Kirkland, *Industry Comes of Age* (Chicago: Quadrangle Books, 1961), p. 238.

23. Asa Briggs, *Victorian Cities* (New York: Harper and Row, 1970), pp. 16–17.

24. Eric Lampard, "Historical Contours of Contemporary Urban Society," *Journal of Contemporary History* 4, no. 3 (July 1969):20.

25. Milton Barron, "Intermediacy: Conceptualization of Irish Status in America." *Social Forces* 27, no. 3 (March 1949):256–63.

26. Joyce, *The Story of Philadelphia*, p. 474.

27. Newspaper coverage of McNichol at the time was extensive. See *Philadelphia North American*, January 2, 9, 1908; *Philadelphia Public Ledger*, January 3, 1908; *Philadelphia Record*, January 6, 1908; *Philadelphia Inquirer*, April 12, 1908; *Philadelphia Evening Bulletin*, April 15, 1980; and Edward Morgan, *City of Firsts* (Philadelphia: City of Philadelphia, 1919), p. 291.

28. Joyce, *The Story of Philadelphia*, p. 474. Sam Bass Warner sees the urban landmarks of this period as part of a commerce-dominated city culture reflecting "privatism" and an inability of city leaders to confront the problems of dealing with urban disorder. See Warner, *The Private City*, pp. 205–7.

29. Interview with James Duffin, grandson of David J. Duffin, Philadelphia, June 11, 1970.

30. *Philadelphia Evening Bulletin*, October 29, 1934.

31. Ibid.

32. James Reichley, *The Art of Reform* (New York: The Fund for the Republic, 1959), p. 6.

33. *Philadelphia Evening Bulletin*, March 10, 1936; June 10, 1962; February 25, 1968.

34. Ibid.

35. Ibid., May 29, 1963; Thomas O'Malley, "John McShain: Builder," *Columbia* (February 1955).

36. *Philadelphia Evening Bulletin*, May 29, 1963; October 3, 1962.

37. Reichley, *The Art of Reform*, pp. 9 and 20.

38. *Philadelphia Evening Bulletin*, September 21, 1935. Spring Garden Institute was a vocational and technical school.

39. Ibid., February 25, 1968.

40. O'Malley, "John McShain." E. Digby Baltzell in his book *The Protestant Establishment: Aristocracy and Caste in America* (New York: Random House, 1946), p. 122, has written of the educational and social-class barriers that insulated the Philadelphia old-family socialites, and the exclusionary practices that worked against men like the Irish contractors. See also Nathaniel Burt, *The Perennial Philadelphians* (Boston: Little, Brown and Company, 1963).

41. In their individualism and self-reliance these contractors of the Gilded Age resembled the dynamic boosters of the new cities of the West. See Daniel Boorstin, *The*

Americans: The National Experience (New York: Random House, 1965), pp. 115–23. The prevailing spirit is summarized by Thomas C. Cochran and William Miller, *The Age of Enterprise* (New York: Harper and Row), pp. 119–35.

42. For views of the changes in building in the late nineteenth century, see Charles N. Glaab and A. Theodore Brown, *A History of Urban America* (New York: Macmillan Company, 1967), p. 146; Kirkland, *Industry Comes of Age*, p. 261.

43. John G. Cawelti, *Apostles of the Self-Made Man* (Chicago: University of Chicago Press, 1965), p. 178.

44. Some attention devoted to the topic of ethnic influences by Edward J. Logue in his essay "The impact of Political and Social Forces on Design in America," in *Who Designs America*, ed. by L. R. Holland (New York: Doubleday Books, 1966), pp. 236–56.

PART III: **Wrap the Green Flag Round Me, Boys**

Agitation for Irish liberty from the sanctuary of the United States is one of the strongest themes of the Irish-American tradition from the eighteenth century forward. The plots, intrigues, dedicated careers, and campaigns involved with this agitation are a fascinating feature of ethnic experience in the United States. Although some studies have been compiled showing how Irish patriotic groups worked on the national scene, most of the organizing, fund raising, and propaganda activity was carried out on a local level.

Examples of Irish activity in behalf of the political liberation of Ireland are provided in the next three chapters. The first deals with the Fenian Brotherhood, a group formed in America that became the fountainhead of much of modern Irish nationalism. The second chapter contrasts the careers of two Irish nationalist activists, one a moderate, the other a dynamic revolutionary who had an extraordinary career. The persistence of nationalist agitation is illustrated by the work of John Reilly and his circle in the third chapter.

7   The Philadelphia Fenians

The history of any secret organization presents a particularly difficult field of inquiry. One of the legacies of secret societies is a mass of contradictions and pitfalls for historians. Oaths of secrecy, subterfuge, aliases, code words, and wildly exaggerated perceptions conspire against the historian. They add another vexing dimension to the ordinary difficulty of tracing and evaluating documentary sources.[1] The Fenian Brotherhood, an international revolutionary organization active in Ireland, England, and the United States a century ago, is a case in point. Founded in Dublin in 1858, the organization underwent many vicissitudes. Harried by British police and agents, split by factionalism, buffeted by failures, reverses, and defections, the Fenians created a vivid and romantic Irish nationalist legend. Part of their notoriety derived from spectacular exploits that received sensational publicity, and part derived from the intrepid character of some of the leaders. Modern historians credit the Fenians with the preservation of Irish national identity and idealism during one of the darkest periods of Irish national life.[2]

Although some general studies of the Fenians have been written, there are few studies of local branches of the brotherhood. Just how such a group operating in several countries functioned amid problems of hostile surveillance, difficulties of communication, and political disruptions raises numerous questions that the historian finds difficult to answer.[3] This chapter will examine some phases of Fenian activity in one American city, Philadelphia, and will show some of the problems of the local Fenians and something about the kind of men who made up the leadership of the local circles of the organization.

This article was originally published in *The Pennsylvania Magazine of History and Biography*, 95, no. 1 (January 1971), and is reprinted with the permission of that journal.

The generation of Irish who survived the disaster of the great potato famine in 1846–47 was a generation shadowed by tragic memories. The famine caused the population of Ireland to fall dramatically. In 1841 there were more than 8,000,000 inhabitants, but in 1851 there were only 6,500,000.[4] The hunger-stricken people of the island emigrated by the thousands. Following the famine, in the year of revolutions, 1848, a hapless flicker of attempted armed risings by the "Young Ireland" movement was stifled almost casually by powerful British forces. The fate of these risings was symbolic of the despair and disarray of the Irish nationalist cause. However, the grim panorama of wholesale emigration to America was to have unanticipated results for the Irish nationalist tradition. The bitter memories of English rule in Ireland carried in the hearts of the emigrants would inspire an American brand of Irish nationalism with which England would have to contend for seventy-five years.[5]   In the cities of the United States the Irish communities constituted ready reservoirs of nationalist sentiment.[6] By 1850 the remnants of the "Young Ireland" movement in Dublin were asking the aid of their brethren in America.[7] In Philadelphia such pleas would be heard by responsive men. The Irish in Philadelphia formed a large segment of the city's population. In 1850 there were 72,000 Irish-born people in the city.[8] Their churches, schools, and organizations were growing rapidly.[9] Some of the organizations had long records of support for causes in the old country. The local branch of the Repeal Association had collected $2,000 in one week for Daniel O'Connell's fruitless drive to sever the connection between England and Ireland through parliamentary means.[10] During and after the famine Philadelphians had worked in campaigns for famine relief and emigrant aid.[11] Ignatius Donnelly, a Philadelphia-born Irishman who would become a fiery Populist leader in later years, testified to the Irish devotion to liberation of the old country in a speech at Independence Hall in 1855.[12]

By the late 1850s Philadelphia Irish had become engaged in actively setting up a far-flung agency of conspiracy and revolution, the Fenian Brotherhood. Chief among the revolutionaries was James Gibbons, owner of a printing business at 333 Chestnut Street. He joined the Fenian organization in 1859 by taking its secret oath to "labor with earnest zeal for the liberation of Ireland from the yoke of England and for the establishment of a free and independent government on Irish soil."[14] He may have been one of the Irish Americans who first urged the formation of a secret revolutionary society as early as 1857. In the ensuing years Gibbons worked strenuously for the Fenian cause. As one of the earliest Fenians in the country, he became a member of the first national governing council of the organization. As such, he knew James Stephens, the "Fenian Chief," a Limerick man, survivor of the 1848 failure. Stephens was the prime organizer of the Brotherhood. After having become acquainted with Parisian revolutionary circles, Stephens visited the United States in 1859 to further his dream of providing Ireland with a revolutionary cadre on the continental model. Gibbons's association with such men as Stephens and John O'Mahony, American head of the Brotherhood, confirmed him in his commitment to revolutionary work. The diligent printer rose to be president of the Fenian Senate and remained an indefatigable member of its higher councils through numerous plots and misadventures.

One of the tasks of the local Fenians was to promote events and gatherings to air Irish grievances, stimulate public opinion against England, and rally Irish-Americans to the cause. One of the first occasions was provided by the "Trent Affair" in November 1861, when an American naval vessel stopped a British mail steamer and removed two agents of the rebellious Confederacy. Anglo-American relations were thrown into turmoil by the act, and the Fenians sought to heighten the feeling against England. They promoted a well-attended mass meeting in Philadelphia, which was addressed by Michael Doheny, another of the leaders of the 1848 rising who had fled to the United States.[15] In 1861 the Philadelphia Fenians also contributed $300 to the fund used to stage memorial demonstrations for Terence Bellew McManus, one of the "Forty-Eighters" who had died after release from the convict camps of Australia, to which he had been banished by the British.[16] These demonstrations, culminating in a vast funeral procession when the body of McManus was carried through Dublin, were the first public manifestation of the organized power of the Fenian Brotherhood.

James Gibbons was responsible for calling the first national convention of the Fenians. It was held in Philadelphia in 1863, and Gibbons was again elected a member of the directorate controlling the organization.[17] Plans were laid to recruit members of the Union Army into the Brotherhood with an eye to making use of the military experience they were gaining in the Civil War. The intention was to prepare for military forays against England after the Civil War, The Union forces included thousands of Irish, and men such as Thomas Francis Meagher, another veteran of the 1848 rising and head of the Union's Irish Brigade, were sympathetic to the Fenian efforts. In 1864, James Stephens came to America from Ireland once more and toured Union army encampments, recruiting Irish men into the organization. These recruits added an experienced dimension of military abilities to the burning commitment of the Fenian conspirators.

However, the Brotherhood faced increasing difficulties as it grew. On February 13, 1864, Archbishop James Wood, the Roman Catholic primate of Philadelphia, along with other bishops, issued an episcopal circular condemning the Fenians. The opposition of the bishops to secret societies was part of a long-standing policy.[18] There were other clergy, however, who were close to the Fenians. Father Patrick Moriarty, in particular, was sympathetic to them. This outspoken priest, pastor of Saint Augustine's Church at Fourth and Vine streets, was widely known as a colorful orator, an ardent Irish nationalist, and a leonine personality.[19] Perhaps in an effort to counter the episcopal condemnation, a mass meeting was arranged for the Academy of Music. Father Moriarty was scheduled to speak on the topic "What Right Has England to Rule Ireland?" When Archbishop Wood, a man of English background, forbade Moriarty to give his oration, the priest defied his superior and delivered a roaring broadside, calling Britain "tyrant, robber, murderer . . . infidel England," and stating, with respect to violence, that "Ireland may well return all that she has received from her Caesar."[29] The priest subsequently wrote a public apology to Archbishop Wood, but his speech was widely circulated. Significantly, the copies of it were printed by James Gibbons.

Episcopal opposition, which posed serious questions of conscience for Catholic Fenians, was not the only problem besetting the Brotherhood. John O'Mahony, the head center or highest leader of the American Fenians, had launched the sale of bonds issued in the name of the "Irish Republic." This action, taken without appropriate consultation with the other leaders of the organization, plus the fact that O'Mahony was felt to be dilatory about preparing for the proposed military ventures planned by the organization, angered many of the militant Brotherhood members. The Fenian Senate, with Gibbons presiding, repudiated O'Mahony on these and other counts in late 1865.[21] As president of the senate, Gibbons was one of the leaders of the agitation of the American wing of the Brotherhood for prompt and aggressive action against the British Leviathan.

The *Catholic Herald*, official newspaper of the Philadelphia Archdiocese, continued to excoriate the Fenians. On Saint Patrick's Day, 1866, it charged them with "anarchy and bloodshed," alleging that "nothing but trouble and misery has been created both in America and Ireland" by the Brotherhood.[22] *The Press*, a Philadelphia democratic paper, maintained a mildly reproachful tone on the Fenians, but such sober periodicals as the *Commercial and Financial Chronicle* saw "little of intelligent purpose" in the movement and the capability for "much mischief."[23]

With the Brotherhood split by factionalism, the "immediate action" wing planned a raid on Canada as a more expedient alternative to a rising in Ireland. Although Stephens and O'Mahony adhered to a policy of placing priority on a rising in Ireland, the senate wing under William R. Roberts of New York and Gibbons felt that swift action was needed to hold the loyalty of the American militants. Through the winter and spring of 1866 furious preparations were made to further the Canadian invasion. In January 1866 Charles Carroll Tevis, a Philadelphian and a graduate of West Point, visited the city to arrange for a purchase of muskets from Jenks and Mitchell Company, arms manufacturers. In April, 4,200 guns were purchased from the Bridesburg Arsenal, a government installation. Efforts to buy artillery at the arsenal failed.[24]

James O'Reilly, who had attained the rank of colonel in the Union Army and had fought with dashing bravery in many battles, raised the Twentieth Regiment of the Irish-American Brotherhood in Philadelphia. In company with contingents from throughout the Midwest and the northeastern states, he went to upper New York at the end of May 1866.[25] There, on June 2, the Fenians crossed the border to confront the Canadian "Queen's Own Volunteers." After some skirmishing the Fenian plan miscarried, and United States officials intervened, confiscating arms and disbanding Fenian units. Amid harsh criticism, Gibbons convened the senate on July 1 and berated the United States government for its intervention.[26] Undaunted by the invasion failure, Gibbons issued an address to the Brotherhood in Philadelphia, urging more organization and reminding the members of England's continued ascendancy over the Irish homeland.[27]

The Canadian venture caused a sensation in the United States and England far out of proportion to its limited tactical success. By August 1866 the tireless Gibbons was helping to plot more Canadian raids. The Fenians were bitter that some of those who took part in the June raids were imprisoned in Canada like criminals.[28] A Tammany Hall chieftain informed the Brotherhood, after a meeting in October 1866 with President Andrew Johnson, that he had the assurance of high officials that these men would soon be freed.[29]

Disagreement about priorities did not diminish the interest of the senate wing of the Brotherhood in events in Ireland. The militants there were planning a rising for 1867. As early as 1865 Irish-Americans were entering Ireland for the purpose of furthering this plan. One of these was Col. Michael Kerwin, a Wexford-born man who had lived most of his life in Philadelphia. He had served with Gen. Philip Sheridan's cavalry in the Civil War. Sent to Ireland in 1865 by John O'Mahony, he was one of 300 Fenian officers and men from America who took part in the 1867 outbreaks.[30]

Gibbons was aware of the impending rising. The strain of anticipation is reflected in a letter he wrote to a fellow Fenian in January 1867. He observed that "we are in the midst of Fearful events."[31] The risings in January and March 1867, were a grim failure, and hundreds of Fenians were seized and imprisoned, among them Kerwin.[32] Once again, sensational publicity attended the militarily disastrous outbreaks.

Although dismayed, the Brotherhood leaders, men who had

constantly contended with adversity, would not relent. In July 1867 Gibbons was busy with new recruiting and the acquisition of Springfield rifles.[33] He was sustained by the conviction that even if efforts in Ireland had been smashed, there was another Irish nation outside of Ireland numbering in the millions, and it was his duty to work with it in continual conflict with England and her interests.[34]

In September 1867 an attempt to rescue Fenian prisoners in Manchester, England, led to bloodshed, and three of the prisoners were condemned to death.[35] The three, William Allen, Michael Larkin, and Michael O'Brien, became the subject of huge Irish demonstrations for clemency in American cities. Upon the execution of the "Manchester Martyrs," a great funeral cortege with mock coffins was assembled in Philadelphia and marched to Broad and Chestnut Street as a public commemoration. Col. James O'Reilly organized thirteen Fenian circles and thousands of sympathizers for the demonstration, which ended with a raging speech by John O'Byrne, a lawyer and political figure, calling for vengeance against England.[36]

Another national gathering of the Brotherhood was called by Gibbons for November 1868 in Philadelphia. One of the senate members wrote of him as "full of ideas."[37] Factionalism was as rife as ever, however, and Gibbons was disheartened by failures and defections. In April 1869 he wrote to a friend, "Ah, but we are sorry revolutionists," a plaintive outcry from a man whose dedication had been tested often.[38] "Oh, if our people could understand, but they are too selfish and too jealous," he wrote.[39] For all the charges of atheism and godlessness hurled against them, many of the Fenians were sincere Christians. "God in his wisdom" would advance the cause of Irish liberty, Gibbons insisted.[40]

Gibbons deplored the failings of his countrymen, viewing some of the Irish as "blind and helpless slaves." He pleaded for brave and honest men to further the revolution.[41] At the end of 1869 he was circulating orders warning against renegades and attending meetings in Philadelphia to set up a secret project referred to by the code word "Red River."[42]

The year 1870 was a time of further reverses. The bitter internal wrangling resulted in an assault on the Brotherhood's treasurer, P.

J. Meehan, in which he was seriously wounded. Although Gen.
John O'Neill, president of the Brotherhood in 1870, was planning
further attacks on Canada, such a course was now recognized as
futile by the senate. Gibbons, as the chairman of the Executive
Council, sent out orders countermanding O'Neill's designs. The
circular on this subject confessed that the affairs of the organization were "out of joint" but called the faithful militants to "close
ranks."[43]

Thus, the Philadelphia Fenians ended a decade of stormy and
frustrated activity. Gibbons might plead toward the end of the
decade that "now is the hour to keep militancy," but the heyday of
the Fenians was over.[44] Although the brotherhood would continue
its underground efforts, a new vehicle was forming. The Clan na
Gael (Brotherhood of the Gael), founded in 1867, would gradually
supplant the Fenians as the largest Irish revolutionary society.[45]

The Philadelphia Fenians, theoretically embracing thirteen
"circles" of 800 men each in 1868, gave expression to an Irish
nationalism that had been systematically suppressed for generations by the strongest empire of the nineteenth century.[46] It helped
to focus American opinion on the plight of Ireland. As Father
William D'Arcy in the most exhaustive study of the American
portion of the movement concluded, the members were largely
sincere and honest men, motivated by a deep sense of justice, and
committed to taking the only course accessible to them to secure
Irish freedom, that of conspiracy and revolution.[47]

Work for the Irish cause continued in Philadelphia through the
rest of the 1800s and into the twentieth century. As Gibbons and
his generation faded from the scene, a new group of men took up
the torch. The most remarkable of these was Dr. William Carroll,
who began his revolutionary work as a Fenian. Carroll was a
Presbyterian from Donegal. He was a confidant of the exiled
Fenian John O'Leary, immortalized by William Butler Yeats as the
symbol of romantic Irish nationalism.[48] Working closely with
Charles Stewart Parnell and the indomitable John Devoy of New
York, Carroll would extend his work to his death in 1926, long
enough to see the partial fulfillment of that Fenian dream to which
so much sacrifice and effort had been devoted, an "independent
government on Irish soil."[49]

NOTES

1. One student of Irish secret societies, who wrote a history of the "Invincibles," a terrorist group of the 1880s, found the evidence "riddled with doubt and untruth, vagueness and confusion." See Tom Corfe, *The Phoenix Park Murders* (London: Routledge and Kegan Paul, 1968), p. 135.

2. T. W. Moody of Trinity College, Dublin, holds this view. See his *The Fenian Movement* (Cork, Ireland: Mercier Press, 1967), p. 111. J. C. Beckett of Queens University, Belfast, writes: "The famine left Ireland politically as well as economically exhausted." See his *A Short History of Ireland* (New York: Alfred A. Knopf, 1966), p. 146. Beckett also credits the Fenians with preserving the nationalist ideal of a republic and causing the British government under Gladstone to take up the Irish question, ibid., p. 148.

3. Moody, in *The Fenian Movement*, p. 9, points out that there has been little scholarly writing on the Fenians and that most of what we know is based on accounts of participants. There have been some works published recently dealing with the organization, including Brian Jenkins, *Fenians and Anglo-American Relations during Reconstruction* (Ithaca, N.Y.: Cornell University Press, 1969), a study of the impact of the movement on diplomatic relations; and Mabel Gregory Walker, *The Fenian Movement* (Colorado Springs, Colo.: Ralph Myles, 1969).

4. Cecil Woodham-Smith, *The Great Hunger* (New York: Macmillan Co., 1962), p. 411.

5. Thomas N. Brown, *Irish-American Nationalism: 1870–1890* (Philadelphia: J. B. Lippincott Co., 1966), pp. 178–82; also Alan J. Ward, *Ireland and Anglo-American Relations* (London: Weidenfeld and Nicolson, 1969), p. 262.

6. William E. Lecky noted the profound alienation from England among those who fled Ireland in famine times, in his *Leaders of Public Opinion in Ireland* (New York: Appleton Co., 1912), vol. 2, p. 177.

7. *The Irishman* (Dublin), March 9, 1850.

8. J. B. D. De Bow, *A Statistical View of the United States Being a Compendium of the Seventh Census* (Brooklyn, N.Y.: Central Book Co., 1854), Table IV, p. 399.

9. Daniel Mahony, *Historical Sketches of Catholic Churches and Institutions* (Philadelphia: D. J. Mahony, 1895), pp. 67–104.

10. Charles Gavan Duffy, *Young Ireland: A Fragment of Irish History* (New York: D. Appleton Co., 1881), p. 318.

11. John H. Campbell, *History of the Friendly Sons of St. Patrick and the Hibernian Society* (Philadelphia: The Hibernian Society, 1892), p. 206.

12. Martin Ridge, *Ignatius Donnelly: A Political Portrait* (Chicago: University of Chicago Press, 1962), p. 11.

13. The Rev. William D'Arcy, *The Fenian Movement in the United States* (Washington, D.C.: The Catholic University of America Press, 1947), p. 33. Gibbons's address is listed in *McElroy's Philadelphia Directory* (Philadelphia: McElroy Co., 1859).

14. D'Arcy, *The Fenian Movement*, p. 37.

15. Joseph Denieffe, *A Personal Narrative of the Irish Revolutionary Brotherhood: 1855–67* (New York: Gael Publishing Co., 1906), p. 74.

16. *Irish American* (New York), October 21, 1861.

17. D'Arcy, *The Fenian Movement*, pp. 33, 50.

18. As early as 1851 the Catholics of Philadelphia were warned by their Catholic newspaper about secret societies. See Philadelphia *Catholic Herald*, January 3, 1851. For a note on Archbishop Wood's condemnation, see The Rev. T. C. Middleton, "Some Memories of Our Lady's Shrine," *Records of the American Catholic Historical Society* 12 (1901): 271.

19. Ibid., pp. 271–83. Father Moriarty had traveled widely in Europe and Asia before

coming to Philadelphia. Saint Augustine's was one of the churches that was involved in the violence against Irish Catholics in 1844.

20. A copy of this address is in the Archives of the American Catholic Historical Society, Saint Charles Seminary, Overbrook, Pa.

21. Circular of the Fenian Brotherhood, December 7, 1863. This circular is contained in a collection of Fenian Papers in the Archives of the American Catholic Historical Society. This collection of more than 200 letters, telegrams, circulars, and treasury reports, referred to hereinafter as FP/ACHS, has not been listed previously in any bibliographies on Fenianism to the author's knowledge. These bibliographies include those in D'Arcy, *The Fenian Movement*, pp. 412–28; Jenkins, *Fenians and Anglo-American Relations*, pp. 329–40; Moody, *The Fenian Movement*, pp. 113–26; James W. Hurst, "The Fenians: A Bibliography," *Eire-Ireland* 4 , no. 4 (Winter 1969): 90–106; Breandan Mac Giolla Choille, "Fenian Documents in the State Paper Office," *Irish Historical Studies* 16, no. 63 (March 1969): 258–84. None of these bibliographies list the ACHS collection, which was apparently a file owned by James B. Gallagher of Buffalo, N.Y., a member of the Fenian Senate. How the papers came into the possession of the American Catholic Historical Society is not known. The materials are in good condition, are mostly written in a clear script, and have been classified and numbered. The papers have also been placed on microfilm (ACHS Roll B-13). They offer an insight into various key personalities involved in the upper levels of the movement and the political intrigues that were part of the inner life of the Brotherhood.

22. *Catholic Herald*, March 17, 1866.

23. *The Press*, October 24, 26, 1865; *Commercial and Financial Chronicle* (New York), April 21, 1866.

24. D'Arcy, *The Fenian Movement*, p. 145.

25. Campbell, *History of the Friendly Sons*, p. 493.

26. D'Arcy, *The Fenian Movement*, pp. 158–68. The *Evening Bulletin* excoriated the Fenians, charging that they were criminals, remnants of the Confederacy, and cowards. See Philadelphia *Evening Bulletin*, June 1, 2, 4, 1866.

27. Circular of the Fenian Brotherhood dated Fall 1866, FP/ACHS. Philadelphia, unlike New York, had no Irish-American newspapers of its own. It was necessary, therefore, for Gibbons to print the brotherhood's addresses and orders for circulation to the members.

28. William R. Roberts, president of the Fenian Brotherhood and former head of the Fenian Senate, to Francis B. Gallagher, November 22, 1866, FP/ACHS.

29. Michael B. Murphy to Francis B. Gallagher, Oct. 30, 1866, ibid.

30. Denieffe, *A Personal Narrative*, p. 281.

31. James Gibbons to Francis B. Gallagher, January 18, 1867, FP/ACHS.

32. Denieffe, *A Personal Narrative*, p. 282.

33. Telegram from James Gibbons to Francis B. Gallagher, July 18, 1867, FP/ACHS.

34. James Gibbons to Francis B. Gallagher, August 6, 1867, ibid.

35. Anthony Glynn, *High upon the Gallows Tree* (Tralee, Ireland: Anvil Books, Ltd., 1967), pp. 38–42.

36. Campbell, *History of the Friendly Sons*, p. 493. A copy of the O'Byrne speech is in the Archives of the American Catholic Historical Society.

37. D. O'Sullivan to Francis B. Gallagher, September 24, 1868, FP/ACHS.

38. James Gibbons to Francis B. Gallagher, April 10, 1869, ibid.

39. James Gibbons to Francis B. Gallagher, April 17, 1869, ibid.

40. Ibid.

41. James Gibbons to Francis B. Gallagher, June 10, 1869, ibid.

42. Gen. John O'Neill to Francis B. Gallagher, December 22, 1869, ibid. There is no clarification of the nature of this project in the sources cited here.

43. Circular of the Fenian Brotherhood, April 7, 1870, ibid.

44. Ibid.

45. Moody, *The Fenian Movement*, pp. 93–94.

46. The number of Philadelphia circles is reflected in the Treasury Reports of the Brotherhood. FP/ACHS.

47. D'Arcy, *The Fenian Movement*, p. 411.

48. Marcus Bourke, *John O'Leary: a Study in Irish Separatism* (Tralee, Ireland: Anvil Books, Ltd., 1967), p. 163. Dr. William Carroll is listed as having lived at 617 S. Sixteenth St. in 1867, in *McElroy's Philadelphia Directory*, 1867.

49. For a biographical note on Dr. William Carroll, see Desmond Ryan, *The Fenian Chief* (Coral Gables, Fla.: University of Miami Press. 1967), p. 305. See also D'Arcy, *The Fenian Movement*, p. 33.

8   Martin Ignatius and Dynamite Luke: Two Patriots

The panorama of Irish nationalism both in Ireland and overseas is replete with an amazing array of characters engaged in struggles to attain the liberation of the motherland. Zealots, martyrs, adventurers, spies, traitors, orators, writers, soldiers, and terrorists all mingle in the historical throng of "the patriot game." Some of the agitators for Irish liberation who worked for the cause in America share the tradition of dedication and eccentricity that marked the careers of so many nationalist leaders in the nineteenth century. There was, for instance, Fenian Charlie Collins, who mined the goldfields of the Dakotas and circulated Irish nationalist pamphlets throughout the Far West. His thesis was that if enough Irish could be brought to prospect in the West, enough gold would be found to finance a full-scale revolution in Ireland. There was also John P. Holland who invented the first practical submarine prior to the Civil War, with the intention of ramming and sinking British ships in American harbors. Another, Gen. John O'Neill, after a distinguished career in the Union Army led a spectacularly unsuccessful Irish revolutionary force in an abortive invasion of Canada. The cast is widely varied.

In the United States the Irish nationalist movement was broad enough to have both widespread radical and extensive conservative wings. Some men began as radicals in their younger days and gradually became more conservative. An example is Patrick Ford, editor of *The Irish World*, published in New York. From an early position as agitator and fiery critic, Ford moved to a right-wing stance in his later years. Other Irish-Americans adopted an early posture and varied very little in their approach to the nationalist struggle throughout their lives. Although individual campaigns and tactics may have varied, their basic orientation remained the same. This radical-conservative divergence is, as Thomas N. Brown has shown, one of the central themes of Irish exile nationalism.[1] It is partly a reflection of the different social positions of Irish figures in American life, partly a reflection of personality differences, and partly attributable to irreconcilable views of Irish history and political development.

It is useful to trace this nationalist dualism to have an understanding of what influences came to bear upon Irish-American leaders and how they, in turn, shaped powerful elements of Irish opinion and organization. The careers of Martin Ignatius J. Griffin, publisher, and "Dynamite" Luke Dillon, revolutionary, both of Philadelphia, illustrate the distinctly American forces acting on Irish nationalists in the second half of the nineteenth century.

Martin I. J. Griffin, as he would invariably style himself with Victorian propriety, was born October 23, 1842, the son of parents from County Wicklow in Ireland. His boyhood scholarship earned him entry into Philadelphia Central High School, an unusual advantage for an Irish Catholic in the 1850s. After secondary school he became a correspondent for various Catholic newspapers, a job that taught him the growing power of printed media. In an age of organizational proliferation when Americans became renowned as joiners, Griffin belonged to a number of Catholic societies. His energy advanced him steadily until in 1872 he became national secretary of the Irish Catholic Benevolent Union, an organization founded in 1869 to unify and expand charitable efforts. The I.C.B.U. superseded the older Emigrant Aid Societies that had been set up in various cities earlier in the century. As secretary the enterprising Griffin boosted the membership to 20,000.[2]

Using his journalist background, Griffin launched the *I.C.B.U. Journal* in 1873. The *Journal* provided news of Ireland, of immigration conditions, and of Catholic affairs for a huge audience of Irish people who were hungry for news of the old country and very interested in charitable schemes to relieve immigrant suffering. The *Journal*, later to be called *Griffin's Journal*, was to be the chief sounding board for the editor's views on Irish and American affairs.

The president of the I.C.B.U. from 1873 to 1875 was Anthony
M. Keiley, a Democratic mayor of Richmond, Va. His interest in
colonization plans to remove the Irish from the grim living
conditions of the cities inspired Griffin to espouse the colonization
cause. In 1876 Griffin led in the founding of the Philadelphia
Colonization Society. Plans were drawn up for an Irish settlement
in Charlotte County, Va., to be called Keileyville, and the venture
was promoted with the typical enthusiasm of the colonizer. Bishop
John Ireland of Saint Paul, Minn., was also engaged in colonization
schemes in the West, and for a time such ventures seemed to offer
the two things felt to be most needed by the Irish, escape from the
misery of the city slums, and land for a fresh start in America.[3]
Griffin extolled the glories of rural life and hailed the Keileyville
settlement in one *Journal* issue after another. By 1880, however, it
was clear that the practical problems of such a colony were very
serious.

The eventual turnabout on colonization was signaled in 1881
when Griffin used a letter from Thomas A. Butler of Saint Louis on
the front page of the *Journal*, in which the writer decried colony
schemes for the Irish immigrants. He urged instead that the Irish
go to the root of their own problem and recapture the land of their
home island from English landlordism.[4] Griffin was already far
along in this direction, but it was not until November 1883 that he
formally confessed to readers the demise of the Keileyville
scheme. Thereafter, Griffin was to rely on the gradualist improvement plans of the I.C.B.U. to elevate the lot of the Irish in
America.

The I.C.B.U. was an amalgam of more than 200 charitable
organizations functioning at the state and local level. The strains in
such a broad array were constant, and Griffin editorialized frequently about the need for unity. Because the I.C.B.U. was to be
his central organizational experience, this necessity to achieve
unity by consent from among a far-flung representation would have
a long-term impact on Griffin over the years. It led him in 1879 to
inveigh against secret societies and to reprint episcopal pro-
nouncements against them. Revolutionary groups like the Fenian
Brotherhood and the spasmodic Mollie Maguires in the mine
districts of Pennsylvania were not organized for charitable pur-

poses, he wrote, but as direct-action groups bent on using violence to secure their ends.

Although wary of secret organizations and animated by a vision of social progress through the uplift activities of the I.C.B.U., Griffin was nevertheless aware of the desperately abject conditions of the bulk of the Irish people. The poverty of rural Ireland constantly threatened the landless with hunger. In January 1880 Griffin was a member of the committee that arranged a Philadelphia reception for Charles Stewart Parnell and John Dillon, chief apostles of the Irish National Land League. Parnell declaimed:

> We must break down this odious land system which has been a horrible miasma over our land. We must give Irishmen at home a chance to show that energy that has been shown to such an extent in this country. They must own their land, and govern their land, free from all foreign influences.[5]

Griffin was stirred by this address to the closest approximation to advocating violence that he ever uttered. In the February 1880 issue of the *Journal* he editorialized:

> Help, brothers! Give Ireland to eat and to be strong—strong in body, in mind, in soul. No nation determined can be thwarted! The Roman Emperors trembled upon the throne of the world when their people shouted *Panis vel Sanguis!* Bread or Blood![6]

Although these sentiments were expressed in 1880, a year later Griffin encountered an Irish leader at a Total Abstinence Brotherhood meeting in Scranton, Pa., who spurred him to prodigious organizational feats in behalf of the Land League. That leader was Michael Davitt, the most widely admired Irishman of his time, next to Parnell. Davitt was born to an Irish-speaking family in the bitter poverty of County Mayo. During his childhood he lost one arm in a factory in England. He spent years in prison for his agitation against English rule. Davitt's ideas about land reform and social development inspired his involvement with the Land League and his tours of Irish communities in America to gain support for it. His speech to the Scranton convention galvanized Griffin to more than cries for "Bread or Blood!"

In the following months Griffin organized in Philadelphia alone twenty-four branches of the American Land League, and these in turn generated nine ladies' auxiliary groups. One was named for Parnell's grandfather, Adm. Charles Stewart of Philadelphia. "The Land League must have money to extend the agitation, and the lovers of justice must furnish it," wrote Griffin.[7] In each of the issues of the *Journal* the activities of the branches were reported. In 1881 Parnell and his colleagues in Ireland issued a "No Rent Manifesto," calling for the withholding of rents by tenants until their grievances were satisfied. Griffin and his followers were driven to even greater exertions when Parnell was imprisoned by English authorities. Fund raising was avidly pursued, and $100,000 was obtained from Americans of many backgrounds. The idea of land for the people had a strong appeal to American audiences, who saw land redistribution as a key to the pacification of Ireland's troubled life. Unlike many other communities, Philadelphia did not experience rancorous disputes about the handling of the funds collected. Griffin's long-time friend, Patrick O'Neill, a municipal council member in Philadelphia, was a scrupulous and exceedingly honest treasurer of the Irish National League.

Martin Griffin took a vigorous part in American Land League conventions and fund raising and helped organized the Parnell Testimonial in 1883, the Parnell Parliamentary Fund Demonstration, and the Mrs. Parnell Testimonial in 1885. As the Land League was merged with the Irish National League to broaden the base of Irish power in the United States, Griffin played a role in the latter organization. Throughout this period he continued to promote and publicize the Irish Catholic Benevolent Union. In 1884 he founded the American Catholic Historical Society, which did a great deal of valuable archival and publishing work relating to Irish-American history.

The Irish land agitations of the 1880s eventuated in a drive for Home Rule in Ireland in 1886, and Griffin took part in developing support for this political goal. Again, the goal was congenial to American ideals in which self-government was an accepted principle of political life. The sheer extent of Irish organizational effort, however, generated problems and conflicts. One of these conflicts was over the Total Abstinence Brotherhood and its campaign for a nonalcoholic Irish constituency. Griffin was a T.A.B. stalwart. Saloon keepers were big contributors to Irish and Catholic causes, and they resented the T.A.B. attempts to dominate the Irish Catholic Benevolent Union. That organization finally split over this issue in 1894, and Griffin's power began to fade. The Ancient Order of Hibernians extended its influence, as did the Irish National League.[8] Griffin's years of national sway were past, but in 1904 he was active in planning the Irish Exhibition at the Saint Louis Exposition. In 1908 Griffin at last visited the birthplace of his parents in Ireland. Three years later he died, and his passing was noted in Ireland and America with the recollection that he had organized more branches of the Land League than any other Irishman in the United States.

Griffin's career was grounded in his role as a journalist for Catholic publications. His work in behalf of Irish causes was consonant with the conservatism of Catholic bishops and most organization leaders. When a dispute arose as to the morality of Irish tenants' withholding rent from landlords, Griffin researched the Catholic teaching on the issue and found moral justification for the action. Yet, he decried secret societies and abhorred violence. He was a model Victorian organizer, tremendously energetic, capable and filled with a sense of righteous purpose.

The career of another Philadelphian born of Irish parents stands in striking contrast to that of Griffin. A course of Irish nationalist dedication of quite a different kind was followed in the life of Luke Dillon, known to the Irish revolutionary underground as "Dynamite Luke." Dillon's parents had emigrated from famine-wracked County Sligo in the mountainous West of Ireland to Leeds in England. Luke Dillon was born in Leeds in 1848 and brought to the United States at the age of six. The family lived in Trenton, N.J. Like many young Irish men with slim prospects, Dillon enlisted in the U.S. Infantry Regiment in Montana and Wyoming. He left the army in 1870 as a corporal with a service rating of "excellent."[9]

After army service Dillon took up residence in Philadelphia. In the 1870s he came into association with the Fenian Brotherhood in the city led by such men as James Gibbons, a printer, and Dr. William Carroll, a physician. The 1870s were a period of disillusionment for the Irish revolutionaries. The bold plans of the Fenians for an invasion of Canada and an uprising in Ireland in earlier years had been thwarted, as I have shown in Chapter 7. But planning was always under way, for the protagonists of Irish independence were deeply committed men. Violence as a form of protest was a tool of political revolutionaries among various suppressed national groups in Europe, and their exiled agitators constantly spurred its use from bases in America and elsewhere.

The Fenian Brotherhood was gradually replaced by the Clan na Gael (Children of the Gael) in the 1880s, and the Clan developed plans for a bombing campaign in England. In 1884 Luke Dillon and Roger O'Neill went to London and carried out bombings that wrecked the Junior Carleton Club, an upper-class political resort, and the office of Scotland Yard. These daring acts were followed in 1885 by explosions at the House of Commons. An attempt to mine London Bridge, however, resulted in an accidental explosion and the deaths of two of Dillon's companions, and he returned to the United States still unknown and unsuspected by British authorities.[10]

The late 1880s were a time of deep plotting and internal discord for the physical-force elements of the Irish nationalist movement.[11] The partisans of violence had built up a formidable underground membership of thousands in the United States, and the strains within the Clan resulted in a split into two bitterly opposed factions. One group was headed by Alexander Sullivan, a Chicago lawyer. The other, which included Dillon and most of the Philadelphia contingent, was led by John Devoy of New York. Unknown to either group was the fact that the British secret service had infiltrated the Clan, and a remarkably skillful agent acting under the name of Major Henri Le Caron was steadily funneling reports on Irish-American affairs to officials in London.

In 1888 Le Caron reported renewed interest in the Clan in dynamite schemes. He mentioned a number of prominent Philadelphia Irish men involved in Clan activities, including John Walsh; Michael J. Ryan; Dr. Peter McCahey; Dr. William Carroll; Hugh McCaffrey, a wealthy hardware manufacturer; Bernard McCready, a textile manufacturer; Miles Carr; John J. Bradley; and Roger O'Neill, the companion of Luke Dillon in the London bombings of

1884. Dillon was named at various times in Le Caron's secret dispatches.[12]

The split in the Clan became deadly serious when Alexander Sullivan was charged with embezzling more than $300,000 in organizational funds. The Clan set up a Trial Committee to convene in Buffalo, N.Y., to investigate the matter. Dillon gave crucial evidence there, accusing Sullivan of trying to bribe him with Clan funds and, even more damaging, with having betrayed one of the London bomb plots to British officials. Such testimony certainly earned the enmity of Sullivan, which was not to be taken lightly, for one of Sullivan's critics, Dr. Patrick H. Cronin of Chicago, was subsequently murdered in that city by Sullivan's henchmen. Dillon and Dr. Peter McCahey, who was also on the Trial Committee, were marked men in the murky underground of Irish intrigue. Sullivan, however, became discredited and gradually lost his power.

Prior to leaving the United States and "blowing his cover," the agent Le Caron visited Luke Dillon in Philadelphia and heard him describe a new explosive device that he hoped to use in the future. It was Le Caron's opinion that in 1888 the strongest center of Irish revolutionary activity in America was located in Philadelphia, and one of his last acts before leaving for England was to send a photograph of Dillon to the authorities there.[13]

Through the 1890s Dillon continued his work as a revolutionary, helping to organize meetings and local fund-raising events, providing refuge for men "on the run" from Ireland, and generally propagandizing for his cause. By 1899, when England became involved in the Boer War in South Africa, Dillon was ready for another escapade. It took the form of a bombing venture against Canada's Welland Canal, a very strategic waterway linking the Great Lakes to the Saint Lawrence River. The facility was generally important for shipping but especially important because England needed war materials from Canada. On April 21, 1900, at 6:30 P.M. an explosion occurred at the locks of the Welland Canal. Three men, John Walsh, John Nolan, and "Karl Dullman" were apprehended by Canadian police in Thorold, Ontario, in connection with the explosion, which had not sealed off the canal but had damaged it. "Karl Dullman" was Luke Dillon. Despite the fact that

Dillon was never placed at the actual scene of the explosion, a Canadian jury in thrity-five minutes found the three men guilty after a trial in which the evidence against Dillon was flimsy. All got life sentences. Nolan went insane in prison. Walsh was released after some years, but persistent efforts by Irish-American groups to free Dillon were unavailing. He remained in prison until July 12, 1914. It was believed by Irish-American leaders that he was kept imprisoned for fourteen years because Canadian officials were fearful that his release would antagonize the Loyal Orange Order, a secret society which was very strong in Lower Canada, and which was bitterly opposed to Irish independence and its protagonists. [13]

After his eventual release from prison Dillon returned to Philadelphia. He resumed work for the Clan na Gael, this time in behalf of the Easter Rising of 1916, which was to lead to the war for Irish independence. That struggle, financed in large part from America, resulted in the setting up of an Irish Free State under a 1921 treaty imposed by England. This was far short of the Irish Republic sought by men like Dillon, and he continued in his old age to work for a full republic until his death in 1926.

The memory of Luke Dillon persists in the Philadelphia community, especially among members of the Clan na Gael. A ballad about him was taught to me by the late Owen B. Hunt, but Hunt was unable to tell me who composed it:

The Ballad of Luke Dillon—
The Hardest Man of All

My name it is Luke Dillon
From a lovely Irish glen.
My parents they were driven forth
By greedy Englishmen.
They came here to America
In sorrow and despair,
And raised me up in poverty
On the banks of the Delaware.

They taught me to love Ireland
And hate her ancient foe.
They worked me hard and taught me well

And a strong lad I did grow.
I worked upon the railway.
You could hear the foreman bawl,
"You work like twenty engines, Luke,
You're the hardest man of all."

In eighteen hundred sixty-six
For the army I did sign
And fought the savage Indian
On the bloody frontier line.
One day I fought as others died
And my captain he did call,
"You've killed their chief, Luke Dillon!
You're the hardest man of all!"

I came to Philadelphia
And joined the Clan na Gael,
A secret band of Irishmen
Who would twist old England's tail.
We swore to bomb proud London town
Right up to the palace wall,
And they sent me there to do the job
As the hardest man of all.

With bold old Mack Lomosney
We bombed proud London town,
And made our way to London Bridge
To blow its pilings down.
Mack Lomosney lit the fuse
But it blew a fiery ball.
He died as I swam from the flaming boat
As the hardest man of all.

In England I did bomb and burn
So the Queen could never say
She kept her foot on Ireland's neck
And never had to pay.
For England and her army
Kept Ireland in her thrall,
But Ireland had Luke Dillon
Oh, the hardest man of all.

Eighteen eighties, eighteen nineties,
Then England fought the Boer,
And sought to crush out freedom
In another bloody war.
The Clan sent me to Canada
To bomb canals and all,
And burn the guns of England's sons
As the hardest man of all.

At the Welland Canal they captured me
My secrets I would not tell.
The Orange warden cursed me hard
As I sang in my prison cell,
"Go to hell you Limey warden,
You can screw me to the wall!
You'll never break Luke Dillon!
I'm the hardest man of all."

For fourteen years I heard their jeers
In the prisons of the Crown,
But I did not have a minute's doubt
We would bring old England down.
I was free in nineteen sixteen
When Ireland's lads stood tall,
Drinking: "Here's to old Luke Dillon!
He's the hardest man of all!"

The careers of Martin Ignatius J. Griffin and Luke Dillon
contrasted strongly. Griffin, respectable and prominent, was identified with conservative Catholicism. Dillon, a member of a secret
society banned by the church, was a lifelong radical. In one
respect their careers paralleled. Both failed in their plans to chart
the future of the Irish in America. Griffin, after seeing that
colonization would not be the road to improvement, pinned his
hopes on a Catholic-sponsored social-uplift organization. This
movement was upstaged by the variegated course of Irish progress
in the country that brought improvement through trade unionism,
social mobility, and political organization. Dillon sought to commit
the Irish in the United States to a violent course against England,
but the interest of the group in its own advancement, and the

acceptance by it of the half-a-loaf settlement in 1921 leaving a partitioned Ireland, undercut his radical aspirations.

The careers of both men illustrate the moderate versus radical tension that polarized Irish-American organizational life intermittently over the generations.[15] However, both of these Irish-American nationalists came in the end to face that complex condition that confronts all idealists, the contradictory history of one's own people.

NOTES

1. Thomas N. Brown, *Irish-American Nationalism, 1870–1890* (Philadelphia: J. B. Lippincott Co., 1966), pp. 63–84.

2. These and other facts of Griffin's life are documented in the Griffin papers in the Archives of the American Catholic Historical Society, Saint Charles Seminary, Overbrook, Pa.

3. Carl Wittke, *The Irish in America* (Baton Rouge, La.: Louisiana State University Press, 1956), p. 73.

4. *I.C.B.U. Journal*, Jan. 1881.

5. *I.C.B.U. Journal*, June 1880.

6. *I.C.B.U. Journal*, Feb. 1880.

7. *Griffin Papers*, R.C. 8, Boxes 7 and 8.

8. Brown, *Irish-American Nationalism*, p. 161.

9. Quoted in Colm Brannigan, "The Luke Dillon Case and the Welland Canal Explosion of 1900," *Niagara Frontier* 24, no. 2 (Summer 1977): 36–44.

10. Leon O'Broin, *Revolutionary Underground: The Story of the Irish Republican Brotherhood 1858–1924* (Totowa, N.J.: Rowman and Littlefield, 1976), pp. 5–61.

11. Brown, *Irish-American Nationalism*, pp. 172–78.

12. This information was obtained from Le Caron's letter book, a copy of which is in the possession of the author.

13. Letter of Le Caron to Sir Robert Anderson, October 12, 1888, Le Caron letter-book.

14. Brannigan, "The Luke Dillon Case and the Welland Canal Explosion of 1900," pp. 40–44.

15. Philip Foner, "Radicalism in the Gilded Age: The Land League and Irish-America," *Marxist Perspectives* (Summer 1978), pp. 6–55.

9 John Reilly's Fight against Partition

When disorders erupted in 1969 in Northern Ireland, a further chapter was begun in the long struggle between Irish nationalists and British loyalists on Irish soil. The recurrence of violence in Northern Ireland in 1969 was a manifestation of a political, cultural, and religious cleavage in Ulster that had deep roots in the economy and history of the area. To students of Irish affairs the 1969 disruptions in the British-dominated six counties of Northern Ireland were simply an extension of a long-festering Irish nationalist resentment against the partition of Ireland. The formal division of the island grew out of British actions at the time of the 1921 treaty that followed the successful Irish guerrilla war establishing the independent Irish Free State, later designated the Republic of Ireland. Hard-line nationalists never accepted the compromises involved with the 1921 treaty, especially the continued British rule of the province of Northern Ireland created at that time.[1] Even the moderate government of the Irish Free State never juridically accepted partition of the Northern six counties of the country. British arguments favoring the "Protestant state for a Protestant people" created in Ulster were impugned not only by the Irish at home but also by Irish emigrants and allies in the United States. Irish-Americans used their influence to counter British maintenance of partition in a way that would not let the matter rest and that forecast the activity in behalf of dissent in Ulster in the decade following 1969.

The broad Irish-American community that had been instrumental in marshaling American opinion in support of an independent Ireland became quiescent after the treaty of 1921.[2] A civil war in Ireland between hard-line nationalists and proponents of the Free State from 1921 to 1924 disillusioned many. Through the late 1920s and 1930s the problems of American life and the Great

Depression preoccupied most Irish-Americans. They maintained their social and fraternal groups and a few national organizations, but the coming of World War II left little time for Irish-American attention to the old country.

After World War II the potential for the use of Irish-American influence against partition began to emerge. The strong wartime alliance of England and the United States made any opposition to British interests difficult, but the Irish nationalists had never been deterred by the ascendancy of British prestige. There still existed in major American cities extensive Irish constituencies with a long tradition of political participation and concern for conditions in Ireland. In the past this Irish-American constituency had exerted a powerful influence on Irish leadership and nationalist under-takings.[3] The city of Philadelphia had long been a center of such Irish-American interest and in the post–World War II period would become the focus of much antipartition agitation.[4]

After World War II the Irish government in Dublin was faced with some difficult problems of opinion in the United States as well as serious postwar economic issues. Despite the enlistment of several hundred thousand Irish in British military forces, Winston Churchill upbraided Ireland for remaining neutral in the face of the Nazi threat to all of Europe and England. Eamon De Valera, head of the Dublin government during the war years and after, believed that Ireland had been scrupulously neutral and argued that partition of his nation by England forbade an Irish alliance with England.[5] Many people in the United States shared Churchill's resentment of Irish neutrality. In postwar years the De Valera government and leading Irish-Americans were anxious to have Ireland's case presented to American opinion and to take up the argument against partition once more in a period when many boundaries were being redrawn and the United Nations was being developed as a forum for international problems.

Leaders in the Irish community in Philadelphia had remained faithfully engaged in activity in behalf of the old country even in the hard years of the 1930s. The local base of the efforts was the Federation of American Societies for Irish Independence founded in 1933. This federation united some twenty-five organizations, including societies representing those with ties to various Irish counties, fraternal groups, and such groups as the Commodore John Barry Society, which memorialized the Wexford sailor who founded the American navy. Because of the prestige and dedication of several Philadelphians, the city was also a center for the activities of the American Association for the Recognition of the Irish Republic. This organization had been founded by De Valera in 1919 when, as a young revolutionary, he visited the United States seeking aid for the fledgling Irish state. Over the years the organization had survived the factionalism and strains of Irish-American life and had also survived the twists and turns of De Valera's tortuous political alterations in the years when he rose to head successive Irish governments.

The Irish groups met in a constellation of meeting halls in the older neighborhoods of the city to plan a whole cycle of annual events. Some of these events required liaison with the Irish in other cities. In 1939, for instance, De Valera planned to visit the United States, and a National De Valera Reception Committee was set up in New York. A committee in Philadelphia busied itself with plans for the visit. Looking toward the future, J. C. Walsh of the national committee urged the Philadelphians to carefully preserve the lists of invites developed for the De Valera visit. The visit never came off, however, because growing tensions in Europe induced De Valera to cancel it. The tour by the Irish leader was to have ended with an "International Irish Congress" in Chicago, at which a huge petition would have been presented to the U.S. government urging it to formally oppose the partition of Ireland.[6]

A key figure in the persistent activist network was John J. Reilly, a Philadelphian who conducted a successful real-estate business. Born in Doylestown, Pa., in 1899, Reilly had served in the American navy and had visited Ireland after World War I.[7] He was widely acquainted with Irish-Americans who were involved in the drive to obtain Irish independence in the period following the Dublin uprising of 1916. Quiet, astute, and with an inventive sense of political and propaganda tactics, Reilly was an impressive figure. Of medium height, bald, with a steady gaze and an ever-present pipe, he communicated solid confidence and a swift intelligence. He had come to know most of the major figures in Irish affairs who had intermittently visited America, including De

Valera, Frank Aiken, Sean Lemass, Sean MacBride, and others. Having worked with them through the 1920s, he maintained his ties and became president of the American Association for the Recognition of the Irish Republic. By 1944 he was also a board member of the American Congress for the Unity and Independence of Ireland based in Chicago and later vice-president of the American League for an Undivided Ireland. Through these groups Reilly carried out a very long campaign to advance the prestige of Ireland and to oppose partition. By 1954 Reilly had become president of the Friendly Sons of Saint Patrick, the nation's most prestigious Irish organization, founded in 1771.

The war years presented the Irish-American organization heads with an array of difficult issues concerning Irish interests. Many of their constituents were in the military forces, the news was dominated by the great events on the battlefronts, and England's fight for survival endowed her with enormous prestige in America. John Reilly and his colleagues were not deterred by these conditions from keeping up a small but continuous propaganda campaign to counter British policy. In 1940 Reilly and David R. Roche published a pamphlet, *Partition in Ireland,* that recited the history of the division of Ireland in 1920 and stated, "An artificial boundary, a subsidized puppet government, and the continued persecution of those within that boundary are assurances that neither England nor Ireland can be at peace." In July 1941 he wrote to President Franklin Roosevelt concerning Irish neutrality and its justification. He also excoriated a priest, Rev. Maurice S. Sheehy, who on becoming a chaplain in the U.S. Navy reproached Ireland for her wartime neutrality, saying that "the cause of England is the cause of freedom." Reilly emphasized England's imperial aims that were mingled with the aims of the Allies in the war on the Axis.[8]

Irish organizations in Philadelphia through their federation purchased $100,000 in defense bonds, while criticizing Britain for spreading propaganda supporting the partition of Ireland through American armed-forces libraries.[9] The British Information Service was a constant source of irritation to the Irish-Americans. John Coyle, president of the Federation of American Societies for Irish Independence, issued a statement urging the United States to send arms to the Irish government so that Irish neutrality could be defended against threats from Germany or England. The Philadelphia activists publicized a speech by Judge Clare Gerald Fenerty, a gifted speaker, criticizing the United States for providing Lend-Lease and, later, Marshall Plan aid for England without pressing for a redress of Irish grievances. In 1942 Reilly and others sent to members of Congress a resolution urging that any postwar international conference include Irish partition as one of the issues to be resolved. Later, Reilly circulated De Valera's statement that "Peace is dependent upon the will of the great states. All the small states can do, if the great states fail in their duty, is resolutely to determine that they will not become the tools of any great Power and that they will resist . . . every attempt to force them into a war against their will."

The years after 1945 may have been "postwar," but they were hardly peaceful. Eric Goldman describes them as "worried . . . yearning . . . exhilarated," beset by strikes and internal discord domestically and expanding Communism abroad.[10] The Irish-Americans were sharing in the economic growth, suburbanization, and higher-education boom of the time. The men who worked with John Reilly, however, were developing their publicity and lobbying network to press their arguments against partition. Two of Reilly's collaborators were Robert V. Clarke and Capt. David Roche. Clarke was a government employee and a journalist by avocation. Born in County Mayo, he was full of humor and stories about Irish politics and nationalist episodes. Roche, who had served in the U.S. Army during the war, was a County Cork man, short, good-looking, and witty, with a sharp flair for satire. These men met frequently at Reilly's center-city office to manipulate a wide selection of lobbying and pressure tactics. Reilly kept in touch with the Irish legation in Washington. Correspondence with senators and representatives was generated. Political figures with close Irish ties, such as former U.S. attorney general James P. McGranery and Philadelphia Congressman Michael Bradley, were always ready to try to be helpful. Reprints of materials about Ireland from the *Congressional Record* were freely distributed. News releases to Irish-American and metropolitan newspapers were produced, and letters of praise or refutation of such columnists as Dorothy Thompson, Anne O'Hare McCormick, or Arthur Krock were prepared.[11] Local events, such as the annual mass and speechmaking in honor of Commodore John Barry, were used as occasions to decry partition. Visits of Irish dignitaries to the city were also used to emphasize the issue. This was all done by Reilly and his colleagues without any remuneration. Indeed, the organizational work cost all of them money and a heavy commitment of time. "Ireland is a small country. She requires big sacrifice," was one of the traditional nationalist canons.

Though such contacts and old friends as Sean T. O'Kelly, elected president of Eire in 1945, Reilly and his network were aware of the desire of the Irish leaders to mount a major refutation of British indictments of Irish neutrality. In 1945 De Valera made a stern speech in response to Winston Churchill. Reilly had copies of the speech reproduced, and he himself made a radio speech in Philadelphia, following De Valera's line of argument that offered the partition of Ireland as the justification for keeping the country out of war. On Saint Patrick's Day Reilly broadcast a talk, pointing out that as early as 1935 De Valera had given notice of Irish neutrality to European powers. He refuted allegations that German submarines had refueled in Ireland and that the German legation in Dublin was an espionage center. He stated that 175,000 Irish men and women had served in the forces of the Allies, that 100,000 performed direct war work in Britain, and that many Britons were given refuge in Ireland, while 150 million dollars worth of food a year was supplied England from the Irish sanctuary. The speech was inserted in the *Congressional Record* by Representative Bradley, and copies were distributed to Irish groups.[12]

On August 4–5, 1945, Reilly brought together Irish leaders from throughout the eastern states at the Hotel Pennsylvania in New York City. Judge Robert Mahoney (New York), Dr. Joseph P. Tynan (Boston), Katherine Kane (Hartford), and others convened to review the work of the American Association for Recognition of the Irish Republic. Reports were presented from California, Illinois, Ohio, and other states. Recommendations of the meeting included a membership drive, work with other organizations, and a better flow of information from the Irish government.[13]

In 1946 Reilly made arrangements to distribute widely a pamphlet reprinted from articles in the *Derry Journal*, a newspaper in Northern Ireland. The pamphlet, by Cahir Healy, set forth many references to how Irish partition emerged and provided statistics on Northern Ireland's "gerrymandering of electoral districts and persecutions of Nationalists." Another exposé of the injustices under partition was written in 1946 by Eddie MacAteer, entitled *Ireland's Fascist City*, and this detailed account of the disfranchisement of the Catholic minority in Derry was distributed through Reilly's office.[14] Reilly also served as treasurer of the Green Cross Committee of Philadelphia, a fund begun under an Irish bishop to aid families of those imprisoned by the British in their periodic roundups of nationalists in Northern Ireland. Hon. Michael Donohoe, Judge Clare Gerald Fenerty, and Hon. John L. Coyle were officers of the group. Through this organization meetings were sponsored to keep the conditions in Ulster before the local Irish community.

With such organization and publicity work underway locally, attention was shifted to the national level to prepare for a planned visit by DeValera in 1948. On November 23, 1947, an "Irish Race Convention" was convened at the Commodore Hotel in New York City, under the auspices of the American League for an Undivided Ireland. Presiding was former Philadelphia congressman Donohoe, who as a young schoolteacher in County Roscommon had been driven out of Ireland for his nationalist views. Seamus MacDermott, brother of the martyr of the 1916 rebellion, Thomas MacDermott, was secretary, and such figures as Sean Keating, James J. Comerford, Charles T. Rice, and New York mayor William O'Dwyer were involved. Through Donohoe, one of the grand old men of the Irish network, Reilly had a strong hand in the gathering.[15]

Through this convention and other work the Committee on Foreign Affairs of the House of Representatives was persuaded to hold hearings on the subject of Irish partition. A delegation from the American League for an Undivided Ireland appeared before the committee on February 5, 1948. Reilly was part of the group, along with representatives from San Francisco, Chicago, Boston, and various eastern cities. Heads of the national Irish organizations, such as the Ancient Order of Hibernians, were present. Hon. Joseph Scott of Los Angeles delivered a strong appeal, stating that "we shall continue to speak and we shall continue to protest . . . against the sending of a single dollar of American Taxpayers' Money to Britain while the government at 10 Downing Street persists in the insane division of Ireland."[16]

Following this event arrangements began in earnest for the De Valera visit. The Irish statesman, who had been smuggled into the United States as a hunted revolutionary in 1919, was larger than life in the minds of many Irish people. The sole survivor of the original leaders who led the 1916 uprising, he had survived a British attempt to execute him by having proof of his American birth and citizenship discovered by the brilliant Philadelphia lawyer Michael F. Doyle. As chief of the Irish government through the 1930s and the years of World War II, he had inveighed against partition but had never chosen to actually bring the issue to an all-out conflict with England. He was conscious of the liabilities that a dissident Protestant minority of one million Ulster inhabitants loyal to Britain would mean for a united Ireland. Temporarily out of office from 1948 to 1951, however, he would use his time to denounce the injustices of partition.

In the spring of 1948 De Valera toured the major American cities with his exhortations to those of Irish background and all people interested in international understanding to heed Ireland's case. Never a good platform orator, the aging chief of Irish politics delivered reasoned and dignified speeches. His largely Irish audiences were really ready for more fire than the restrained De Valera could provide, so more stirring speakers usually preceded him at the podium to set the mood.

De Valera's appearance in Philadelphia was typical. A very large hall, the opulent Academy of Music with 3,000 seats, was rented by Reilly's organization. The chairman of the mass meeting was former U.S. attorney general James P. McGranery. Reilly made introductory remarks, and the redoubtedly eloquent Judge Clare Gerald Fenerty introduced De Valera. The Irish leader recounted the long and twisted history of the partition issue and made an appeal for British participation in a moderate settlement looking toward some kind of unity for Ireland. He asserted that the

six Northeastern Irish counties had been sequestered from the rest
of Ireland against the will of the overwhelming majority of the Irish
people and had been retained in British control by both force and
fraud. Recalling Abraham Lincoln and the war to maintain
American national unity, he asked Americans to promote Irish
unity. De Valera said with respect to loyalist fears in Northern
Ireland:

> We don't mind giving a local Parliament, in fact, we provided
> for it in our Constitution. We can leave to the six counties the
> powers which they locally possess, that is, all the powers they
> have, provided that Britain transfers to an all-Ireland Parliament
> in which these people in the North would be proportionately
> represented . . . the powers which Britain has.

He insisted that gerrymandering, however, would have to be
corrected so that the franchise in Ulster could be exercised
equally.[17]

Following the De Valera tour, activity among Irish organizations
incrased on the partition issue. The United Irish Counties Association in New York held a large meeting on the subject in October
1949. In that same month Ed Flynn, powerful political leader of
the Bronx, gave a widely circulated speech hailing the creation of
Israel and highlighting its fight against British domination while
urging attention to Irish efforts against partition.[18]

In March 1950 Irish ambassador John J. Hearne visited Philadelphia and conferred with Reilly and others.[19] A speaking tour
was arranged for Denis Ireland, a Protestant nationalist from
Belfast who was willing to speak in behalf of the unity of Ireland.[20]
In April 1950 the Philadelphia antipartition cohort was protesting
vigorously to the Chamber of Commerce the reception planned for
Sir Basil Brooke, a proponent of British sovereignty over Northern
Ireland who was seeking American aid for industrial development
there.

Having gained access to the forum of Congress, the Irish
activists were not slow to capitalize on it fully. Hearings of the
House Committee on Foreign Affairs were again held in April
1950, and at this session the testimony was detailed and extensive.
A young congressman from Massachusetts, John F. Kennedy,

made a brief statement saying: "I believe that justice will be served if all the people of Ireland are given the opportunity to choose their own form of government." Congressman Kennedy supported a House resolution urging a plebiscite in all of Ireland on the partition issue.[21] In 1949 Congressman John E. Fogarty, a Rhode Island Democrat, had introduced a resolution favoring the political federation of Northern Ireland and the Republic of Ireland unless a clear majority of all the people of Ireland in a free plebiscite declared to the contrary.

The Philadelphia delegation was well prepared for the hearings. John Reilly's testimony recalling his experience in the strife-torn Ireland after World War I was modestly presented. The more extensive argument was given by Robert Clarke, Capt. David Roche, and others. Clarke testified that the British government in 1949 had adopted an "Ireland Act," which:

> guarantees that the partition boundary cannot be changed without the consent of the puppet government of that area. The word "government" here is significant. If the people of the subjugated area should ever want to join with the free portion of the country—and in four of the six partitioned counties a majority of them want to do just that—the Ireland Act is there to prevent them. It is, therefore, apparent that the policy of the present British Labor Government is not one iota different from that of its Tory predecessor of 1920, when the original crime was perpetrated. The Ireland Act is reminiscent of the secret message written by Lloyd George in 1916 to Sir Edward Carson. "We must make it clear," the letter said, "that Ulster does not, whether she wills it or not, merge in the rest of Ireland."

Captain Roche testified that:

> Britain's actions in Ireland are the antithesis of all the principles in which every American firmly believes. Five unassailable facts characterize her program of imperialism:
>
> 1. Northern Ireland is a puppet state, established by an act of the British Parliament alone, and imposed on Ireland by the superiority of British armed forces.
>
> 2. The institution of this state was imposed on the Irish people under the threat of "immediate and terrible war."

3. From the time of its inception in 1920 Britain has continued its support and maintenance.

4. The basic rights of democracy have been denied to over 30 percent of the population of that area.

5. There has been a very effective disfranchisement of the same proportion of the population by gerrymandering and by highly restrictive voting qualifications, both of which have been carefully framed to insure a continuation of British power by the same sectarian party.

Since this partition of Ireland was planned by Britain, established by Britain, is maintained by Britain, and guaranteed of continuance by that same power, it is obvious that only direct action by Britain can end this unnatural division of a country. Any different premise or any different viewpoint cannot be other than evasion and a refusal to appraise the situation in the light of existing facts. As long as the Congress of the United States appropriates funds to aid British recovery, then the Congress, in effect, is subsidizing the repression and persecution of 420,000 Irish men and women in Northern Ireland.[22]

Such testimony, circulated through reprints and stories in Irish-American newspapers and repeated at further meetings, built support for Congressman Fogarty's resolution. Sympathetic members of Congress echoed the testimony on the floor of the House and elsewhere through 1951 and 1952.

In 1951 on Saint Patrick's Day a reception and luncheon in honor of Sean MacBride, Irish minister of external affairs, was held in Philadelphia. Attending were Dennis Cardinal Dougherty, the local bishops, and an array of Irish-American leaders.[23] MacBride was a strong nationalist, the son of one of the executed rebels of 1916 and the extraordinarily beautiful Maude Gonne MacBride. Such Irish officials esteemed John Reilly highly. As MacBride stated, "I was particularly gratified at the splendid press and radio coverage which was obtained, and I feel that, thanks to you particularly and to those other 'faithful few' of the old guard who have worked so hard in the cause over many years past, my visit was well worth while." Sean Nunan, minister of the Irish legation in Washington, wrote Reilly that he was "deeply thankful for the wonderful cooperation you have always given me in making better known to the American people the intolerable wrong which has been inflicted upon Ireland by the partitioning of that ancient land, and for your unremitting efforts to right that wrong."[24]

On September 27, 1951, the Fogarty resolution came to the floor of Congress for a vote and lost by 206 to 139. Those opposed to the resolution claimed that Northern Ireland was none of the United States' business in the one-hour floor discussion on a motion to schedule the resolution for formal House debate.[25] Congressman John W. McCormack, the Massachusetts Democrat, resented some of the arguments used against the resolution. "Some of the arguments just make me sick," he said. "We are for a free and democratic nation in Palestine, and I'm for that. And here we merely express our opinion that the people (of Ireland) should have a right to determine their future."[26] The Fogarty resolution lost support after that defeat. By May 1953 Congressman Fogarty was able to muster only seventy-five signatures of the 218 needed to get the resolution out of the House Foreign Affairs Committee.

Reilly and his collaborators continued their work of agitation about Irish partition, and Clarke and Roche even established a short-lived newspaper, the *Irish-American,* in 1952 to keep up the campaign.[27] The paper, which opposed Senator Joseph McCarthy's strident anti-Communism, could not support itself. The Korean War again focused public opinion on a nation-wrenching conflict, and pleas for Irish unity were brushed to one side. The Irish-Americans were dispersing ever farther from their old neighborhoods, and the revival of interest in ethnic roots had not yet arrived. Antipartition became a neglected issue even though an Irish Republican Army bombing and raiding campaign in the mid-1950s forecast the violent events that would tear Northern Ireland apart after 1969.

The antipartition work of John Reilly and the organizations he sided was one campaign among many seeking to move American opinion and policy. Haitians, Cubans, Armenians, Africans, and Jews all engaged in such lobbying. Most Americans did not take the zealous arguments of the various activists very seriously. Ironically, the nation blundered into a tragic Vietnam war for which there was no ethnic lobbying. Yet, thoughtful citizens now rue the manner in which such activists were ignored, and years of tragedy in Northern Ireland are a grim reminder that more intelligent attention to such long-standing injustices as that in a divided Ireland might have avoided the bloodshed and bitterness there. The antipartition activists of the 1940s and 1950s knew their Irish history and saw the potential for tragedy in the long-ignored partition problem. Their strenuous lobbying for a moderate solution failed. Conditions in the 1960s deteriorated in Northern Ireland, and violence tore apart a stagnant and vulnerable Northern Ireland regime.[28]

NOTES

1. Calton Younger, *Ireland's Civil War* (New York: Taplinger Publishing Company, 1969). A history of the partition problem is given by Michael Farrell, *Northern Ireland: The Orange State* (London: Pluto Publishers, 1976).

2. Joseph O'Grady, *How the Irish Became Americans* (New York: Twayne Publishers, 1973), p. 137.

3. Sean Cronin, *The McGarrity Papers* (Tralee, Ireland: The Anvil Press, 1972), details this contribution in the twentieth century. In Philadelphia in 1939 John J. Reilly's files listed twenty-four Irish organizations meeting regularly. Much of the information that follows is derived from Reilly's personal papers, which contain correspondence, lists, pamphlets, clippings, radio scripts, conference proceedings, and other materials. These papers will be identified hereafter as the JJR Papers. They are now in the collection of the Historical Society of Pennsylvania, Philadelphia.

4. Dennis Clark, *The Irish in Philadelphia: Ten Generations of Urban Experience* (Philadelphia: Temple University Press, 1974).

5. F. S. L. Lyons, *Ireland since the Famine: 1850 to the Present* (London: Weidenfeld and Nicholson, 1971), pp. 580–82.

6. Letter of April 8, 1939, John J. Reilly to De Valera Reception Committee members; Petition form, May 19–21, 1939. JJR Papers.

7. Biographical note, JJR Papers.

8. Reilly to Roosevelt, July 6, 1941, stating, "Irish neutrality is an accepted fact, and on numerous occasions the Irish government has stated it will fight the moment that neutrality is violated by either belligerent."

9. *Philadelphia Record*, November 26, 1945.

10. Eric F. Goldman, *The Crucial Decade and After: America 1945–1960* (New York: Vintage Books, 1956), p. 45.

11. Correspondence and notes dealing with all these figures are in the JJR Papers.

12. Radio talk reprint, March 17, 1945, JJR Papers.

13. Proceedings of the American Association for the Recognition of the Irish Republic, New York, August 4–5, 1945, JJR Papers.

14. Copies in JJR Papers.

15. Program of the Irish Race Convention, New York, November 23, 1947, JJR Papers.

16. Extension of remarks of Hon. Joseph Scott, president of the American League for an

Undivided Ireland, before the Committee on Foreign Affairs of the United States House of Representatives, February 5, 1948.

17. Transcript of address by Eamon De Valera, Academy of Music, Philadelphia, April 4, 1948, JJR Papers.

18. Speech by Edward Flynn, Irish Information Bulletin, October 27, 1949, JJR Papers.

19. *Philadelphia Daily News*, March 30, 1950.

20. Ireland to Reilly, January 11, 1950, JJR Papers.

21. Hearing before the Committee on Foreign Affairs, House of Representatives, 81st Congress, Second Session, April 28, 1950, p. 89.

22. Ibid., pp. 124, 127.

23. Program, JJR Papers.

24. MacBride to Reilly, April 25, 1951, and Nunan to Reilly, March 18, 1950, JJR Papers.

25. News release by Sean Kelly, Washington, D.C., September 27, 1951, JJR Papers.

26. Ibid., p. 3; *Congressional Quarterly* (1953), p. 702.

27. A copy of the first issue of this paper is in the JJR Papers.

28. For an interpretation of Irish-American reaction to events in Ireland in 1969 and after the date, see Dennis Clark, *Irish Blood: Northern Ireland and the American Conscience* (Port Washington, N.Y.: Kennikat Press, 1977).

PART IV: # Them and Us

Those who write about ethnic history usually focus on one ethnic group and do not relate that group to other ethnic communities to which it is socially connected. An exception is to be found in studies of slavery, where interaction between blacks and whites is most frequently the framework for analysis. The three chapters that follow focus on the relations of the Irish and other urban groups in Philadelphia neighborhoods. The relations of the Irish and adjacent blacks constitute a long and troubled story summarized in chapter 10. The ties between an elite Anglo upper-class area and the large Irish community of working-class people nearby is the subject of the chapter about the Rittenhouse Square district. Links between the Irish and the Jews, the subject of the third chapter in intergroup history in the city, are part of the shifting pattern of social interaction to which each of the ethnic groups in local communities had to adjust.

10   Urban Blacks and Irishmen

Of all the ethnic antagonisms that have arisen in the turbulence of American social development, few have such a distinctively rancorous history as that between black and Irish. Only the white versus Indian and English versus French antagonisms have a longer span of intergroup hostility. Indeed, the enmity between blacks and Irish has become sufficiently proverbial in historical reference that its patent acceptance has served to discourage analysis.[1]

It is important to examine somewhat more closely this long-standing minority conflict, for unlike the other ethnic duels that have plagued this country, it has distinctive features. It has been largely an internal conflict lodged in the centers of national life, not an external one located on the periphery or frontier. It has for most of its course involved two ethnic minorities, not a dominant majority group and an ethnic subgroup. Much of the interpretive literature on our sorry racial history deals with the latter kind of adversary relationship. The Irish-black conflict has also been an almost exclusively urban phenomenon. In a period when we are devoting increasing attention to our urban situation, past and present, this persistent tradition of group strife should be of special interest to us. As an intraurban contention, much of the hostility has political implications in a time of rising black political aspirations. The Irish have been an avidly political group, and the rise of black power now impinges with climactic force on a system of political organization that the Irish had a big part in constructing.[2]

Any attempt to gain insight into a problem with such a lengthy

This article was originally published in Miriam Ershkowitz and Joseph Zikmund, eds., *Black Politics in Philadelphia* (New York: Basic Books, 1973), and is reprinted here with the permission of the original publisher.

history demands some limitation of the topic. This chapter will deal with black-Irish conflict in only one city, Philadelphia. I have resorted to such a restriction of the topic in the hope that it may prompt broader inquiries merited by the scope of the subject.

To understand the social realities underlying and contributing to the legacy of black-Irish antagonism, one must first identify the similarities and differences between the two groups. Both have long traditions of minority status in Philadelphia. Free blacks were present in the city before the American Revolution, and Irish were a part of the colonial population as laborers, indentured servants, and refugee political exiles.[3] Both groups spoke English, a fact that did not help them to surmount ethnic barriers as might have been expected. Both blacks and Irish came to Philadelphia from distinctively rural backgrounds, for the slave-holding South and rack-rented Ireland were each dominated by agriculture. Blacks and Irish entered the industrial city largely as unskilled labor, and this fact had important consequences for their social development. Both had a deep tradition of having been exploited by hereditary overlords, and the psychological results of this similarity have added to their respective histories of alienation and minority consciousness. Both were stigmatized as violence prone by nature. Indeed, both were viewed as separate races, for in the nineteenth century the Irish were viewed as "Celts" and so considered themselves. However, the attribution was not so damaging in America as that of being black.[4]

The histories of the two groups diverge in a number of significant respects. The Irish were pioneers in mass ghetto living and could be said to have founded the ghetto as a Philadelphia urban residential institution under the pressure of nativist discrimination. After a period of initial social disorganization due to emigration in the 1840s, the Irish stabilized family life in conformity with the authority-centered pattern set forth in Roman Catholic teachings. The Irish had as a resource, and used with prodigious energy, the elaborate juridical and institutional structure of the Catholic church. Teachers, leadership, funds, and designs for self-improvement were obtained through this medium. Finally, this group handily attached itself to government and utilized public jobs, programs, and processes for its advancement.[5]

In contrast, blacks, traditionally segregated, came to full-fledged ghetto status in great number after the Irish influx. The Irish ghettos formed before the Civil War, whereas the black population did not begin to increase heavily until after the Civil War. Black family life, evolving within the rural culture of the South after the depredations of slavery, was disrupted again in the migrations to the northern cities. Its adaptations to urban conditions were not strongly shaped by any highly codified and supervised system of religious teaching. A looser structure with more matriarchal influence developed. Black churches, though pervasive in Negro life, were not coordinated and were more democratic than the Catholic structure. With respect to government, the record of repression by public authorities in the South and the disfranchisement and intimidation of blacks in the North even after the Civil War prevented the use of government for Negro advancement until well into the twentieth century. This was 100 years after the Irish infiltrations into the political processes had produced swift naturalization, patronage, and public contracts. In addition, the factor of skin color was ineradicable and worked to reinforce minority status despite any gains in social or economic mobility for blacks.[6]

Within the framework of the economic and social growth of the city, the histories of the two minorities represent courses of development that are different chronologically and demographically but that involve engagement with many of the same problems of urban life. The Irish Catholics began to increase substantially in the city's population in the 1830s. The great wave of Irish immigration in the 1840s constituted a profound shock to the Philadelphia social order because it was the largest single concentrated influx of strangers the city had known since its foundation. By 1850 there were 72,000 Irish-born residents in Philadelphia County. In 1860 this group had increased to 95,000. Four major areas on the outer edges of the city were heavily Irish: Southwark-Moyamensing and Grays Ferry–Schuylkill in South Philadelphia; and lower Kensington and Port Richmond in North Philadelphia. The entry of Irish immigrants continued throughout the nineteenth century, and the Irish remained the largest foreign-born group in the city between 1860 and 1910, composing about 15 percent of the total population. After World War I the group began to decline until by 1960 Irish-born Philadelphians numbered only 58,000 in a population of more than two million. Throughout this long cycle of minority status, the Irish experience notable shifts in residential and occupational life. Their original mid-nineteenth-century areas of concentration persisted until the 1890s. Steady accessions of new Irish immigrants replaced those dispersing to newer residential areas with the momentum of the social mobility of the expanding city. The original Irish areas also received influxes of Jews, Italians, and Eastern Europeans during the "New Immigration" after 1880. The Irish dispersion was broad, extended over the second half of the nineteenth century, and included penetration of upper- and middle-class areas. The erosion of the old Irish areas continued in the twentieth century until the group lost any real residential focus in the city.[7]

Blacks in Philadelphia numbered only a few thousand at the beginning of the nineteenth century, but by 1840 there were more than 20,000 in the county. This total remained fairly stable until after the Civil War, when it began to rise with migration from the South. By 1890 there were 40,000 Philadelphia Negros. In the succeeding decades there was a dramatic increase from 84,000 in 1910 to 134,000 in 1920. The massive increases of the Negro population during and after World War II led to the present vast concentration that all but dominates the inner city in a configuration surrounding the central business district. From a tiny ghetto at the eastern edge of South Philadelphia in the early nineteenth century, blacks moved west behind Cedar (now South) Street, forming the axis for the later enlarged black area across the southern edge of the downtown district. From a nucleus around Tenth Street and Columbia Avenue in North Philadelphia, blacks moved west along Columbia Avenue and then obliquely northwest along Ridge Avenue, thus extending a residential angle that served as the arms to embrace a large area of that section of the city. In the 1890s middle-class blacks moved to West Philadelphia, north of Market Street, in a concentration forecasting a greater black residential shift in this direction after the 1940s.[8]

With respect to the growth of the city, the development of the two minorities offers some fundamental contrasts. The Irish increased their numbers swiftly and heavily between 1830 and 1860 when the industrial character of Philadelphia was being formed. They were thus able to become part of the railroad, metals, and textile industries that were central to the urban economy. This fact, plus Irish small-business activity in an age of expanding free enterprise, permitted large numbers of participate in the outward residential expansion of the city and to achieve a flexible social position within it. Blacks increase less rapidly in relation to Philadelphia's total population. They confronted a post–Civil War economy that was moving beyond the takeoff stage to a more rigid composition. When great tides of black workers entered the city during the periods of the two world wars, the need for unskilled labor, though strong in wartime, was not nearly so consistent as during the early period of industrialization. To the difference of economic mobility was added the difference of color with all the superstitions attached to it. These two factors restricted black penetration of the broader urban fabric, resulting an in intensive segregation more thorough and more enduring than that which the white immigrants experienced.[9]

Sam Bass Warner, in one of the few historical articles that attempts to provide more than a chronological framework for the city's past, gives a convenient typology for viewing Philadelphia development. Three major periods may be discerned: a preindustrial period that yielded to industry as the nineteenth century unfolded; a period of rapid industrialization after 1830, consolidating in the Victorian era; and a time of extension and dispersion of economic and residential life leading to the current pattern. It is helpful to consider the interaction of blacks and Irish against this three-phase background.[10]

In the preindustrial city Negroes were a minority that, like German-speaking Philadelphians and the Irish, lived in a position of clustered subordination in the British-dominated city. The situation was not one of continuous tension. The American Revolution and then the French Revolution disseminated ideas of liberal civil practices that functioned within a class system and a Whiggish economic hegemony. The scattered residential makeup of the city somewhat insulated one group from the other. Free blacks developed a number of skilled pursuits and businesses, but their numbers were limited, and poor Negroes made up the majority of those populating the alley dwellings near South Street. The strong personality of Richard Allen created the Bethel African Methodist Episcopal Church at Sixth and Lombard streets and later the Zoar African Methodist Episcopal Church at Fourth and Brown streets. The location of these churches is significant, for it indicates an early propinquity of blacks and Irish. The Irish immigrants were concentrated near both of these locations in the early nineteenth century. [11]

The Irish of the eighteenth and early nineteenth centuries were composed of two groups, the poor, including the indentured, and an articulate cadre of liberal leaders, many of whom were political exiles. The poor lived on the margin of the city's life, socially and economically. The leadership group took a vigorous and at times flamboyant part in local affairs. Regarded with hostility or skepticism by the dominant families of British lineage, the Irish nevertheless thrust themselves into prominence and controversy. In addition to leaders of the revolutionary period, such as Thomas Fitzsimons, Stephan Moylan, John Barry, and George Meade, the early nineteenth century had such gifted men as Mathew Carey, the political economist, and the litterateur Robert Walsh. These men were Catholic, but the city also contained a host of fiery and democratic Irish Protestants. Such a group established the Irish as a distinctively active public influence in the city in a way that was not paralleled for the black population. Some of the Irish leadership were part of the pioneer abolitionist opinion in the city. Robert Walsh was a strong advocate of such sentiment, and such abolitionist agitators as Thomas Brannagan became well-known antislavery controversialists. Irish attachment to the ideals of the French Revolution disposed educated figures toward an antislavery view. [12]

Within the loose fabric of the preindustrial city, blacks and Irish shared a disadvantaged position, but they were able to coexist with one another without consistent friction. In addition, the libertarian political stance of prominent Irish permitted a sympathetic view of black aspirations of freedom. This period of estranged coexistence, relative tolerance, and mutual subordination, broken only occasionally by hoodlum elements, did not produce any definite pattern of relationships between blacks and Irish. Both were largely excluded from higher political life, and both were accorded only grudging tolerance by the dominant elements of the city.

The period of rapid industrialization that began in the Jacksonian years produced severe strains within Philadelphia. Dislocation of traditional institutions, increased economic competition, depression, and massive immigration taxed the capacity of the city to maintain order and stability.[13] While the black population grew, it did not grow rapidly enough to make a dramatic impact on the social geography of the city in the way that the incoming tide of Irish did. The Irish influx of the 1840s caused a broad challenge to Anglo-Saxon domination of the city. The Irish slum areas proliferating along the southern and northern edges of the city seemed to threaten to surround it. The tumultuous Irish identification with the Democratic party identified them with proslavery opinion. The Irish immigrants, jammed into overcrowded housing, laboring under a memory of oppression in Ireland, and confronted by nativist hostility in the city, were appropriate tinder for intergroup conflagration. The anti-Catholic riots of 1844 only heightened their restiveness. Jostling with blacks who competed for slum space and menial jobs prompted an antagonism toward blacks among the Irish that was stimulated by their own insecurity.

In the turbulence of the industrializing city, clashes between gangs of unemployed or competing workers were not unusual. There were black versus Irish race riots in 1832 and again in 1842 in Southwark and Schuylkill and in 1849 near Sixty and Lombard streets.[15] Later, political rivalry set Irish Democrats against abolitionist Republicans.[16] An urban folk tradition of black-Irish antagonism grew up, marked by street fighting and countless bloody encounters in the dim half-world of the slums.

There were some Irish who still adhered to the libertarian principle. John B. Colohan, a lawyer married to a Quaker, was an officer of the Irish Repeal Association's auxiliary in Philadelphia. This group was dedicated to aiding Daniel O'Connell's campaign to separate Ireland from British parliamentary control. The organization in Philadelphia was torn apart in 1843 by a bitter dispute over remarks O'Connell made expressing his opposition to slavery. O'Connell's espousal of universal liberty was rejected by the majority of his followers, but John B. Colohan and a few others stood firm.[17]

The furious debates of the Civil War period found the city deeply split over the issues that the conflict symbolized. Negroes won sympathy from some, aid via the "Underground Railway" from a few, and, finally, wartime support from the overwhelming majority when an antislavery attitude became synonymous with the defense of the Union. The Irish largely anti-Negro, still volunteered to fight for the Union in great numbers under St. Clair Mulholland, James O'Reilly, and Thomas Francis Meagher.[18] Their wartime response helped to dispel the suspicions about their loyalty to the country that nativist prejudices had propagated. Daniel Dougherty, a lawyer and orator, was a founding member of the Union League and a favorite speaker on the Union cause.[19] The Irish Democrats, however, fell into a permanent limbo because of the identification of their party with the South. They did not recover for generations. The Republican party became so powerful in the city and state that its sovereignty went unchallenged for decades. Blacks had lost the franchise in the state as a result of court decisions in 1838. In the wake of the Civil War, as their numbers grew due to in-migration from the South, they regained it. This sparked murderous election brawls in the 1870s as the Irish sought to keep blacks from voting in areas they controlled. As W.E.B. Du Bois wrote, "As the Irishman had been the tool of the Democrats, the Negro became the tool of the Republicans."[20]

The Irish-black vendetta that grew between 1830 and 1870 practically amounted to an accepted communal pathology. Like so much of the mid-nineteenth century experience of the Irish, it was strongly determinant. Unable themselves to gain control of the city politically, they treated with resentment the attempts of others to gain power. Though politically hamstrung, they were able to make social and economic advances.[21] One of the chief media for their educational and social rise was the Roman Catholic network of schools and self-help organizations that the Irish built with impressive energy and then dominated.[22] The Catholic church, by definition an interethnic and transcultural entity in the scope of its mission, sponsored various activities in behalf of Negroes. Saint Peter Claver Church was built in 1891 at Twelfth and Lombard streets. The heiress Katherine Drexel, daughter of one of the city's wealthiest families, founded an order of nuns to work with Negroes and Indians and devoted her life and fortune to institutions she set up, several of which served Philadelphia. Additional bequests from Irish men, such as Patrick Quinn, and the conduct of missionary work by Irish priests and nuns did not alter the deep cleavage between the Irish and blacks. Protestant Negroes caught in a static web of urban privation and discrimination were rarely compatible with Irish Catholics, more mobile, more accepted, but themselves still alienated from many channels of social life by the memory and persistence of religious and ethnic barriers. As the city entered its mature period of industrialized metropolitan status, black segregation increased as Irish concentration diminished.

In 1880 Philadelphia Negroes briefly deserted the Republicans in a hotly contested mayoralty campaign. William Still, Robert Purvis, and James Forten led the black revolt, tempted by police jobs held out to them by Democrats. As the nineteenth century closed, blacks had built a political redoubt in the Seventh Ward between Spruce and South streets in South Philadelphia. From this ward came the first black Common Council members, and Harry Bass won a seat in the Pennsylvania Assembly from the ward. The center of black political activity was the Citizens Republican Club founded by Andrew Stevens, a caterer, in 1895. Such men as Dr. N. P. Mossell launched much of their early civil-rights work from it. Eventually, the Negro politicians moved their influence into the Thirtieth Ward between South and Christian streets west of Broad Street. With the aid of a newspaper, The *Philadelphia Tribune,* founded in 1887, the black community finally began to navigate politically in the 1890s.[24]

The Irish, split between those who remained doggedly loyal to the hapless and outnumbered Democrats and those who sought their fortunes in the Republican party, contested black inroads into their traditional South Philadelphia territory. Democratic ward bosses resisted every inch of encroachment. The most notable Irish leader to emerge in Republican circles was James P. "Sunny Jim" McNichol, a contractor-politico who headed the Republican City Committee and wielded enormous power in the early twentieth century (see chapter 6). In a more liberal city McNichol would

probably have gone on to become mayor, but in a Republican city
in an imperiously Republican state, he rose only to the state
Senate.[25]

The friction in the South Philadelphia area continued for
decades. At the time of World War I the increase in the black
population in the area's Thirtieth and Thirty-sixty wards caused
acute tension. In 1917 the use of blacks as scab labor during
strikes caused racial brawls. Competition for housing, entry of
blacks into "white" occupational categories, and neighborhood
resentments set the stage for violence. In the summer of 1918 a
mob rioted outside a house newly occupied by a Negro woman on
Ellsworth Street. Disorder spread. The *Philadelphia Tribune*
alleged that Irish police and rioters worked together against
Negroes. The other Philadelphia papers displayed little tolerance
of Negro complaints in the aftermath of the rioting. The political
fortunes of numerous ward bosses and party chieftains were deeply
threatened by the growth of the black population from 84,000 in
1910 to more than 134,000 in 1920.[26]

As the black population swelled in the twentieth century, it
covered ever greater areas in the inner city in South, North, and
West Philadelphia. The Irish, continuing the residential dispersion they had begun so early, gradually evacuated the older areas.
Paradoxically, however, their political prominence increased as
they lost any definable residential base for themselves as a group.
They achieved in Philadelphia, as they had elsewhere, a special
identification with political roles, assuming a generalized political
function as intermediaries, monitors, and strategists. Upon the
basis of political experience begun in representation of their own
ghetto interests, they built a broader framework of urban political
aptitude based on interethnic alliances and professionalized political leadership. On this basis, long after they had lost demographic
concentration, the Irish broke through in the twentieth century in
Philadelphia.[27]

The city's blacks under J. C. Asbury were vassals of the
powerful machine of William S. Vare until 1928. The Democrats
made little or no effort to capture their allegiance for decades. The
memory that it was the Republicans who had restored the franchise
to Negroes and the facts that Democrats ruled the racist South and

were ineffectual in Philadelphia bound blacks to the G.O.P. in 1928, however, the black vote became fluid, with Al Smith getting more black votes than any previous Democrat in the city. In 1932 the Democrats were rallied at last by the handsome and popular John B. Kelly, who lost by a narrow margin. In 1932 the Democrats got 30 percent of the black vote, while getting 42 percent of the city-wide vote. The next year the Democrats went out to register black voters in earnest. Thus, the shift of the Negro vote, once begun, increased.[28] Still, in 1937, 2,500 Negroes were reportedly employed in city and county government jobs under the Republicans, a powerful patronage hold that retarded Democratic progress.[29]

The break in the Republican hold on the city did not really come until 1951, when Mayor Joseph S. Clark and City Controller Richardson Dilworth, two socialite reformers, led a Democratic surge into City Hall, the first Democratic municipal administration in the city in sixty-seven years. Behind it was a keenly managed ward-level effort tended by James Finnegan and Congressman William J. Green, two unabashedly professional Irish politicians. Blacks, who then represented more than one-fourth of the city's population, shared in the victory after returning solid Democratic majorities in their wards.[30] As something of an anticlimax, the first Irish Catholic was elected mayor in 1962, when James H. J. Tate took office as a Democrat. Under the reform administration and the Tate regime, blacks moved into numerous high city posts, becoming deputy mayor, department heads, and heads of antipoverty and urban-improvement programs. Irish and blacks collaborated in city government and politics after generations of estrangement.

The racial crisis of the 1960s, however, fiercely tested the new alliance. Blacks were attempting to penetrate beyond their ghetto areas, and intermittent neighborhood disorders accompanied housing changes. Black rioting and militancy in the ghetto produced bitter confrontations with the police, a portion of the municipal service still strongly Irish in personnel and spirit. As the reform glow faded from the Democratic machine, racial polarization increased.[31] Many white neighborhoods where the Irish had lived changed their population in a few years and became totally black. Portraits of John and Robert Kennedy could appear beside that of

Martin Luther King in ghetto windows, but the sneering racism of hard-hat Irish blue-collar workers left little room for interethnic sentimentality in the age of the Black Panthers.

A "new breed" of younger Irish Democrats arose, including Congressman William Green, Jr., son of the William Green who had been the architect of the Democratic machine that underlay the reform of the 1950s. These men, such as housing coordinator Gordon Cavanaugh and School Board member Gerald Gleeson, held fast to political careers despite the intense pressures of urban problems and black militancy. The Republicans, headed by William Meehan and William Devlin, also showed younger Irish leadership. Although far removed from the old ward-heeler image, these men still had to contend with ever-growing demands from blacks for patronage and control. By the end of the 1960s there were three black city councilmen out of seventeen, a share that did not match the fact that blacks constituted almost one-third of the city's population. With black mayors appearing in Cleveland, Gary, and Newark, the possibility of a black mayor for Philadelphia was widely discussed. The prospect for an Italian mayor seemed real also. An eclipse of Irish power that had been so long in the making by a black political power that had been kept in the wilderness for an even longer period offered an anomalous situation in the distinctive ethnic history of the city.

The Irish had long maintained their vigorous anti-Negro posture despite such influences of liberal Catholicism as were exercised on them in a notably conservative archdiocese. The Catholic Inter-racial Council under Judge Gerald Flood, Robert Callahan, and Mrs. Anna McGarry was unequal to the glacial prejudice that prevailed.[32] These leaders tried to ameliorate such conflicts as the race violence accompanying integration of the transit-system operators during World War II, when the transit workers were a heavily Irish group. Matthew McCloskey, the powerful Democratic national finance chairman and Philadelphia contractor, could set up a Martin de Porres Foundation to provide blacks with scholarships, but the curse could not be taken off the old tradition. Politics was a more expedient and successful meeting ground than religion, but the rising militancy of blacks, decrying "the system" and repudiating the gradualism of electoral politics, threatened to undermine black political leadership. [33]

What seems evident from this review of Black-Irish relations over an extended period is that urban conditions constituted an exacerbating background for this minority conflict. Beginning with industrialization, what Seymour Lipset has termed "working class authoritarianism" infected the black-Irish relationship. [34] The insecurity and resentment generated by a harsh industrial system played on both minority groups, with blacks suffering most. Their raucous and intolerant prejudice undercut counsels of civic, religious, and political prudence for generations. It was the primary force in a long ethnic duel. Second, the marginal and subservient status of both blacks and Irish within the broader framework of the city's politics and social structure made each group mutually uncertain and highly protective of their political vested interests in the wards and public offices. [35] Neither group could work with the other without feeling tainted. Negro Republicans saw Irish Catholics as intractable foes dating from before the Civil War, even if they could not state this view safely. The Irish saw the blacks as rivals for political control over the bottom of the city's society, a control that could be lucrative and lead to higher things. Third, the spatial and social ecology of the city placed the groups in adjacent positions where they were bound to clash given the circumstances of their competition for housing and facilities. When two groups live along borders of rigidly segregated territory under conditions of mutual hostility, conflict is to be expected. [36] The Irish outnumbered blacks and were strongly represented in police work after the 1880s, and this added to their propensity for aggression toward blacks. Negroes occupied older areas as their population swelled and responded with their own cult of violence.

The aggravating influences of urban life that beset these two groups formed a troubled subculture of conflict underlying political life in Philadelphia. The assumptions of mutual respect and justice required for democratic intercourse were simply absent amid the poverty, struggle, and cynicism of lower-class life in the city. When the opportunity for political interaction for positive goals did present itself in the twentieth century, the legacy of past injury was still intimidating. Black and Irish had each survived the ravages of ghetto life and industrial cruelty, but each was scarred and seared in spirit.

NOTES

1. Carl Wittke devotes a chapter to early Black-Irish conflict in *The Irish in America* (Baton Rouge, La.: Louisiana State University Press, 1952), pp. 125–34. John Higham in *Strangers in the Land* (New York: Atheneum, 1970), p. 26 notes the combative conditions of immigrant life. The persistence of traditions of competition and conflict have belied earlier assumptions of rapid assimilation and have escaped thorough analysis. See Lawrence H. Fuchs, ed., *American Ethnic Politics* (New York: Harper and Row, 1968), p. i.

2. The prominence of the Irish in American politics is summarized well by Bruce M. Stave, *The New Deal and the Last Hurrah* (Pittsubrgh, Pa.: Pittsburgh University Press, 1970), pp. 7–8. Also Fuchs, *American Ethnic Politics*, p. 6.

3. This article deals almost exclusively with Irish Catholics. Irish Protestants, the "Scotch-Irish" so active in the eighteenth century in Pennsylvania, occupied a social position that made them more rural and less exposed to conflict with blacks, although their epic battles with Indians were terrible. See James Leyburn, *The Scotch-Irish: A Social History* (Chapel Hill, N.C.: University of North Carolina Press, 1962), p. i.

4. For background on black Philadelphians see Thomas J. Woofter, *Negroes in Cities* (New York: Doubleday and Company, 1928), Carter G. Woodson, *A Century of Negro Migration* (Washington, D.C.: Association for the Study of Negro Life and History, 1918), Richard B. Sherman, ed., *The Negro and the City* (Englewood Cliffs, N.J.: Prentice-Hall, 1970), and W.E.B. Du Bois, *The Philadelphia Negro* (Philadelphia: University of Pennsylvania Press, 1899).

Background on Irish immigrants is contained in William Forbes Adams, *Ireland and the Irish Emigration to America* (New Haven, Conn.: Yale University Press, 1932), Marcus Lee Hansen, *The Atlantic Migration* (Cambridge, Mass.: Harvard University Press, 1940), Wittke, *Irish in America*, William A. Shannon, *The American Irish* (New York: Macmillan Co., 1963) and L. P. Curtis, *Anglo-Saxons and Celts* (New York: New York University Press, 1968).

5. Irish adaptation to Philadelphia is detailed in Dennis Clark, "The Adjustment of Irish Immigrants to Urban Life: The Philadelphia Experience" (Ph.D. diss., Temple University, 1970).

6. Negro life in the city is reflected in Du Bois, *Philadelphia Negro*, and George F. Simpson, *The Negro in the Philadelphia Press* (Philadelphia: University of Pennsylvania Press, 1936), and James Erroll Miller, "The Negro in Pennsylvania Politics" (Ph.D. diss, University of Pennsylvania, 1945), pp. 69–78.

7. Irish population figures are presented in Irwin Sears, "Growth of Population in Philadelphia: 1860–1910" (Ph.D. diss., New York University, 1960), pp. 67–68, and Clark, "Adjustment of Irish Immigrants," pp. 29–30. Figures for 1960 are from the *Eighteenth Census of the United States, Census of Population*, Part 40, Pa., Table 79 (Washington, D.C.: Government Printing Office, 1963), pp. 40–437. Figures are rounded to the nearest thousand. See also Sam Bass Warner, *The Private City: Philadelphia* (Philadelphia: University of Pennsylvania Press, 1968), Table VII, p. 55.

8. Black population figures are given in Miller, "Negro in Pennsylvania Politics," pp.

57, 77, 86; Leonard Blumberg, *Negroes in Metropolitan Philadelphia* (Philadelphia: The Urban League of Philadelphia, 1959), pp. 31–33; *Philadelphia's Non-White Populations, Report no. 1* (Philadelphia: City Commission on Human Relations, 1961), p. 3.

9. Irish job and residential mobility is described in Clark, "Adjustment of Irish Immigrants," pp. 39–45 and 75–81, and Warner, *Private City*, pp. 55–58.

10. Sam Bass Warner, "If All the World Were Philadelphia: A Scaffolding for Urban History," *American Historical Review* 74, no. 1 (October 1968): 26–43.

11. Clark, "Adjustment of Irish Immigrants," pp. 54–58; J. T. Scharf and Thompson Westcott, *History of Philadelphia: 1609–1884*. (Philadelphia: L. H. Everts Co., 1884), vol. 2, p. 1397; and Works Progress Administration, *Philadelphia: A Guide to the Nation's Birthplace* (Philadelphia: William Penn Association, 1937), p. 107.

12. George O'Brien, *A Hidden Phase of American History* (New York: Dodd-Mead Co., 1920), and John Tracy Ellis, *Catholics in Colonial America* (Baltimore, Md.: Helicon Press, 1965), p. 398. For post-Revolutionary Irish leaders see Edward C. Carter II, "A Wild Irishman under Every Federalist's Bed," *Pennsylvania Magazine of History and Biography* 94, no. 3 (July 1970): 342; Lewis Leary, "Thomas Brannagan: An American Romantic" *Pennsylvania Magazine of History and Biography* 78, no. 3 (July 1953): 332–80. For Robert Walsh see M. H. Rice, *American Catholic Opinion and the Anti-Slavery Controversy* (New York: Columbia University Press, 1944), p. 111.

13. Warner, *Private City*, pp. 125–60. See also Michael Feldberg, "The Philadelphia Riots of 1844," Ph.D. diss., University of Rochester, 1970.

14. Warren F. Hewitt, "The Know Nothing Party in Pennsylvania," *Pennsylvania History* 2, no. 2 (April 1935): 69–85, and Ray Allen Billington, *The Protestant Crusade: 1800–1860* (Chicago: University of Chicago Press, 1964), p. 183.

15. Elizabeth M. Geffen, "Violence in Philadelphia in the 1840's and 1850's," *Pennsylvania History* 34, no. 4 (October 1969): 381, and Woodson, *Negro Migration*, pp. 45–48.

16. Irwin Greenberg, "Charles Ingersoll: the Aristocrat as Copperhead," *Pennsylvania Magazine of History and Biography* 93, no. 2 (April 1969): 194.

17. Accounts of this dispute are in the Philadelphia *Public Ledger* for June 3, 6, 12, 15, 23, 28, and July 20, 1843.

18. John H. Campbell, *History of the Friendly Sons of St. Patrick and the Hibernian Society* (Philadelphia: Hibernian Society, 1892), pp. 273–74, 493, and Ella Lonn, *Foreigners in the Union Army and Navy* (Baton Rouge, La.: Louisiana State University Press, 1951), pp. 124–25, 253, 257.

19. *Biographical Encylopaedia of Pennsylvania in the Nineteenth Century* (Philadelphia: Galaxy Publishing Co., 1874), p. 276.

20. Du Bois, *Philadelphia Negro*, p. 373 and pp. 38–39.

21. Dennis Clark, "Hamstrung Hibernians," in *Greater Philadelphia Magazine* (March 1960). The resistance of Philadelphia class structure to change is explored in Nathaniel Burt, *The Perennial Philadelphians* (Boston: Little, Brown and Co., 1963), and E. Digby Baltzell, *The Protestant Establishment* (New York: Random House, 1964).

22. Thomas McAvoy, *History of the Catholic Church in the United States* (Notre Dame, Ind.: University of Notre Dame Press, 1969), pp. 226–65.

23. Daniel J. Mahony, *Historical Sketches of Catholic Churches and Institutions in Philadelphia* (Philadelphia: Daniel J. Mahony, 1895), pp. 146–47 and 211.

24. WPA, *Philadelphia: A Guide*, p. 107, and Miller, "Negro in Pennsylvania Politics," pp. 77 and 84–86.

25. Edward Morgan, *City of Firsts* (Philadelphia: City of Philadelphia, 1919), p. 291.

26. I am indebted to Irwin Greenberg of Temple University for making available to me

data on this period. For newspaper accounts of the rioting see the Philadelphia *Inquirer* and the Philadelphia *Evening Bulletin* for July 29, 1918, and the Philadelphia *Record* for July 29, 1918.

27. Edward Levine, *The Irish and Irish Politicians* (Notre Dame, Ind.: University of Notre Dame Press, 1966), pp. 188–89. See also Milton Barron, "Intermediacy: Conceptualization of Irish Status in America," *Social Forces* 27, no. 3 (March 1949), pp. 256–63, and Daniel P. Moynihan and Nathan Glazer, *Beyond the Melting Pot* (Cambridge, Mass.: MIT Press, 1970), pp. 250–74.

28. Miller, "Negro in Pennsylvania Politics," pp. 195–210.

29. WPA, *Philadelphia: A Guide*, p. 107.

30. James Reichley, *The Art of Reform* (New York: Fund for the Republic, 1959), and Edward C. Banfield, *Big City Politics* (New York: Random House, 1967), pp. 107–20.

31. Dennis Clark, "Post-Kennedy Irish: The American Decline," *Hibernia* (Dublin, Ireland: March 1967). Black resentment against the Irish, especially the Irish police, became fully expressed in the 1960s. Anti-Irish sentiment erupted even in the Catholic church. See Rev. Lawrence Lucas, *Black Priest, White Church* (New York: Random House, 1970), pp. 98–99 and 240.

32. William Osborne, *Segregated Covenant* (New York: Herder and Herder, 1967), pp. 152–79.

33. As Philip Foner writes: "Blacks, unlike immigrant groups, are achieving local power at a time when the cities are bankrupt, and effective political power, not to mention tax revenues, has shifted from localities to Washington." See his "In Search of Black History," *New York Review of Books* 15, no. 7 (October 22, 1970): 14.

34. Seymour Lipset, *Political Man* (Garden City, N.Y.: Doubleday and Company, 1960), pp. 109–13.

35. The tension between black unity goals and the quid pro quo of politics is indicated by James Q. Wilson, *Negro Politics* (Glencoe, Ill.: Free Press, 1960), p. 169, where black goals are seen as a continuing theme, and Sherman, *The Negro in the City*, p. 159, where expedient machine politics are seen as the tradition.

36. Alan D. Grimshaw, ed., *Racial Violence in the United States* (Chicago: Aldine Publishing Co., 1969), pp. 289–98.

11 Ramcat and Rittenhouse Square

The precincts of privilege exercise a powerful fascination on people who have never shared the life-style of the upper class. From Beacon Hill in Boston to Nob Hill in San Francisco the preserves of wealth and snobbery have had a magnetic effect on the imagination of an otherwise democratic America. This curiosity and interest apply especially to the residential domains of the elite in the Victorian age when bejeweled matrons in resplendent coaches were trotted up to the graceful doorways of Fifth Avenue mansions or stately Philadelphia town houses. Indeed, Philadelphia's Rittenhouse Square in the second half of the last century was something of a synonym for upper-class status. It came to symbolize architectural elegance, aristocratic demeanor, and elite opulence. However, this symbol that we have known is only a partial reflection of reality.[1] It is no accident that our vision of upper-class communities in urban America has been distorted. The dazzling image of their rich and powerful residents has kept us from placing such neighborhoods in the same context with the industrial disorder and swelling urbanism that surrounded them. They have been described more often in romantic than analytic terms. We have really seen only one level of areas like Rittenhouse Square—the "Upstairs" and not the "Downstairs."[2]

Two broad conditions have retarded the historical study of urban community life and prevented the development of a complete perspective on wealthy areas. The speed with which many neighborhoods grew and the disorder of the American urban experience in general have blurred our view of the process of community

Material reprinted from "The Divided Metropolis: Social and Spatial Dimensions of Philadelphia, 1800–1975", edited by William W. Cutler III and Howard Gillette, Jr. and used with the permission of the publisher, Greenwood Press, a division of Congressional Information Service, Inc., Westport, Connecticut.

establishment and growth. In addition, most American historians in the twentieth century have emphasized the broad, integrating aspects of life in the United States, concentrating, as they have, on the political and military scene at the national level. Only recently have they begun to appreciate the extraordinary range of communities in America that were for too long the exclusive province of the provincial, indeed eccentric, writer. Hence, Charles Dickens, James Bryce, and Henry James could all recoil from the apparent chaos and polyglot vitality of American cityscapes while patriotic scholars stood by, unprepared to substitute informed and thoughtful commentaries for the negative observations of such eminent authors.

The growth of sociology and then of social history has done much to eliminate this scholarly oversight. From such pioneering works as Harvey Zorbough's *The Gold Coast and the Slum*, published in 1929, we have progressed to computerized studies of community change.[3] Despite its title, however, Zorbaugh's early book did little to compare the Gold Coast and the slum, and we still lack studies that trace the relationship between one kind of community and another. Analyses of ethnic enclaves, so important for an understanding of our urban past, have tended to fix on one group at a time. The complexity and interrelations of pluralism have not often been shown.[4]

What has been written about Rittenhouse Square and the large Irish area adjacent to it constitutes a clear example of the imbalance in our social history of the nineteenth century and urban studies today. The square itself has been the subject of an impressive literature. There are books on its notable residents, its architecture, and its social structure. E. Digby Baltzell's classic, *Philadelphia Gentlemen: The Making of a National Upper Class*, devotes considerable space to it. Because memoirs, biographies, and guidebooks refer to it repeatedly, we have much material on its wealthy families and their Victorian life-style.[5] However, we know all too little about the area behind Rittenhouse Square to the south and west, and yet this neighborhood was as extraordinary in its own way as the square itself. It was the site of an Irish community that formed in the 1830s and persisted for more than a century with remnants still present today. The history of this neighborhood testifies to the endurance of an ethnic identity even in a rapidly changing American city. Only one book deals with the area to any extent, and it is a fine novel of working-class failure, *John Fury* by Jack Dunphy.[6]

The Irish neighborhood behind Rittenhouse Square is known as Schuylkill, the name of one of Philadelphia's two rivers. The river borders the central business district on the west and loops around this Irish enclave like an enfolding arm. A nineteenth-century crossing called Gray's Ferry also imparts its name to a portion of the area, but the more colorful appellation of "Ramcat" has been used by local people with casual imprecision to refer to the entire neighborhood.

Early histories of the city record that the Schuylkill riverfront was a transfer point for trade with the rich hinterlands to the west and south of Philadelphia. Wagon routes led to Gray's Ferry, and the river shore soon became a mooring area for barges and flatboats as well as vessels in the coastwise trade that sailed up the river from Delaware Bay and the Atlantic. Thus, while Philadelphia proper was growing along the Delaware riverbank and moving westward across empty fields, the Schuylkill settlement was expanding and extending eastward to meet it.[7]

In the 1830s the booming city of Philadelphia was caught up in the first full pulse of its industrialization. Workers were busy on the docks on the Schuylkill River unloading coal and wood to fuel homes and factories all over the city. River-front employers required unskilled hands and strong backs, and since the 1820s the Irish had provided more and more of both. Just as in other areas at the edge of the growing city, the foreign-born were increasing in Schuylkill, and they crowded into jerry-built frame houses and shantytown districts.

The Irish women of the neighborhood took in washing, gathered bones and dung, or worked as ill-paid seamstresses or menial servants, while the men performed the heavy dockside labor of coal heavers and longshoremen. In 1835 these men staged one of the first strikes of unskilled labor in American history, but the reaction of the Philadelphia elite was so swift and hostile that all the city's unions felt threatened.[8] In the Irish community children were always expected to work. Some were indentured for seven or fourteen years as tannery boys, hostlers, or carters; others were put out simply to acquire some discipline, especially if they were orphans, runaways, or delinquents. As early as 1837 a soup society was providing nourishment of body as well as soul to the poor of the area. The Census of 1841 showed 47 percent of the workers in Schuylkill to be unskilled or semiskilled. Many worked in the numerous brickyards that had sprung up in the district.[9]

During the great influx following the famine of 1845–46 the Irish population of Philadelphia grew swiftly from about 40,000 to 70,000.[10] In the Schuylkill neighborhood the 1850 Census listed more than 1700 as Irish born, 43 percent of the total population. Most lived between Lombard Street and Shippen (now Bainbridge), Eighteenth Street and the riverbank.[11] Others lived adjacent to the United States Naval Asylum or the Federal Arsenal near the river. In addition to the many who worked as stevedores, some were employed as weavers, woolsorters, stonecutters, carpenters, and shoemakers. There was even a doctor, J. F. Galey, who lived in the area, as well as a chemist-pharmacist named John Murry.[12] According to a sample of taxpayers whose ratables were recorded in 1850, some Irish had also begun to accumulate land. "General B. Riley" held 21 acres south of the built-up area. Mary Lafferty owned 9 acres, and Christianna Lafferty owned 2½ along with a dwelling and a barn, while James Lafferty kept an inn. John K. Kane counted 110 acres among his possessions, and John McConnell owned some brick kilns. Landowners were exceptional, however. Of the 35 Irish males listed in the surviving tax assessment ledger, 15 were laborers and others were dairymen, basket makers, or small farmers living at the city's edge.[13] Still, these holders of skilled jobs and real property reveal an important feature of the Irish urban condition in 1850. By the middle of the nineteenth century there was a nucleus of example and leadership in the Irish community on the Schuylkill. Originally composed largely of coal heavers, it had diversified and expanded. It was still primarily working class, but by 1850 it had developed some economic variety and a social structure of its own.

However, the growth of the Irish population represented an incremental social threat to the acustomed order of cities like Philadelphia. To the native American the Irish represented disease, especially tuberculosis and cholera, afflictions that were commonly considered to be the scourge of the Great Jehovah on the superstitious Papists. The Irish were manifestly partial to alcohol, a vice terrible to the mind of the Protestant leadership. They were in need of education yet would not send their children to the public schools where Protestantism prevailed. They were unskilled in cities where industrial development demanded not only strong bodies but also new skills. As voters they were enthusiastically democratic, thus imperiling upper-class control of local government. The Irish were also deeply entangled with crime; they were identified not only with gang violence and other disorder but also with the gambling circles of horse racing and illegal boxing. Secret societies and anti-English nationalist groups added a further dimension to the danger that their presence supplied. Finally, they were conceived by educated people to be a separate race, inherently different and inferior. A group alien and intractable, they were fitted for servitude but little else. Perhaps most vexatious of all, they refused to accept their public image and contested it with a vanity only exceeded by the vigor of their protest. Their growing numbers were a deeply unsettling intrusion on the social stability of Philadelphia and other American cities.[13]

In the 1840s anti-Irish and anti-Catholic feelings rose dramatically in Philadelphia, in part because of the famous riots of 1844. In April of that year Catholic weavers fired on a Protestant political rally in Kensington, and in retaliation Protestant attackers burned two Catholic churches near the Delaware River and later beseiged another in South Philadelphia. The riots were a serious manifestation of the social dislocations that industrialization was causing in the city. They were an outgrowth of the competition between hard-pressed native-born artisans and Irish factory laborers. They have also been credited with weakening the important workers' movement of the 1830s by further polarizing workers around cultural loyalties and undercutting their common concern for economic issues. To the Irish Catholics the disorders were simply the most flagrant example of their alienation from the general community.[14] In Schuylkill one response was the formation of the Rangers, the city's first large-scale criminal gang. More than the poverty and harsh dockside conditions of the area, the Rangers

came to signify this Irish community to the rest of the city. Under
the leadership of Billy Keating and Jim Haggerty the gang engaged
in petty thievery, mugging, burglary, intimidation, and prostitution
and controlled the neighborhood. It extorted payments from barge
and ship owners along the waterfront and was energetically
successful until 1857, when Mayor Richard Vaux and a tough local
police lieutenant named John Flaherty drove Keating from the city
and broke the reign of the Schuylkill Rangers.[15]

During the mid-nineteenth century privation and struggle profoundly influenced the Schuylkill area, giving it a tough image and
a strong memory of immigrant suffering. Unemployment and low
wages took their toll on both family life and individual opportunity,
especially when the pace of the city's economy slackened during
hard times. To go "over the River" in "Ramcat" meant being sent
to the Philadelphia Almshouse at Blockley in nearby West
Philadelphia. In 1855 the *Evening Bulletin* observed that an "army
of paupers" afflicted the city, requiring a chain of soup kitchens to
stave off starvation. "The Irish," the paper said, "generally
compose more than two thirds of the population of the Almshouse."[16] In "Ramcat," however, no one had to read the *Bulletin* to
know how bad it was.

To view the Schuylkill community in 1880 is to see it greatly
enlarged but still with many of the same problems. The number of
blocks occupied by houses and businesses had expanded fivefold.
The district now spread between Broad Street and the Schuylkill
River for thirteen blocks south of Lombard Street instead of just six
as in 1850. Not 4,000 but 40,000 people lived in the area, and
more than 22,000 of these were Irish-born or the children of
Irish-born. Doubtless, many others were of Irish background
further back in their families. The heaviest concentration of Irish
had settled from the eastern edge of the area above Fitzwater Street
to the bend in the river above Grays Ferry Avenue. With more than
9,000 Irish-born and their relatives in a neighborhood only a mile
square, the ethnic identity of the district was patent. It was the
most thoroughly Irish section of the city.[17]

Mingled with the row houses in "Ramcat" were many industrial
and commercial activities that helped give Philadelphia its manufacturing and business character in the second half of the nine-

teenth century. Eighteen textile and fabric-processing mills were scattered throughout the district. Coal and lumber yards were still very important; there were 38 such fuel and wood businesses. Ninety-eight building and construction enterprises gave work to local men. More than 300 food outlets dotted the streets, and no less than 174 liquor purveyors catered to the thirst of the workers and residents.[18]

Despite all this economic activity, however, "Ramcat" still had many poor people. The Western Soup Society at 1613 South Street was busy in the area, and its register for 1878–79 contained mostly Irish names. Catherine Kane and her four children of 2023 Federal Street received two and half quarts of soup that winter; Catherine McIlhenny and her five children, who lived at 1815 Naudain Street, got a similar portion. Barney Clark of 507 South Twenty-first Street brought his eight children to obtain eight quarts, and Annie Conway and her one child took soup home to their ironic address, 202 Prosperous Alley.[19]

To be a "souper" was to risk the contempt of the rest of the Irish community. The charter of the Western Soup Society bound it to give "helpful instructions and guidance," which were usually religious in nature. The pride of these Irish Catholics was doubly offended by having some of their number going as supplicants to a charity that put Protestantism in its soup. According to its subscription book, the society's supporters were Wanamakers and Lippincotts, Yarnalls and Lewises, the same fashionable Philadelphians who lived around Rittenhouse Square.[20] To be forced to take Protestant soup after having resisted all manner of anti-Catholic intimidation in both Ireland and the United States was to accept a potion laced with gall.

As Philadelphia became more prosperous and more intensively developed its prime land, more employment became available, even for the Irish. After the Civil War the downtown greatly expanded its retail and entertainment functions, which opened opportunities for the Irish to work in a variety of jobs within walking distance of the Schuylkill neighborhood. The Irish took positions as singing waiters, doormen, bartenders, hotel maids, telegraph runners, cabdrivers, firemen, and policemen. Such service jobs supplemented the hard labor in industry with which the Irish were identified and that was swelling the fortunes of the city's most successful entrepreneurs.

The neighborhood was now also linked with the transportation industry in Philadelphia. In addition to working in the factories of Schuylkill, the Irish were fixtures on the railroads by 1880; they were employed in the track gangs and as switchmen, trainmen, freight handlers, and engineers. The Philadelphia, Wilmington and Baltimore Railroad ran across Washington AVenue from Gray's Ferry. Later, the Baltimore and Ohio would have a terminal beside the Schuylkill at Chestnut Street. The mighty Pennsylvania Railroad owned and operated a huge terminal and switching yard west of the Schuylkill above Market Street. These railroads provided jobs for many of "Ramcat's" males.[21]

At Twenty-sixth and South streets there were horse-car "turn arounds" and carbarns. The Irish were numerous on the horse-car lines as drivers, conductors, and maintenance men. The 1880s were a terrible period for labor unrest on these lines, and many Schuylkill residents suffered accordingly. There were numerous strikes as traction magnates P. A. B. Widener and William L. Elkins unified the city's seventeen transit companies into a transportation empire. Working conditions on the lines were abominable. The daily wage for drivers who worked fifteen to eighteen hours was a mere $1.50. No time off for meals was allowed. Any labor-union activity meant instant dismissal. In 1886 a twelve-hour day was achieved as well as some other improvements, but more strikes lay ahead and they would be both bitter and violent.[22]

Catholic parishes in the Schuylkill area grew with the Irish population. Founded in 1839, Saint Patrick's predated the extensive development of either Rittenhouse Square or "Ramcat." It began in a makeshift chapel converted from a warehouse. A lot at Twentieth and Rittenhouse streets was secured in 1841, but it took twenty-three years to pay the mortgage. As the new church was being erected money was so scarce that the struggling parish school had to be closed. Saint Charles parish at Twentieth and Christian streets was begun in 1868 in surroundings described by one writer as having "more brick-clay ponds and frogs" than parishioners. By 1876, however, so great was the post–Civil War housing boom that the area was mostly built up, and the church was the third largest in the city. Further south a third parish, Saint Anthony's, was launched in 1857 at Grays Ferry Road and Carpenter Street. By 1893 a Romanesque structure with sculptures imported from Paris was dedicated in ceremonies illuminated by new devices using electricity.[23]

Through these churches active charitable work helped those hard-pressed in the community. In each parish the Saint Vincent dePaul Society distributed food, clothing, and furniture, while the church "poor box" supported additional aid. The parish gave Irish families access to Catholic schools, hospitals, orphanages, and mutual-aid societies. The House of the Good Shepherd, located in Saint Patrick's parish from 1850 to 1880, was a refuge for those girls who had fallen into a "life of shame," for in Philadelphia prostitution was still a predominantly Irish pursuit at this time.[24]

As early as 1836 there was a little schoolhouse in the Schuylkill area, but public schools did not attract large numbers of area children until the second half of the nineteenth century. By 1880 various public schools in the neighborhood each enrolled between 400 and 600 children. The Pollock School at Twenty-fourth and Christian streets was the local secondary school, and it drew students from Primary School No. 5 at Twentieth and Catharine streets and No. 7 at Twenty-fourth and Christian. Saint Patrick's parish opened a day school under Dr. Daniel Devitt in 1839, and later a free school for boys was begun under the same auspices by Richard Patrick McCunney, a graduate of the Irish college in Salamanca. His wife, Bridget Kearney McCunney, instituted a dormitory for girls in her home at Nineteenth and Sansom streets and taught her pupils reading and sewing. The largest parochial school in the city in 1853, Saint Patrick's remained one of the most popular for the balance of the nineteenth century. In 1880 only 4 other parish schools reported more students than the 900 enrolled at Saint Patrick's, and, together with the nearby schools of Saint Charles and Saint Anthony's, it educated the great majority of the Irish Catholic children in the downtown area.

Progress beyond the elementary level was slow for the children of working-class Irish families in Philadelphia. In 1850 only 4 boys from Schuylkill with Irish names were among the 180

admitted to Central High School, the city's leading postelementary
school. Thirty years later only 2 boys from this ethnic neighborhood were among the 134 Central entrants. The desire for
advanced education among the Irish grew, however, and Schuylkill
children eventually began to make their way to such Catholic high
schools as Saint Joseph's and La Salle in the central city.[25]

Thus the Schuylkill community pursued its own well-being at a
time when no aid could be expected from government and when the
toll on working people from economic insecurity was harsh.
However, with the multiplication of employment opportunities and
the gradual improvement of their relative job position, the Irish
increased their chances for stability. An urban life-style developed
that included merry christening celebrations at O'Brien's Hall at
Twentieth and Federal streets. There were also political meetings,
picnics, and sports at outings of the five local divisions of the
Ancient Order of Hibernians. Parish celebrations were frequent.
The swift gossip and mocking banter so much a part of Irish life
provided daily amusement. Through it all the more serious striving
for betterment continued. Education and respectability became the
goals of an increasing number of Irish families.

While the drama of working-class community life was being
unfolded south of Lombard Street, the land immediately adjacent to
Rittenhouse Square was also being developed. Actually, some of
the earliest residents of the square were Irish. When its borders
were still a jumble of brickyards, stables, and open lots, some
shrewd businessmen seem to have sensed its promise, for they
built themselves good homes on what was then inexpensive land.
Thomas Hunter, Irish-born, Protestant, and founder of the Acme
Tea Company that would later succeed so handsomely, erected a
"mansion" on the square in the 1820s. In the 1840s William
Devine, a textile manufacturer of similar background, lived at
1800–1802 Rittenhouse Square. One of the earliest to put up a
home on the square was John O'Fallon, American agent for the
Queen of Spain, whose legal fees made him wealthy. He, like the
Philadelphia family of Baron John Keating, had ties to the
numerous Irish men who served in the armed forces of France and
Spain. Purchasing a brickyard, he built a large home at 216 South

Nineteenth Street. These men preceded the wave of fashionable Philadelphians who migrated west of Broad Street after 1850.[26]

The growth of commercial activity east of Broad Street in the mid-nineteenth century made the old city less and less attractive to families that could afford to choose their residential locations. As a result, a movement west along Walnut Street began. Born in Ireland, John A. Brown became a wealthy banker and president of the American Sunday School Union; he lived at Twelfth and Chestnut streets in 1828 but later moved to Rittenhouse Square. His Episcopalian, Presbyterian, and Methodist peers did the same. E. Digby Baltzell has skillfully described this migration and analyzed upper-class neighborhood concentration in Philadelphia. He has listed Rittenhouse Square property holders between 1850 and 1900, and this catalogue is replete with the name of people of enormous wealth—railroad barons, merchant bankers, industrial tycoons, and "old Philadelphia" families with roots in the city's colonial history.

On South Rittenhouse Square, Thomas Scott, president of the Pennsylvania Railroad, lived only a few steps from the banker Francis Drexel and Thomas Wanamaker, the son of the founder of the great department store. Diagonally across the square on Nineteenth Street, Tench Coxe, descendent of an eighteenth-century Philadelphia family, shared a block with Samuel Bodine, president of the city's gas monopoly; S. Weir Lewis, China merchant and banker; Joshua Lippincott, publisher; and A. J. Cassatt, another president of the Pennsylvania Railroad. A self-made millionaire in cotton manufacturing, John McFadden resided along the Walnut Street edge of the square, hoping no doubt that his Episcopalianism and his art collection might make his neighbors overlook his Irish name. Nearby were Charles Edward Ingersoll, lawyer; George S. Pepper, philanthropist; Algernon Sidney Roberts, heir to an iron fortune; and Thomas Dolan, owner of the Keystone Knitting Mills. On the Eighteenth Street side of the square, Joseph Harrison, railroad entrepreneur, built his huge and ornate mansion. "At no time in the city's history before or since," wrote Baltzell, "have so many wealthy and fashionable families lived so near one another."[27] These were the men who dominated a

Philadelphia in which, as early as 1860, 50 percent of the wealth was owned by 1 percent of the population, while the lower 80 percent owned only 3 percent of the city's real and personal property. This aggregation of money and power was more diverse in its background than might be presumed. Irish Protestants, Germans, and Dutch among others were included, but the standards and manners of Rittenhouse Square were set by the Anglo culture that characterized upper-class life in Victorian America.

It is difficult for Americans today to imagine the grandeur of the elite life-style of Rittenhouse Square at the end of the nineteenth century. Because of geographic dispersal by the "better sort" and the concomitant inner-city poverty, the extraordinary baroque monuments of that age have steadily disappeared from our city streets. The class culture of such wealthy neighborhoods created what amounted to a fairyland of elegance and display protected by Victorian codes of civility and discrimination. These enclaves of privilege combined architectural eclecticism with passionate embellishment, lavish furnishings, and an adoration of English upper-class family etiquette. Flamboyant architects such as Frank Furness and Theophilus Chandler, designed edifices for an almost hysterical display of wealth—here a mansion for the sugar baron James Scott, there a Renaissance palace for Mrs. Sarah Drexel Fell. The structures on the square became wildly adorned shrines to aggressive vanity and the obsessive flaunting of riches.[28]

However, an aristocratic way of life requires much more than money and manners if it is to remain in ascendancy. It demands presumptions of superiority, the exercise of assured authority, and the collaboration of a servant class to do the thousands of jobs necessary to guarantee an elaborate system of personal comforts and princely appointments. The "haute monde" of the Victorian elite was perhaps a contradiction in a democratic society, but that society was not yet competent to act on any such judgment. The working people who served were often from such impoverished backgrounds that they had no choice but to serve, and some may even have been beguiled into servility by the mere thought of association with the elegance that they labored to support.

In the 1880s Rittenhouse Square was the scene of an interdependent relationship between rich and poor. A wealthy matron going about her morning's business of directing and maintaining her household would have had to deal with Mary Ellen in the nursery, Catharine, the upstairs maid, and Bridget in the kitchen. In addition, she would probably have had recourse to the services of a variety of others in the neighborhood. Maria Moran of 2008 Lombard Street might have been summoned to do the heavy laundry. Mary O'Brien of 1938 Locust Street, a dressmaker, might have been engaged to alter a ball gown. Ed McKeown of 521 South Twenty-fourth Street would have come as arranged to drive madam to the print shop of Stephen Farrelly at 248 South Twenty-first Street to choose designs for an invitation to a musical gala. If madam's nose told her that the privy in the rear used by the servants needed attention, she would send for McAnanny and Brannan of the Quaker City Odorless Excavating Company on South Street. Meanwhile, the household maids would have been pressed to get on with the ironing—approximately 200,000 square feet of wrinkle-free curtains, linens, clothes, and oddments each year.[29]

The servants required to prepare and serve the meals, shop, clean the household, do the laundry, and care for all the details of the privilege establishments on Rittenhouse Square were drawn for the most part from the South Philadelphia Irish community. After 1850 "Irish" in Philadelphia became virtually synonymous with "servant." According to the United States Census of 1870, there were 254,108 domestic servants in the city, of whom 10,044 were born in Ireland. Among the remainder a large portion were of Irish parentage.[30] This concentration of Irish in household occupations was believed by most educated people to be inevitable. Sidney George Fisher, a Philadelphia diarist, observed that the Irish had "taken the position of an inferior race in the business of life, because by nature and education [they were] fitted for it."[31] Although the presence of "Bridget" in American homes may have been expedient, however, it was not necessarily a blessing. From the 1850s forward ladies' magazines and polite journals commonly printed columns and cartoons deprecating the Irish as servants. E. L. Godkin, editor of the *Nation*, saw them as "ignorant, helpless and degraded." Their deportment was often "presumptuous," their culinary skills calamitous, their ideas of cleanliness scandalous.

Not one Irish woman in a hundred, wrote Eunice Beecher, "can by
any amount of care, patience, or indefatigable teaching, be
transformed into a neat, energetic, truth-telling servant."[32] In
addition, being Catholics, these servants were seen as threats to
the religious integrity of the family and a peril to the Protestant
purity of its children.[33]

The great households of Rittenhouse Square were caught in a
social dilemma. It was impossible to pursue the extravagant
life-style of mannered elegance and luxury without servants, but
those most readily available were from a group alien in outlook,
habits, and background. Nevertheless, wealth had to make the
best of it and be served by such poor as there were. The vast
fortunes represented on Rittenhouse Square were created by the
labor supply of the city, and the beneficiaries of those fortunes had
to enjoy their wealth through the ministrations of that labor supply.

For the Irish a similar ambiguity characterized their connection
with Rittenhouse Square. It was demeaning for them to be forced to
serve families whose wealth was founded on notoriously exploitive
mills, factories, and railroads. These same families also supported
those soup and Bible societies which sought to inveigle the Irish
out of their religion by the relief of their hunger. Many a railroad
pick-and-shovel man looked with deeply mixed feelings on his
daughters' employment in the great houses of men whose railroads
had meant for him a lifetime of miserable toil.

Those who served in the households of the elite sometimes found
the extravagance there to be offensive for its great distance from
what so many counted as their meager reality. One man, who later
worked as a doorman at the Union League Club on South Broad
Street, recalled his amazement at the lavish meals served in the
house where he was employed while families he knew three blocks
away in Donnelly's Court were living mostly on bread and
drippings. During a bitter transit strike a woman from County Clare
who worked in a fine house on Spruce Street was able to feed her
brother's family for weeks by using the scraps from her master's
kitchen. Another woman remembered that her employers spoke
French so that the servants would not know what was being said.
When she and her friends "below stairs" then spoke "Irish,"

however, her mistress became furious and told her to cease or face dismissal.[34]

Maps prepared in the 1890s make it clear that in the late nineteenth century the Irish still predominated in the neighborhood behind Rittenhouse Square. The properties around the square continued to be solidly upper class, but west of Twentieth Street and south of Pine the blocks were well over 50 percent Irish. On the north side of Lombard Street, west of Twenty-third, twelve of the fourteen row houses were owned by people with Irish names. The 2400 block of Ashburton Street was almost totally Irish. Worsted mills, the Philadelphia Galvanizing Works, and the unlovely Philadelphia Rubber Works were all scattered throughout this area. Tiny "courts," notorious for their crowding and poor sanitation, were still occupied by the Irish poor. Reaney's Court on Twenty-sixth Street between Pine and Lombard was one such nest of small dwellings. The National Fire Brick Works and the coal yards rimmed the Schuylkill river. Well into the twentieth century this same pattern of ethnic and class concentration remained in the area of Rittenhouse Square.[35]

However, the two worlds of "Ramcat" and Rittenhouse gradually changed. Toward the end of the nineteenth century Irish Catholics created their own wealthy class. Born near Twenty-sixth and South streets, Thomas Cahill struggled as a youth to operate a coal and lumber business along the banks of the Schuylkill. Twice his stocks were washed away by floods, imperiling his efforts to support his widowed mother and her other children. Doggedly, Cahill rebuilt, and eventually he amassed a fortune. Remembering that as a boy he had been rejected by Central High School because he was "too young," even though he had passed the entrance examination, Cahill left his wealth to build Roman Catholic High School, the first such school to be run by a diocese in the nation.[36]

In the early twentieth century some Irish Catholics gravitated into the physical and social orbit of Rittenhouse Square. Constance O'Hara, daughter of a prominent physician, became one of its leading citizens. The Sisters of Notre Dame opened a fashionable finishing school on the west side of the square. Michael Francis Doyle, a brilliant attorney whose work saved the life of Eamon deValera in 1916 when the Irish leader was condemned to death by the British, bought a house on the square. Some say that he vowed to buy the property when he was turned away from the front door as a delivery boy and told to go to the rear. Ultimately, too, John McShain, a wealthy contractor, would purchase the Barclay Hotel, an elite facility best known for debutante parties.[37] But the square was no longer what it once had been.

By the 1930s the great fortunes were under siege. The income tax and the Depression had reduced the ability of the rich to disport themselves as had their fathers and grandfathers before them. In 1928 the Republican party's traditional hegemony in Philadelphia politics had been challenged for the first time, and now a popular Democratic contractor, John B. Kelly, was working furiously for Franklin D. Roosevelt. In "Ramcat" the Republican machine, which had provided jobs and contracts for decades, was not secure. In 1928 almost 40 percent of the voters in its two wards, the Thirtieth and the Thirty-sixth, cast Democratic ballots.[38] A new era was at hand, and the dominance of the "Philadelphia Gentlemen" was passing. Apartment houses were encroaching on Rittenhouse Square, and the elite were leaving the city. Indeed, by 1930 most had already left. The automobile was rapidly eroding many of the old neighborhood identities and altering the geography of class.

As those whose families had reigned resplendent on Rittenhouse Square in the 1880s declined or decamped, the square became drab and unkempt. The great houses were shuttered, demolished, or converted to apartments. The flocks of servants to tend them were no longer affordable or fashionable. The girls from "Ramcat" were becoming secretaries or nurses; some were even going to high school and college. While old ideas about and among the Irish were being modified, however, those in the Social Register still could not bring themselves to actually mingle with them in clubs or social activities. The social distance between wealthy Philadelphians and the workers and servants of "Ramcat" had decreased somewhat, but the memory of the earlier gulf and exploitation persisted. Even as late as the second half of the twentieth century it was not uncommon to hear Philadelphians of Irish heritage refer to the erstwhile area of social privilege west of Broad Street and south of Market as "Rottenhouse Square."

NOTES

1. Charles J. Cohen, *Rittenhouse Square: Past and Present* (Philadelphia: privately printed, 1922), and Nathaniel Burt, *The Perennial Philadelphians: The Anatomy of an American Aristocracy* (Boston: Little, Brown and Co. 1963).

2. Cleveland Amory, *Who Killed Society* (New York: Harper Brothers, 1960).

3. (Chicago University of Chicago Press, 1929).

4. Two recent exceptions to this unilateral treatment of ethnic communities have been Jay Dolan, *The Immigrant Church* (Notre Dame, Ind.: University of Notre Dame Press, 1975) and Kenneth Kusmer, *A Ghetto Takes Shape: Black Cleveland* (Urbana, Ill.: University of Illinois Press, 1976). Although largely in terms of arithmetic variables, Stephan Thernstrom's *The Other Bostonians* (Cambridge, Mass.: Harvard University Press, 1973) also sets ethnic group development against the broader society.

5. (Glencoe, Ill.: The Free Press, 1958).

6. (New York: Arno Press, 1976).

7. Joseph Aberman and Stephen Kozakowski, *History of Development in the Delaware Valley Region* (Philadelphia: Delaware Valley Regional Planning Commission, 1976), pp. 31–46.

8. Dennis Clark, *The Irish in Philadelphia* (Philadelphia: Temple University Press, 1974), p. 18.

9. Sam Bass Warner, *Philadelphia: The Private City*, (Philadelphia: University of Pennsylvania Press, 1968), p. 75.

10. The size of the Irish population of the city in the 1840s is the subject of some dispute. The Sixth Census was a defective one, and 1840 estimates are questionable. These population figures for the Schuylkill area are derived from the computerized grid tabulations of the Philadelphia Social History Project directed by Dr. Theodore Hershberg of the University of Pennsylvania. I must express thanks to Henry Williams of that project for aid in these compilations.

11. Studies of the Irish community in the 1840s were pursued by Dr. Philip Yanella of Temple University in 1975, and his tabulations of census statistics were provided to the Center City Residents Association. The percentage cited above is from the Yanella data.

12. Names in the Seventh Census of the United States, Manuscript Census materials of 1850, Philadelphia Social History Project.

13. Passyunk Township, County, State and Personal Tax Assessment Ledger (1850), Archives of the City of Philadelphia.

14. David Montgomery, "The Shuttle and the Cross; Weavers and Artisans in the Kensington Riots of 1844," *Journal of Social History* 5, no. 4 (Summer 1972): 411–46; Michael Feldberg, *The Philadelphia Riots of 1844* (Westport, Conn.: Greenwood Press, 1975).

15. George Foster, "Philadelphia in Slices," *Pennsylvania Magazine of History and Biography* 43, no. 1 (January 1969): 23–72.

16. Philadelphia *Evening Bulletin*, December 29, 1855.

17. Philadelphia Social History Project, Selected Population Statistics (Schuylkill).

18. Ibid.

19. Register of Recipients (1878–79), Western Soup Society. Urban Archives, Temple University.

20. Subscription Book, Western Soup Society (1850), Urban Archives, Temple University.

21. These lines are shown on the maps of the Philadelphia Social History Project.

22. Sister M. Consuela, "The Church of Philadelphia, 1884–1918," in *The History of*

the Archdiocese of Philadelphia, ed. by James F. Connelly (Philadelphia: The Archdiocese of Philadelphia, 1976), p. 295.

23. Daniel H. Mahony, *Historical Sketches of the Churches and Institutions of Philadelphia* (Philadelphia: Daniel Mahony, 1895), pp. 63, 122, 149.

24. Ibid., p. 198.

25. School enrollment information for the Schuylkill area is not complete for the mid-nineteenth century, thus making comparisons with 1880 difficult. Some information is provided in John Trevor Custis, *The Public Schools of Philadelphia: Historical, Biographical Statistical* (Philadelphia: Burk and McFettridge Co., 1897); *Sixty-Second Annual Report of the Board of Education of Philadelphia* (Philadelphia: Cressey and Markley, 1855), and Semi-Centennial Celebration of the Central High School of Philadelphia (Proceedings of the Public Meeting, October 29, 1888. Information on Catholic schools is in Thomas Donaghy, *Philadelphia's Finest: A History of Education in the Archdiocese of Philadelphia* (Philadelphia: American Catholic Historical Society, 1972), and John O'Breza, "Enrollment Figures: The Growth of the Parochial Schools, 1838–1894," unpublished dissertation on Catholic schools of Philadelphia, Temple University, Philadelphia.

26. Hunter and Divine are mentioned in Cohen, *Rittenhouse Square*, pp. 14 and 81. John A. Brown is mentioned on p. 200. For O'Fallon see Clark, *Irish in Philadelphia*, p. 14.

27. E. Digby Baltzell, *Philadelphia Gentlemen: The Making of a National Upper Class* (Glencoe, Ill.: The Free Press, 1958), pp. 181 and 184–85.

28. Richard Webster, *Philadelphia Preserved* (Philadelphia: Temple University Press, 1976), pp. 108–9.

29. These names and addresses are drawn from city directories for the 1880s.

30. Blaine Edward McKinley, "The Stranger in the Gates: Employer Reactions toward Servants in America, 1825–75," Doctoral thesis, Michigan State University, 1969, p. 155.

31. Ibid., p. 161.

32. Ibid., pp. 162–70.

33. The "Nun of Kenmare," a well-born Irish woman, counseled Irish servants to be very careful of the religious issue. See Mary Frances Cusack, *Advice to Irish Girls in America* (New York: F. Pastet, 1886).

34. Interviews with James Patterson, June 8, 1975; Margaret Dougherty, January 12, 1974; Honora Conn, April 12, 1975.

35. The residential characteristics are clearly seen in the *Atlas of Philadelphia*, vols. 2 and 8 (Philadelphia: G. M. Bromley and Co., 1889 and 1896).

36. Dennis Clark, *Proud Past: Catholic Laypeople of Philadelphia* (Philadelphia: Catholic Philopatrian Literary Institute, 1976), p. 2.

37. Reflections on the decline of the square's residents and their class are provided by E. Digby Baltzell, "The Protestant Establishment Revisited," the *American Scholar* (Autumn 1976), pp. 299–518. Recollections about Rittenhouse Square at the turn of the century are given by Constance O'Hara, "The Square with a Past," Golden Anniversary Lecture, The Philadelphia Art Alliance, Oct. 1965.

38. John L. Shover, "The Emergence of the Two-Party System in Republican Philadelphia, 1924–1936," *Journal of American History* 60 (March 1974): 985–1002.

12   The Irish and the Jews

The Irish Catholics and the Jews would seem to have notably similar legacies. Both trace their histories to pre-Christian cultures. Both share long histories of oppression, long traditions of learning, and distinctive attachments to religion. Both have experienced massive immigration movements to America, and the two groups have been especially concentrated in the urban areas of the United States. As ethnic subgroups in America, Jews and Irish have had to deal with the city conditions that have shaped family and cultural life among urbanites. The Irish were statistically more numerous and shared extensively several cycles of American development in which Jews took part only marginally, such as the westward expansion, the work of early industrialization, and repeated involvement in the nation's earlier wars. The differences, however, do not efface the similarities. They simply coexist as opposite social features of the two group traditions.

As strongly identified religious groups the Jews and the Irish had to deal with the hostility and discrimination aimed at them by mainstream Protestant America. This did not lead them to make common cause in the eighteenth and nineteenth centuries, but Jews and Irish Catholics at different times did help clarify what the constitutional guarantees of freedom of conscience and freedom of association were to mean in American life. Although both groups shared the jeopardy of the country's pluralist interplay, the circumstances of Jewish and Irish group life were too different to permit easy collaboration. The numbers, the cycles of arrival and diffusion, the respective concerns and responsibilities did not usually permit a dovetailing of group interests.

New York City, with its potent concentration of Jews, had, of course, been a phenomenon to itself, and several historians have pointed out the Irish-Jewish ties in that city, particularly in the days of Al Smith and afterward in the New Deal era.[1] Philadelphia, although it has had a large Jewish population in the twentieth century, is more typical of the major American cities in which the Jews and Irish have associated. The Philadelphia Jewish community does trace itself back to colonial times, for Congregation Mikveh Israel was founded in 1740 and counted distinguished Philadelphia families in its membership. The Irish, too, were active in the colonial city and played a vigorous role in the Revolution. As the nineteenth century proceeded, though, there was no mid-century Jewish counterpart to the huge influx of Irish that began in the 1830s and brought hundreds of thousands to the city. Not until the 1880s did heavy Jewish immigration even partially match the Irish flow.

The bitterest anti-Irish hostility had to be confronted in the 1840s and 1850s in Philadelphia, whereas Jews in large numbers did not confront similar extensive community antagonism until their numbers had grown in the late 1800s. Both Irish and Jews were resilient enough to construct their own internal structures for self-defense against discrimination, for getting jobs despite hostility, and for maintaining their own social ties and mutual-assistance activities.

In the 1890s the interaction of Jews and Irish expanded as more and more Jewish immigrants sought opportunities in the city. One of the traditional areas of the Irish—in fact the oldest Irish residential concentration in the city—was in Southwark, a district near the Delaware River docks in the city's Third, Fourth, and Fifth wards. This was a hard area by any standards. Saint Joseph's, Saint Mary's, and Saint Philip's parishes included dockside worlds of brutality and harsh conditions, produce and peddlers' markets, garment lofts and marginal industries of all kinds. By the time large numbers of Jews arrived, the Irish had been dug into the Southwark area for four generations.

On arrival in Philadelphia Jews did what experience and religion taught them was essential. They formed congregations and a community. B'nai Abraham Synagogue at Fifth and Lombard streets and B'nai Jacob at Fourth and Lombard were institutions to which they walked on the Sabbath for worship. At Fifth and Gaskill streets was Congregation Emunath Israel-Pheb Shalom. The Hebrew Education Society conducted English and trade classes at Tauro Hall at Tenth and Carpenter streets, and a Young Women's Union held similar classes for the same Society at 230 Pine Street. These locations were the focus of the immigrant Jews in South Philadelphia in the 1890s. At that time after a decade of heavy immigration there were 30,000 Jews in the six wards in the eastern part of South Philadelphia.[2]

East of Second Street pressed against the docks where they worked was an enclave of Irish. To the west of the Jewish concentration beyond Sixth Street was a larger Irish population that was mingled with Italian, German, and native-born American residents, and numerically it was about equal to the Jewish population in South Philadelphia. The Irish parish churches of Saint Philip's and Saint Teresa's were the east and west poles of this group's local concentration. Thus, the Irish and the Jews were adjacent, intermingled, and interactive in the oldest and least-desirable immigrant area of the city in the 1890s.[3]

From the 1850s forward there were a large number of Irish in small businesses in the city. Tailors, shoemakers, grocers, and butchers were the kinds of craftsmen that could transfer rural and village skills to American settings, and city directories for Philadelphia show that this is what happened. The heavy Jewish immigration into South Philadelphia brought Jews with these same skills into areas where the Irish had been dominant.[4] The strains of competition, displacement, and succession in small businesses were very much a part of the neighborhood friction that could be expected between the two groups.

The more combative elements of each group, for years battled one another in street fights and other confrontations. The surviving Magistrate Court dockets for the early part of the twentieth century list scores of Jewish-Irish conflicts. In many of these Jews were charged as the aggressors. A Jewish community that produced such prizefighters as Benny Leonard and Lew Tendler was not without pugnacious instincts. Thus, in 1909 Magistrate Frank S. Harrison in Court No. 5 had to deal with assault-and-battery cases between Patrick Flynn and Louis Hagnoski, Bessie Weinberg and John Gallen, Julius Plotz and James Sullivan, John Curran and Max Rosenbaum, Herman Kaplan and Lillian Moore, Ada Rosenfelt and Esther Leary. These conflicts and many others listed, of course, were only the ones where the police became involved. There were a multitude of others where no police appeared. The role of the police was a sore point as well. The arresting officers listed were frequently Irish. Mollie Weiss and Ida Kersiver were taken in by Officer Sweeney for disorderly conduct. Patrick O'Brien had Annie Rosenberg and Annie Goldberg arrested for keeping a disorderly house, and Officer McCarthy arrested Max Wexler on a similar charge. Special Officer Barry and Constable Broderick made constant arrests of Jews. Such situations were bound to breed misunderstanding at best and bitter antagonism at worst.[5]

The more responsible leaders of both communities, however, did try to encourage tolerance. To the Irish Catholics, the Jews did seem particularly exclusive. To the Jews, surrounded by Christians, the impulses toward self-defense were second nature. *The Jewish Exponent* in 1893, parroting some of the pseudoscientific racial jargon of the times that in retrospect seems tragically incongruous, wrote of the "very important matter of the preservation of racial Jewry pure and free from unwholesome admixture." Jews were susceptible along with others to the stereotypes so prevalent about the Irish at the time. *The Jewish Exponent* in an article on the British Parliament's debates on Irish home rule noted that the Irish members of Parliament had a "proverbial disposition to internal dissension and ill-timed zeal."[6]

Intermittently, some positive manifestation of goodwill among the Irishmen would be evident. A letter written by Michael Davitt, founder of the Irish Land League and a revered Irish leader, was published in the Jewish press in 1893 and refuted the call of a Mr. Crowley in Belfast who sought to exclude Jews from Ireland. "The Jews, to my knowledge," wrote Davitt, "have never done any injury to Ireland. Like our own race they have endured a persecution the records of which will forever remain a reproach to the 'Christian' nations of Europe." It was to be regretted, he continued, "that any Nationalist or Irishman of any other political conviction should . . . give expression to such reactionary 'know-nothing' views."[7] The work of such spokesmen as Hon. Charles P. Daly, a New York jurist, was well known to informed Jews, for Daly's book, *The*

Settlement of the Jews in North America, originally published in
1872, was republished in 1893.[8] More concrete commitment was
expressed when the steamship *Indiana* was to sail for Russia in
1892 with 3,000 tons of famine-relief stores for the victims of the
czar's pogroms. A dockside prayer and blessing service was held
with Protestant ministers, Archbishop Patrick Ryan, and Rabbi
Marcus Jastrow.[9] The Friendly Sons of Saint Patrick contributed to
the relief drive, and the Irish-born newspaperman Robert Malachi
McWade was especially active in promoting it. The Irish knew
what famine was and could feel deeply for its victims.

As Jews moved beyond their original immigrant ghettos, a new
dimension for relationships with the Irish emerged. The undercur-
rents of anti-Semitism and anti-Catholicism, of course persisted,
but where civility and the decencies of mutual respect were able to
function in stable neighborhoods, relations were tolerant. One
such neighborhood was adjacent to North Broad Street in Our Lady
of Mercy Parish. The large German Jewish concentration east of
this area in North Philadelphia had been notably affected by the
influx of East European Jews beginning in the 1880s. The German
Jews, whose substantial row homes had ranged through streets
around the axis of the Franklin Street market, had viewed the East
European influx as a regrettable invasion and in many cases
recoiled from contact with the newcomers. Economic and social
mobility also induced Jews to move westward toward Broad Street,
a main thoroughfare lined with stately homes. Rabbi Jastrow's
Rodeph Shalom Synagogue at Broad and Mount Vernon streets and
Rabbi Joseph Krauskopf's Keneseth Israel at Broad and
Montgomery Avenue testified to the new status of Jews who had
moved beyond the immigrant districts.

The area along North Broad Street of Our Lady of Mercy Parish
was a heavily Irish neighborhood. The imposing granite church
with its soaring twin steeples at Broad Street and Susquehanna
Avenue had been dedicated in 1893 and was a symbol of Irish
respectability. Monsignor Thomas Drumgoole, the pastor, had
made one of the few attempts ever launched to teach Irish history
in the parish schools by installing it in the curriculum for the
parish children. A few houses away from the ornate rectory of the
parish was the home of Cyrus Adler, publisher and philanthropist,

one of the most notable Jews ever to distinguish Philadelphia. As more Jews moved into the area, the Irish and Jewish families had to accommodate one another in business and social relations. Although there were a few Jews in the neighborhood at the turn of the century, their movement into the area in greater numbers occurred in the 1920s. Many Jewish families still found the most accessible livelihood open to them to be in the conduct of small neighborhood businesses, so that names like Morris Aaron and Louis Goldstein, tailors, appear with the names of Joseph Kelly, tailor, among the businesses on streets bisecting Broad Street. By 1930 Jews shared the main business street of the neighborhood near the church with Irish shopkeepers. West of Twelfth Street and Susquehanna Avenue James Dugan, James Moriarty, and Thomas Gorman had their businesses close to those of Jacob Berkowitz, tailor, and Harry Ravitz, fruit-store proprietor. Margaret Coyne, dressmaker, had the same customers as Max Solomon, hairdresser. On this busy shopping street O. R. Sheridan, grocer, and Mary Gilligan, notary, and James Corkran, upholsterer, did business beside William Glazer, optician, and Isadore Halen's hosiery shop. Elizabeth O'Neill's florist shop was handily close to Morris Blank's fruit store. Residents of the area recalled that the movement of Jews into the local businesses was gradual from 1910 until 1930 and that resentments or antagonisms were rare.[10]

The interplay of Irish and Jews in the 1920s in Philadelphia's neighborhoods was taking place in an environment of changing intergroup attitudes that were slowly altering the isolation of ethnic groups that had been previously separated each in its own ghetto world. In vaudeville teams comedians Gallagher and Sheen were humorously contrasting Irish and Jew. The play "Abie's Irish Rose" on the theme of interreligious romance was breaking records for attendance. If it was American to be tolerant, Irish and Jew would try to be American, although there were misgivings and strains in the background. Jews were still largely excluded from business clubs, from top law firms, banks, and executive posts and from some upper-class neighborhoods. The Irish were still largely unwelcome in such circles where old-line Philadelphia Anglo families dominated. The mobility and social change of the 1920s was opening new pathways, however, and the Irish and the Jews were encountering one another in an increasingly generalized framework. When Owen B. Hunt wanted to locate an office on Chestnut Street for a consulate of the newly independent Irish state in 1921, he was coldly rejected by Anglo property owners but finally obtained an office from a Jew. Young Tommy Regan, fresh from service with the Irish Republican Army in the 1920s, had the same experience in locating a site for the Terence MacSwiney Club.[11]

In the 1920s also an association began between a redoubtable Catholic prelate and the city's leading Jewish real-estate magnate. Dennis Cardinal Dougherty, whose career as archbishop of Philadelphia extended from 1918 to 1951, was for most of this time on very friendly terms with Albert M. Greenfield, a prodigious assembler of land and properties. The cardinal had in trust a great deal of church property and needed much better advice than his priests trained in canon law could provide. Albert Greenfield provided guidance, and a fast friendship developed.[12]

The election of 1928 for the presidency was a flashpoint of interreligious tension in Philadelphia as elsewhere. Al Smith, the Irish politician from New York, not only had to face the religious enthusiasts defending Prohibition, which he had vowed to repeal, but as a Catholic drew forth a virulent stream of nativist anti-Catholic sentiment. The extent of prejudicial rancor in that election led to the formation in the city of a chapter of the National Conference of Christians and Jews. Journalist Constance O'Hara and other Irish Catholics joined in this effort, and this signaled the beginning of a slow development of interreligious collaboration against defamation and prejudice.

An energetic Irish-American broadcaster, Patrick Stanton, launched an Irish radio program in the 1930s and was soon able to charter his own radio station. Whether by design or accident, the station was assigned the call letters WJMJ. The letters *J.M.J.* were a familiar acronym to Catholics. Children in Catholic schools wrote the letters on their classroom papers to dedicate their efforts to "Jesus, Mary, and Joseph." A zealot for civil liberties, who happened to be Jewish, confronted Stanton and insisted that the call letters were an abuse of the public airways and part of a Catholic threat to freedom of information. An Irish lawyer, who was conscious of the seriousness of any such charge before the Federal Communications Commission, was furious. Goaded repeatedly by the civil libertarian, he finally said, "Do you know what those letters stand for? Jews and More Jews!"[13] Thus, there were continuing problems of misunderstanding and alienation to be dealt with as the Irish and Jews became more conscious of the institutional power and social postures each group represented in a complex urban setting.

The Depression years of the 1930s created a desperate ferment as people sought to find some ideas and some leadership that would lift them out of economic disaster. Father Charles Coughlin, through his radio broadcasts and his newspaper *Social Justice*, created a large audience among Irish Catholics for his ideas of economic reconstruction. Unfortunately, he also gave voice to some of the oldest and most discredited stereotypes about Jews, and these were bitterly resented among Jews conscious of the growth of Hitler's anti-Semitic crusade overseas. The repugnance toward Father Coughlin was similar to that generated by Senator Joseph McCarthy in the years after World War II. Jews with liberal opinions were offended both by a cultural style that was demagogic and by the malevolent insinuations in which both these spokesmen indulged. Irish Catholics, for their part, were agitated by the identification of many Jews with what they regarded as atheistic Communist causes, and by the high sensitivity of Jews to any attempts by public authorities to aid the single biggest social and economic community investment of the Irish, the Catholic school system. The fact that liberal Jews were more conditioned by traditions of Europeans socialist thought than by Communism, or the fact that Catholics were voluntarily supporting schools that made an enormous contribution to the public welfare, were facts usually lost in the controversial cross fire.[14]

Despite the strains of the 1930s, which included potent disagreements about the Spanish Civil War, with Jews more often favoring the Spanish Republic and Catholics more often favoring Franco, there was forged a bond around the programs of the New Deal. John B. Kelly, contractor Matthew McCloskey, and Roosevelt's attorney general from Philadelphia, James P. McGranery, had plenty of Jewish confreres in support of Roosevelt. Certain labor unions were especially strong supporters of the New Deal, and these included textile, electrical, and manufacturing-plant unions, Local Jewish politicians, such as Harry Wolov and Joe Gold, could work well with Congressman Jimmy Byrne. The tilt that made more and more Jews Democrats after 1928 was to produce a landslide for Roosevelt in the 1930s, and Albert M. Greenfield, more and more successful as a real-estate tycoon as the Depression waned, was making increasingly heavy campaign contributions. All of this changed the politics of the city from those of a one-party monopoly to those of a two-party system for national elections and a slow erosion of local Republican dominance. Congressman William J. Green, father of the Mayor William Green elected in 1978, was stating a fact when he said in later years that he could manage the political tide in the city's elections if he could just control the Irish, the blacks, and the Jews. The experience of World War II with its atmosphere of patriotic fervor simply served to strengthen these ties.

The increasing integration of American society after World War II led Philadelphians along with other citizens to have more and more recourse to bureaucracy to manage the complexities of life. The social networks of ethnic groups became interwoven with bureaucracy. One example of this condition may be seen in the municipal government of the city during the reform of the 1950s. Under a new City Charter largely composed by lawyer Abraham Freedman, a group of Democratic reformers led by two socialites from distinguished city families, Joseph Sill Clark and Richardson Dilworth, set about to reconstruct a notoriously corrupt local government in 1951. Personnel specialists were brought in to recruit new city employees according to a clean civil-service system. Jewish leaders in the Americans for Democratic Action under Leon Shull vied with one another to draft reform legislation and serve in the new administration. Jewish labor-union leaders, such as Joe Schwartz of the International Ladies Garment Workers and William Ross of the Amalgamated Clothing Workers, worked for the reform ticket. Politicians from heavily Jewish neighborhoods, such as City Councilman Harry Norwich and an array of state representatives and senators, were converted to reform. Victor Blanc as city councilman and later as district attorney, along with other lawyers, aided in drafting new legislation, such as a Fair Employment Practices Act. Abe Rosen, city representative, and Frederick Mann, recreation commissioner, collaborated to rehabilitate the city's image, and William Rafsky and Natalie Saxe in top administrative posts worked hard to guide a turbulent city through change. Real-estate tycoon Greenfield came late to the reform, but he did preside over a City Planning Commission that had transformed the central business district. Thus, liberal ideology, labor unions, Jewish neighborhoods, and professional interests all were represented in the participation in reform that brought ethnics to greater power than ever before in the city.[15]

Mingling with the Jews as the second most prominent group behind the thin phalanx of socialite leaders who were the friends of Mayor Clark and City Controller Dilworth were the meat-and-potatoes platoons of the Irish politicians. Democratic congressman William Green, Col. Jim Finnegan, Councilmen Charles Finley and James Tate, Central Labor Union chief Joseph Kelly, and Congressman Bill Barrett all gathered under the reform movement and put the muscle behind it without which it would have remained a chatty fantasy of the old-line scions at the Rittenhouse and Racquet clubs. The Irish had never had one of their own as mayor of the city, and they would have to wait until 1963 for that to happen, but they were happy meanwhile with the patronage and power that they won in the reform years from 1951 to 1960. On a plane above the ward politics of the working Irish politicians were the very influential figures of John B. Kelly, contractor and father of movie star Grace Kelly, and Matthew McCloskey, a key member of the Democratic National Committee. All together, the Irish political network constituted a formidable cadre in control of the blue-collar electorate without which no election in Philadelphia could be won.[16]

The reform politics of the 1950s was the first opportunity for the Jews and the Irish to collaborate and fraternize in a city-wide movement. They had associated selectively in New Deal activities in the 1930s, but Philadelphia's local politics had remained obstinately Republican except for presidential elections at that time. The political camaraderie of the Democrats in the 1950s helped to generate other kinds of contacts. As the post–World War

II building boom continued to create whole new neighborhoods, both Jews and Irish were moving to them after having fled from or been displaced by blacks in the older areas of the city. Analysts from Temple University viewing this residential resettlement in the huge Northeast section of the city noted that, ethnically, the "Near" Northeast succumbed to the realtor's pitch to settle with "your own kind," and to this day one finds "the segregation of Jews northwest of Roosevelt Boulevard (Route 1—the central spine of the whole Northeast region of the county), and Roman Catholic ethnics on the southeastern side toward the river . . . these neighborhoods can easily be distinguished by the most casual visitor—Catholic areas have a tavern on each block, whereas Jews seem to prefer beauty parlors!"[17]

Collaboration fell short of amity, however, for in various bureaucratic networks, the Irish and the Jews were in uneasy competition. In the School District of the city, for instance, the Irish and Jews had both entered the system as teachers with alacrity in the 1930s. As Italians and blacks moved into teaching there were conflicts about which of the ethnic groups would get supervisory positions. The Philadelphia Federation of Teachers, led for years by a Jewish teacher, Celia Pincus, came to a much stronger position in the 1960s when Frank Sullivan and John Ryan became its leaders. In negotiations, strikes and tough labor pressures, Sullivan and Ryan campaigned through the 1970s to hold the gains teachers had made through the union. Behind the scenes ethnic blocs maneuvered constantly. Italians had a fraternal group as did blacks; the Jews had a Lodge of B'nai B'rith, and the Irish had a branch of the Emerald Society. Caucuses of these groups vigilantly monitored the distribution of supervisory and school principal posts.[18]

The Vatican Council in 1962, which amended Catholic texts to remove passages offensive to Jews and which projected a broader Catholic tolerance and a thrust toward ecumenical understanding, did engage Catholics at the local level with a range of interreligious activities with Jews. While these were usually modest and unspectacular, more informal encounters increased. In 1972 the Donegal Society chose Rhona Weiss as its "Mary of Dungloe" awardee, thus providing this Jewish girl with a free trip and holiday visit to

Ireland. An actor named Shamus Murphy who had attended West Philadelphia Catholic High School came back to the city as a lead star in a Yiddish-speaking theater group. The Jews had not lost their fear of intermarriage, but more and more Jewish-gentile marriages were occurring.[19] In the sphere of informal contacts relations steadily improved, but controversies continued to erupt about such tender issues as abortion and aid to parochial schools, and these frequently pitted Jews against Irish Catholics.

The problems of Israel preoccupied Jews all through the 1970s and were much more intensive than the concern for the crisis in Northern Ireland that distressed a large part of the Irish community. The Irish activists working for the Irish National Caucus envied the solid support among Jews for agitation in behalf of Israel. The Irish community was much more diffuse and diversified than the Jewish population.[20] The Catholic Church had no clear policy on Northern Ireland. Many American Irish ignored the Ulster issue or could not countenance its violence. Irish teachers in the teachers' union resented their inability to divert a small portion of the union's funds to educational work about Ulster, when Jews were able to have very large sums of pension reserves invested in Israel's bonds. The Northern Ireland problem simply did not command the same kind of emotional allegiance as the problem of Israel. A disparity of understanding kept Jews from seeing the Northern Ireland conflict as more than a religious conflict, and many Irish, with their tradition of individualist American patriotism, were uneasy that American interests in the Middle East should be so strongly shaped by Israel and its partisans.

Although the Jewish and Irish communities in the city increased their liaison and respect for one another in the last generation, a considerable social distance remained between them both in association and knowledge of one another. Jews had become overwhelmingly middle and upper class and strongly identified with the professions. The Irish still had a large blue-collar working-class component and involvement with organized labor as well as a professional and managerial class. For many Irish Catholics worries about the subsidence of Catholic allegiance and its effect on their institutions in the 1970s left little time for intergroup diplomacy. Perhaps even more important, however, with an exhuberant Irish cultural revival underway in the 1970s, the Irish were learning more and more about themselves, and concurrently Jews were doing the same.[21] Because each group had so much to learn about itself, and because each group had such rich internal traditions, each was preoccupied with itself. This left scant margin for the Jews and the Irish to examine one another. Considering the extent and vitality of their respective traditions, perhaps such mutual examination would be more than their twentieth-century spirits could bear.

NOTES

1. Nathan Glazer and Daniel P. Moynihan, *Beyond the Melting Pot* (Cambridge, Mass.: MIT Press, 1970).

2. Henry Morais, "Our Jewish Citizens," in *The City of Philadelphia as It Appears in the Year 1893* (Philadelphia: Trades League of Philadelphia, 1893), pp. 145–48. For a description of the slum housing and neighborhood life of the area see Maxwell Whiteman, "Philadelphia's Jewish Neighborhoods," *The Peoples of Philadelphia*, ed. by Allen F. Davis and Mark H. Haller (Philadelphia: Temple University Press, 1973), pp. 236–46.

3. The Irish concentration is shown in Theodore Hershberg, "The Historical Study of Urban Space," *Historical Methods Newsletter* 9, nos. 2 and 3 (Mar.–June 1976), fig. 2, p. 107.

4. *McElroy's City Directory* for 1850 shows that of the 150 people named Kelly listed, the following were in businesses that were for the greater part probably based on skills learned in the old country: weavers (11), tailors (21), dressmakers-milliners (3), shoemakers (7), blacksmiths (4), rope makers (3), saddlers and harness makers (2), and sail maker (1). Of the 123 Doughertys listed four were stonecutters or masons, six were weavers, five were shoemakers, and two were smiths, and there were one butcher, one tailor, and one seamstress. Maxwell Whiteman in his *The Peoples of Philadelphia*, pp. 236–46, notes the kinds of Jewish businesses in the area, as does Henry S. Morais, in his *The Jews of Philadelphia* (Philadelphia: The Levytype Company, 1894), p. 216.

5. Magistrate's Court No. 5, Criminal Docket, 1909–12, Archives of the City of Philadelphia.

6. *The Jewish Exponent* (Philadelphia), April 21, 1893, June 23, 1893.

7. Ibid., September 1, 1893.

8. Charles P. Daly, *The Settlement of the Jews in North America* (New York: Philip Cowen, 1893).

9. *History of Philadelphia: City of Firsts* (New York: Philip Cowen, 1893), p. 399.

10. *Boyd's Combined City and Business Directory–1920* and the same directory for 1930 lists these names. Former residents of the area interviewed by the author include Mrs. Anna McGarry, Mary Kane, Margaret Healy, David Roche, and Max Whiteman.

11. Interviews with Owen B. Hunt, historian of the Society of the Friendly Sons of St. Patrick, July 4, 1976, and Thomas Regan, secretary of the MacSwiney Club, January 20, 1980.

12. Albert Greenfield made handsome donations to the archdiocese. See James F. Connelly, ed., *The History of the Archdiocese of Philadelphia* (Philadelphia: Archdiocese of Philadelphia, 1976), p. 379.

13. Interview with John A. McDermott, February 4, 1980.

14. Arthur M. Schlesinger, Jr., *The Age of Roosevelt: The Politics of Upheaval* (Boston: Houghton-Mifflin Company, 1960), p. 27, and Robert Griffith, *The Politics of Fear: Joseph R. McCarthy and the Senate* (Lexington, Ky.: University of Kentucky Press, 1970), p. 225. The slow changes in city politics are traced in Irwin F. Greenberg, "The Philadelphia Democratic Party, 1911–34," doctoral thesis, Temple University, 1972, Philadelphia.

15. James Reichley, *The Art of Government: Reform and Organization Politics in Philadelphia* (New York: Fund for the Republic, 1959), and Stanley Newman, ed., *The Politics of Utopia* (Philadelphia: Political Science Department, Temple University, 1975).

16. The oddity of Philadelphia Irish retardation in politics is clear from a reading of Bruce M. Stove, *The New Deal and the Last Hurrah: Pittsburgh Machine Politics* (Pittsburgh, Pa.: University of Pittsburgh Press, 1970), pp. 6–7.

17. Peter O. Muller, Kenneth Meyer, and Roman Cybriwsky, *Philadelphia: A Study in Conflicts and Social Cleavages* (Cambridge, Mass.: Ballinger Publishing Company, 1976), p. 40.

18. Daniel Elazar and Murray Friedman, *Moving Up: Ethnic Succession in America* (New York: Institute on Pluralism and Group Identity, 1976), pp. 28–41.

19. Program of the Donegal Society Annual Ball, 1965, collection of the Balch Institute; "Yiddish Theater's Philadelphia Irishman," *Philadelphia Inquirer*, January 10, 1980; "Our Changing Ethnic Society," Philadelphia *Bulletin*, March 9, 1980.

20. In a study of voting in 1978 Dr. Sandra Featherman and William Rosenberg, in their *Jews, Blacks and Ethnics* (New York: The American Jewish Committee, 1979), pp. 9–10, 11–13, found a good deal more consistency in Jewish voting behavior than among the city's Irish.

21. Barbara Crossette, "The Airing of the Green," *New York Times*, March 14, 1980.

PART V: # Hibernian Heritage

One of the chief problems of ethnic life in America is the effort on the part of groups required to maintain their identity in the face of the tremendous power of the mainstream culture that tends to diminish subcultural differences. The extent of this effort over time is impressive, as is shown in the next chapter, which is devoted to the local tradition of Saint Patrick's Day celebrations in Philadelphia, as well as in the following one that describes the evolution of Irish organizations and an immigrant social facility and the strains to which they have been subjected. The final chapter recounts the thin line of scholarship and dedication devoted to the Gaelic language, which is seen as a magnetic talisman of the ancient traditions of the Irish.

13 Saint Patrick's Day Observed

In the very early morning of our country's history, the Irish were already celebrating Saint Patrick's Day in Philadelphia. Before the American republic was founded, Irish men came together in 1771 to pay honor to Ireland's patron as founding members of the Society of the Friendly Sons of Saint Patrick for the Relief of Emigrants from Ireland. George Washington, who had encouraged the many Irish soldiers under his command during the Revolution to fete Saint Patrick's Day, was an honorary member of this society.[1] Thus, the designation of March 17 as a day of special observance was an early Philadelphia custom.

In 1806 on Saint Patrick's Day an audience came together in the city to hear a reading by an Irish actress of the memorable speech made by the Irish patriot Robert Emmett before his execution by the British Crown in Dublin in 1803.[2] In addition to the annual dinner of the Friendly Sons of Saint Patrick, the growing Irish community began planning events on March 17 at which orators could speak out about England's suppression of Irish liberty. In 1837 Joseph M. Doran at the Hall of the Franklin Institute delivered a vigorous patriotic oration:

> Irishmen, naturalized citizens of America! Driven by tyranny and oppression from your own beloved and much injured country, you have come here to enjoy the blessings of civil and religious liberty. . . . A new existence awaits you here, and though the green fields of Erin cover with their verdure the graves of your fathers . . . yet this is now your country—here is all that is dear to you; here are your families, your friends, here are your homes and property. Call forth then your powers, and assist your fellow citizens in perserving those liberties which you are permitted to enjoy . . . cherish, promote and protect the great interests of the country, and show by your conduct that you

are worthy of being naturalized citizens of a prosperous Republic.[3]

Such addresses reminded the Irish in America of the continued need for liberation of the old country.

The swift increase in the Irish population in the 1840s, as victims from the calamity of the Great Famine of 1845–46 sought refuge in America, greatly expanded the activities of Irish-born people. The Irish community, beset by poverty, discrimination, and troubled exile from its homeland, sought to build a new life for itself, a life that included fun and recreation as well as the hard work that the times required. Organizations of all kinds grew up, and one of the most popular was the marching military unit. For centuries the Irish living under foreign domination had had no free military units of their own in Ireland. For generations young Irish men had served in European armies. In America the Irish had the opportunity to form military groups as free men. This they did, and these marching units turned out in full regalia to celebrate the Feast of Patrick. An account in 1859 in the Philadelphia *Public Ledger* told of one such turnout:

St. Patrick's Day was celebrated by a parade of the 2nd Regiment of Infantry, 2nd Brigade, under command of Col. P. W. Conroy. The line was formed on Franklin Street, west of Franklin Square. The following companies participated: Montgomery Guards, Irish Volunteers, Hibernia Greens, Emmett Guards, Meagher Guards, Shields Guards. The companys generally went out in good force. The new Shields Guards, under Capt. Peter Somers, made their first parade with the Regiment and had 44 muskets out. After marching through the principal streets the Regiments proceeded in a body to hear a lecture delivered by Robert Tyler, Esq. at the National Hall for the benefit of the poor of St. Patrick's Church.[4]

Before the Civil War there were many people who doubted the loyalty of the Irish to the American republic, despite the fact that the group had helped establish it. After the Irish Brigade was formed in the Union Army and great numbers of Irish men served the cause of the Union, only the worst bigots could doubt

Irish-American loyalty. After the Civil War parades of all kinds
became a sort of national craze. Veterans of the conflict always
turned out and, in Philadelphia, Gen. St. Clair Mulholland and
other heroes of the war stepped smartly along on Saint Patrick's
Day each year. Temperance organizations became a big component
in the March 17 parades in the 1870s. Of the 10,000-man parade
on Saint Patrick's Day in 1875, the majority parading walked with
the thirty-nine marching units of the Total Abstinence Brotherhood, an organization with strong religious backing and a missionary zeal for temperance crusading.

By 1886 the Philadelphia *Public Ledger* noted that the flags of
both Ireland and the United States were flown from public
buildings on Saint Patrick's Day. Because Ireland was not free at
that time, the flag flown for that country then was the green banner
with a harp of gold, the flag that had been carried by Irish brigades
in the service of France, Spain, and the United States. However,
the newspaper reported that in 1886 the annual March 17 parade
was not held because local Irish leaders decided that conditions of
repression, near famine, and political struggle in the old country
demanded that all energies should be devoted entirely to trying to
relieve the suffering there. At the Academy of Music, however, the
Right Reverend J. J. O'Farrell, bishop of Trenton, gave an address
on "Ireland's Faith and Nationality," while at Villa Nova Hall the
Ancient Order of Hibernians heard a lecture on the leadership of
the Irish patriot Charles Stewart Parnell.[5]

The parades of Saint Patrick's Day had really become an
American institution by the beginning of the twentieth century.
They were a testimony to the contributions of the Irish to American
life and the pride taken in those contributions. The Irish, although
still subject to prejudice, had become part of the American scene
in a particularly vivid way. People affiliated with the schools,
churches, organizations, and fraternities that they had built had
come to look forward annually to the public celebration of their
patron saint's feast. The general public had come to look forward to
the occasion also, for cheering throngs lined the sidewalks as the
marchers strutted along.

The period after 1916 was one of intense activity for the city's
Irish community. On Easter Monday 1916 in Dublin a revolution-

ary rising against British domination of Ireland was suppressed and its leaders executed. This suppression led to a guerrilla war in Ireland, and Irish-Americans worked to aid the revolutionaries to set up an independent Irish state. Huge demonstrations in support of this goal were held in American cities. In October 1920 a massive and solemn March of Mourning took place on Broad Street in honor of Terence MacSwiney, the young Irish mayor of Cork who had died on a hunger strike of protest while imprisoned by English authorities. Such sacrifices did lead to the setting up in 1921, of an independent Irish state for twenty-six of Ireland's thirty-two counties, and Americans rejoiced at the achievement.[6]

By 1927, Saint Patrick's Day in Philadelphia was a very widespread celebration indeed. That year the Ancient Order of Hibernians held a *Feis Ceoil*, or musical competition. The Kerrymen's Patriotic and Beneficial Association rented a hall at Broad Street and Columbia Avenue for its well-attended ball. Saint Columbia's Parish Dramatic Society staged the play "The Wishing Well" along with a concert of Gaelic songs, while other groups held fetes from center city to the suburbs.[7] Later, the Depression years of the 1930s were not good years for parading. The Irish working people of the city were preoccupied with hunger marches, not festive parades. As a result there were no organized parades in the 1930s and 1940s. World War II gave the city many parades, but they were wartime military parades, not ethnic celebrations.

After World War II parading resumed under the auspices of the Saint Patrick's Day Observance Association. The association was incorporated November 5, 1952. There was uncertainty at first as to how the newly organized parade would function. The Irish population of the city had been decreasing since the National Origins Act of 1929 had curtailed immigration, and there was concern about what response a parade could evince in the city. The Ancient Order of Hibernians initiated the first meeting of the association, and its local chaplain, Rev. Thomas Rilley, presided. The Donegal Society, the Kerrymen's Society, the Gaelic Athletic Association, and other fraternal groups were represented. In February 1952 the first parade was planned, and a delegation from the association visited Archbishop John F. O'Hara and requested his cooperation. This cooperation was granted, and the archbishop's aid assured participation by the city's large Catholic school network. This religious orientation of the parade was notable. It set the character of the parade in a definitive way and dictated its spirit and focus for years to come.[8]

The participation of political figures in the committee also assured the inclusion of the Police and Firemen's Band, control of traffic by police, and a wide range of city services. Judge Vincent Carroll, Sheriff William Lennox, and City Councilman James H. J. Tate all worked on the executive committee. A phalanx of the city's Irish leaders were part of the Observance Association. Former Congressman Michael J. Donohoe, grand old man of the Irish community, Magistrate John L. Coyle, Patrick McNelis, Patrick Cavanaugh, and many others assembled each year to plan the fete. A parade director was selected, and the energetic James J. Kissane worked on the hundreds of details required to bring the trouping groups together in some order. Peddlers had to be controlled along the parade route, sheet music procured for bands, and parking space found for buses. After the parade in 1953 the association met and heard a report that 65,000 people had paraded and 100,000 had lined the route of the march. The association congratulated itself on its early success.

The financing of the parade received steady attention at quarterly meetings of the association. Contributions from parishes, Irish organizations, and individuals were solicited by members of the parade committee. Flags and badges were sold to marching organizations. Local businesses formed marching groups. Honoraria were voted for parade marshals, and the most prominent of these was Samuel Karsevar, a Jewish civic leader who had become something of an expert in the organization of local parades. The minutes of the association show consideration of a blizzard of detail. Parade officials had to decide how wide the green line should be that was painted down the middle of the parade route-streets. Should the reviewing stands that held dignitaries be insured? How could people wearing clownish costumes be excluded from the parade? Rest rooms, traffic flow, rising costs—all were debated. In 1957 the parade costs totaled about $3,000. By 1965 this figure had risen to $7,000, and there was a move to increase income. Austin McGreal, a Mayo-born lawyer of great energy, suggested an annual fund-raising luncheon, and his proposal was approved. In 1968 a parade including forty bands was planned, but bad weather forced postponement, and this postponement cost the association $1,800.

In 1959 the Galway Society protested its place toward the end of the parade, so a rotation system was adopted that moved groups successively toward the front of the march each year. The actual number of marchers of the Irish societies was declining by 1962, so they were grouped together among the high school bands and other groups. Some of the participating groups were not even remotely Irish. The Ukrainian American String Band, for instance, had been included since 1957. Peculiar problems, such as obtaining a musical arrangement in marching time for a traditional hymn to St. Patrick, took discussion time. Sheriff William Lennox had visited the Savannah, Ga., Saint Patrick's Day parade and wished to emulate the singing of a hymn to Saint Patrick by all marchers in unison. Others believed that each marching unit should have a chaplain and spiritual director. By the end of 1954 Judge Vincent Carroll proposed that a set of parade rules be drawn up similar to those guiding the New Year's Day Mummers Parade. The annual Parade Orders now embraced city officials, colleges, and high school bands, veterans organizations, fraternal groups, parishes, and Irish societies. Some seventy groups marched off at 2:00 P.M. each year from South Broad Street to Benjamin Franklin Parkway.

In December 1954 rules for the parade were approved by the archbishop's office. Rule One stated that "Any group participating in the parade must be of Catholic character." The rules stated that all floats in the parade had to be of a religious nature. The religious orientation of the parade was to lead to repeated problems about which groups could be appropriately included in the parade.

The route of the parade was never the subject of serious question. All of the major parades in the city followed much the same line of march. Starting on South Broad Street, the parade moved north on that wide thoroughfare and circled around City Hall to Benjamin Franklin Parkway, then marched out the stately Parkway to just beyond the Cathedral of Saints Peter and Paul. The line of march for those who knew the background of the Irish in

Philadelphia recollected some of the history of the city's Hibernian population. The point of departure in South Philadelphia was once the location of the city's largest Irish population in the little row-house streets that housed the workers of the nineteenth century. At Broad Street and Washington Avenue had once stood the big railroad terminal that the Irish had built as poorly paid laborers. From this terminal thousands of Irish men had left to go south to the battlefields of the Civil War. In those days the houses lining Broad Street had employed legions of Irish girls as maids, cooks, and washerwomen. At Broad and Locust is the Academy of Music, where Charles Stewart Parnell, Eamon De Valera, and other Irish leaders had, each in their generation, addressed cheering audiences on the necessity for the independence of Ireland.

At Broad and Walnut streets is the Hotel Bellevue-Stratford. Here the Society of the Friendly Sons of Saint Patrick met for many years. The parade circling around City Hall was able to remind many of the long struggles of the Irish in the city's politics and of the Irish leaders, judges, and lawyers who had distinguished careers in public service. The route up the Parkway treaded a great boulevard built by "Sunny Jim" McNichol, a noted builder of the early part of the twentieth century. Finally, the enormous brown stone Cathedral of Saints Peter and Paul is a monument to the Irish Catholic people of the last century. Begun before the Civil War, it was completed years later. The donations of the poor paid for its erection, and it is said that it lacks side windows because of the fear that they would be broken by stoning. The cathedral was begun only a few years after the city had been torn by the anti-Catholic riots of 1844. Thus, the route of the Saint Patrick's Day parade was a march of memory for many participants. By 1980, however, that had changed. The parade began on the Parkway that year and moved to Chestnut Street and east to Independence Hall. The march had become associated fully with the patriotic affirmation that arriving at the shrine of liberty manifested.

Several personalities strongly influenced the parade in the years after its inception in 1951. Monsignor Thomas J. Rilley was probably the strongest single influence in initiating the parade. As an educator and religious leader he viewed the public demonstration of religious values as an important contribution to community life. Judge Vincent Carroll was prominent in civic and political life for many years, and his interest in the parade was enthusiastic and unflagging. A tall, distinguished man, Judge Carroll not only enjoyed the march itself but took a steady part in all the parade planning year after year. Sheriff William Lennox, a man noted for his strong religious commitment and leadership of charities, also worked actively for the Observance Association. James H. J. Tate, City Council president and later mayor of the city, was especially dedicated to the success of the parade during his career. He was the first Irish Catholic to be elected to the office of mayor of Philadelphia, and therefore he took a special pride in supporting the Saint Patrick's Day festivities.

In recent years younger figures have begun to take part in the Observance Association. Judge Edward Blake and James Cavanaugh, a prominent local leader, have helped with the annual tasks of organizing. In 1980 consideration of televising the parade expanded the publicity potential of the march.

By 1980 the entire Irish community in Philadelphia was undergoing a cultural revival. Concerts, lectures, dances, holiday trips to Ireland, study of local Irish history, and the formation of such groups as the local chapter of the Irish American Cultural Institute and the Irish Teachers Association were all part of the process. "Green roots" were popular, and a new Irish Catholic mayor, the Hon. William J. Green, Jr., brought the city's Irish again into the limelight in civic and political affairs. William Brennan, president of the Federation of Irish Societies of the Delaware Valley, could still recall the story told to him by his mother about how a statue of the Virgin Mary was burned on the steps of Saint Patrick's Church in the Schuylkill section of the city in her girlhood in a spiteful protest against Saint Patrick's Day. "The Irish have had to walk through a bog of misery to achieve their freedom," he said, "and they absolutely must and will continue to have a special day on which to march, walk and dance around to simply enjoy the feeling of it."[9]

The parade, year by year, moved smoothly and without disorder along its celebratory course. Yet, behind the marshaled ranks and smartly dressed bands marching in perfect time there were strains, disagreements, and grievances. The skill of the Observance Association in maneuvering these problems into quiet pacification can hardly be overestimated. Some of the disagreements were monumental from a psychological standpoint, but somehow the leadership always managed to arbitrate them sucessfully.

A few of the issues of contention will illustrate this point. Early in the history of the association, in 1952, it was suggested from the floor of a meeting that the Jewish War Veterans be included in the order of march. Monsignor Thomas Rilley summoned a happy agreement on that suggestion. The point was raised by somebody else, however, that the bagpipe bands of one of the "Orange" lodges might seek the same privilege. This possibility was a more vexatious problem. Dissent was aroused and the question tabled. In 1965 Mickey Cavanaugh, a prestigious leader, Irish-born and a strong nationalist, raised the same issue and urged inclusion of the "Orange" Protestant groups as a gesture of amity. Again dissent arose, and the issue was once more skillfully contained.[10]

The presence in the 1950s of a group of marchers known as "Quinn's Men of Erin" caused another protracted disagreement. Charles Quinn was an affable, respected tavern keeper from the Swampoodle neighborhood. Local marchers from his area carried a banner proclaiming them "Quinn's Men of Erin." Some said that this display was advertising for Quinn's bar. Although some association members sincerely felt that the banner was a business use of the parade, there was some political edge to this dispute. After protracted meetings the group was allowed to march but Quinn's name was removed from the banner. Charles Quinn later was recompensed for any loss of face when he himself was elected to the association after his friend James H. J. Tate became mayor of the city in 1963.

Another example of adeptness is provided by the issue of whether the parade should be aided with public funds. The finances of the parade, always in peril of the weather, could be hurt badly by postponements. Some suggested that a subsidy by the city would solve the problem. Others felt that subsidization would raise controversial issues of separation of church and state. After all, the association did contend that the event was a religious parade. The leadership dissembled on the question, and eventually it solved itself. By 1978 so many other groups of all kinds were receiving aid for public displays and parades that a subsidy was finally accepted. No protests were made.

A highly emotional problem surfaced after the violence in Northern Ireland erupted in 1969. Those with strong nationalist views could see no reason why they could not parade as opponents of the English occupation of Ireland's six northeastern counties with banners exhorting opposition to the English presence there. This opinion was a frankly political view, and others recoiled from such a display and argued that only pleas for peace had a place in what they believed was a strictly religious parade. The association could not be wholly unsympathetic to the nationalist view, for it was advanced amid claims that the Northern Ireland situation was one of historic injustice. As a result, in 1970 "Peace in Northern Ireland" was chosen as the theme for the parade, and after the march those participating were invited to attend a ceremony at Independence Hall to hear Ivan Cooper, a spokesman for the nationalist viewpoint, who was from Ulster. The early 1970s were a period when Catholics were very active in ecumenical affairs in response to the injunctions of the Second Vatican Council, and the efforts to ameliorate any protest in the parade were felt to be important.

By 1980, however, a compromise had been worked out with the nationalist groups, which included the Irish Northern Aid organization and the local chapter of the Irish National Caucus. That year the members of the Irish Northern Aid marched in the parade wrapped in blankets, silently and solemnly, to memorialize Irish prisoners in Northern Ireland who were forced to live with only blankets for covering because of British refusal to accord them the status of political prisoners. This unit was quite a contrast to the festive units of the rest of the parade, and it made the point that a serious issue of justice and suffering needed to be contemplated even on a day of otherwise unbridled good spirits.[11]

These resolutions of conflict were consistent evidence of Irish politesse, a renowned capacity for reaching accord amid opposing views. The gift had been exercised with venerable skill in politics for generations. The affairs of the parade benefited from it. In the case of the requests to include the "Orange Lodge" marchers, the tactic of delay fended off a rancorous conflict. In the case of saloon keeper Charles Quinn and the right of his patrons to march under his banner, the removal of his name from the banner was compensated for by the elevation of Quinn himself to the association at an opportune time. The issue of a city subsidy for the parade, with its thorny church-and-state implications, was carefully debated and then deferred until community conditions permitted it to be solved without controversy. The Northern Ireland problem and its cadre of protesters was deflected by the choice of a peace theme and then later accorded a silent but significant role. Through this kind of maneuverability the parade leaders handled their problems. Their ability was almost second nature, having been developed in ward meetings, labor groups, Irish organizations, and civic affairs. This skillful management was one of the reasons why, in a highly diverse city, the Irish could have the largest ethnic parade despite their declining numbers, and to do so with a completely self-assured aplomb.

The making of Saint Patrick's Day into a fully recognized city institution was symbolized by the incorporation of an association for its celebration. By 1951 when this step was taken the city had been made aware in many ways of the long tradition of the Irish in Philadelphia. The Irish, through the parade, affirmed their identity and the continuity of their presence. Although the religious influence prompting the parade was the strongest stimulus, the political implications of the celebration were almost as strong. During the 1950s the reform administration of the city would have been impossible without such Irish figures as Col. James Finnegan, Congressman William Green, Jr., and City Councilman Charles Finley, who buttressed the political figureheads Joseph S. Clark and Richardson Dilworth. The Irish Catholic leaders of that time welcomed a parade that expressed their tradition. For the thousands of marchers and spectators who shared that tradition, the green-bedecked finery, the trooping bands and floats, and the flags and music constituted one of the oldest pleasures of urban life, and people of all ages and backgrounds simply do love a parade.

NOTES

1. John M. Campbell, *History of the Friendly Sons of St. Patrick and the Hibernian Society* (Philadelphia: The Hibernian Society, 1892), p. 33.

2. Dennis Clark, *The Irish in Philadelphia* (Philadelphia: Temple University Press, 1974), p. 14.

3. Ibid. p. 19.

4. Philadelphia, *Public Ledger*, March 18, 1859.

5. Ibid., March 17, 18, 1886.

6. Interview with Owen B. Hunt, July 4, 1976, Philadelphia.

7. *Philadelphia Inquirer*, March 17, 1927.

8. This information and what follows is based on the Minutes of the Saint Patrick's Day Observance Association, which are in the collection of the Historical Society of Pennsylvania, Philadelphia.

9. Interview with William Brennan, March 13, 1980, Philadelphia.

10. These disputes are recorded in the minutes of the Saint Patrick's Day Observance Association for 1952, 1960, and 1965. Further information was obtained from Mr. Frank Boyle, interview of March 17, 1980, and Robert V. Clarke, interview of January 6, 1979.

11. Minutes of the Saint Patrick's Day Observance Association and the Philadelphia *Evening Bulletin*, March 17, 1980.

14 The Irish Center

Emigration and exile have been the fate of millions of Irish in modern times, and the problem of finding and maintaining community ties has been central to the experience of the Irish people both overseas and in the troubled homeland. Perhaps the most profound novel of the twentieth century, James Joyce's *Ulysses,* is the product of the mind of an Irishman in exile who sought spiritual and cultural understanding in probing relentessly the memories of his native land. The separation of the Irish people from their homeland, and their troubled social history both at home and abroad, has made the cultivation of social bonds among them an acute problem. The yearning for community has been a passionate theme among this gregarious people, and in the last two centuries this yearning has taken the form of religious organization, nationalist fervor, and international fraternity.

Ireland is a country with a history of clan affiliations that extends into modern times. The ruins of great institutions founded on clan fidelity and religious community haunt the landscape of the island homeland. These ruins testify to the ancient struggle among this people to find a focus for social life and to maintain symbolic centers for that most deeply felt of human needs, the craving for social fraternity.

In the United States the chief centers of Irish communal achievement have been the institutions of the Roman Catholic church. Secular institutions, such as New York's Tammany Hall, however, have strongly complemented religious facilities. Indeed, there is substance to the argument that the Irish have played a special role in the socialization and political development of the nation.[1]

The problem of finding congenial community associations in American cities has become more difficult for most Americans in

the twentieth century, and for Irish-Americans this has been true
as well. The days of the massive immigrant presence of the Irish in
the nineteenth century are past. Since the 1920s immigration
restrictions have diminished the numbers of Irish in American
cities. According to the U.S. Census of 1970, however, there were
still about 250,000 Irish-born people in the United States.[2] The
complexity of American cities—where most of these people
lived—and the mobility and diversity of American life have made
it difficult for them to enjoy stable relations with persons of similar
backgrounds who had a common fund of experience that could be
mutually shared. Distinctly Irish residential areas have become a
thing of the past. Older fraternal organizations are fading into
obscurity. Even the Catholic church in the wake of reforms and
changes after the Ecumenical Council (Vatican II) is much less an
Irish medium than had been true in the past. Nevertheless, the
Irish-born and the American-born of Irish background have
continued to maintain their own identity and continued to seek
common goals and associations through local and national organizations reflecting their heritage. The Irish have found their most
meaningful ties in local organizations, for both convenience and a
strong Irish sense of localism have made such groups the most
rewarding in terms of direct social experience.

In Philadelphia Irish fraternal groups flourished in the second
half of the nineteenth century when the Irish, like most Americans,
became enthusiastic joiners of organizations on a large scale. Dr.
Dale Light, in a perceptive study of the history of Irish organizations in Philadelphia, has compiled a list of dozens of such groups
existing in the 1880s and 1890s. They range from the prestigious
associations of the well-to-do and professional men who were
members of the Society of the Friendly Sons of Saint Patrick to the
local chapters of the Irish Catholic Benevolent Union founded by
Martin I. J. Griffin. There were fire companies, marching and
military societies, musical aggregations, chapters of the Irish Land
League, literary societies, death-benefit and beneficial societies,
revolutionary underground secret societies, clubs for drink and
clubs against drink, religious and charitable societies, and even
organizations to promote trade with Ireland—all with an annual
cycle of activity. Light's research is focused on groups that made

the Irish community in the city a veritable hive of organizational interaction. The study shows that the range of Irish organizations in the city was stratified by economic status, with the wealthier Irish gravitating to prestige groups and the working-class Irish contenting themselves with membership in helpful fraternal and beneficial organizations. The major exception was the Irish Land League of the 1880s. This national effort, with dozens of local chapters in Philadelphia and strong clerical backing, gathered support for land reform in Ireland from all segments of the community. The Light study also shows that economic mobility, far from diminishing Irish identity as might be expected, resulted in the clearest expression of ethnic identity through nationalist activity along moderate lines.[3]

In the nineteenth century, when various city neighborhoods were heavily Irish, it was not unusual to have Irish meeting halls serving the organization network conveniently located at the local community level. Philadelphia always had a high level of home ownership even among workers, and this characteristic imparted a stability to its neighborhoods. The halls were used for weddings, christening celebrations, political meetings, concerts, charitable fund-raising dances, and all the gatherings of nationalist groups. The Ancient Order of Hibernians had a number of its local "divisions" in the city, and these usually had their own halls and club facilities. The Total Abstinence Brotherhood, the Knights of the Red Branch, and similar national organizations had such halls. Kenny's Hall, a typical neighborhood hall, served its area in the Kensington mill district well into the twentieth century. Founded by a County Roscommon blacksmith, it was the meeting place of the Roscommon Men's Patriotic and Beneficial Society.

Members of nationalist organizations learned that their political aims at times made them unwelcome in the Catholic halls and church facilities. In 1880 Archbishop Frederick Wood, a churchman of English background, forbade the Ancient Order of Hibernians from meeting on Catholic premises because of his belief that the group was in league with the famous Mollie Maguires, a workers' protest network in the Pennsylvania coal regions.[4] This ban was one factor in promoting the trend toward organizations' obtaining their own halls. There was also prestige attached to a groups' having its own meeting rooms. The fact that Philadelphia until recent years had local ordinances called "blue laws" was a further stimulus. These ordinances, dating from colonial times, prevented the selling of alcoholic beverages on Sunday but exempted private clubs. As a result clubs of all kinds for Sunday drinking flourished. Irish societies knew a good thing when they saw it, and Irish society meetings on Sunday afternoons became a feature of the city's life for many decades.

The Cavan Men's Catholic Social and Beneficial Association provided social contacts and direct assistance to wage-earning men, who were very vulnerable to occupational accidents, unemployment, and exploitation by employers. Sickness and death benefits were highly important to the laboring members. Almost as important was the opportunity for recreation. The earliest minutes show that the group rented halls for dances and raffles, provided occasions for speeches on Irish nationalist topics, and voted to purchase ice cream for the Cavan Ladies Society. Later, a building and loan association was chartered to aid members to build equity toward the purchase of houses.

The county organizations, such as the Cavan Men's Association, were not fully approved by all. Congressman Michael Donohoe, who for a generation was something of an elder statesman in the Philadelphia Irish community, did not entirely approve of the county groups. Himself a Cavan man, he thought such societies divisive. County loyalties and rivalries did cause friction, but even Mike Donohoe freely admitted that Irish Catholics in the city needed organizations to insure themselves against religious discrimination, for up until the 1920s some companies in Philadelphia sternly avoided hiring Irish Catholics.[5]

The Irish-American Club, originally located at 1421 Arch Street, provides an example of a very active nineteenth-century organization located in center city. The club was largely a creation of the militant secret society, the Clan na Gael (Children of the Gael; see chapter 8). Through it the Clan gave its activity a central focus, exercised influence, and made funds by charging rental fees for events held in the club facilities. The surviving minutes of the Clan meetings from the 1880s and 1890s show an impressive sense of organization, a businesslike conduct of affairs, and a steady commitment to propaganda and agitation in behalf of Irish liberation. Immigrants from organization branches in England and Ireland were received into the Clan as local members on security clearance and certification of their previous affiliations. The Clan printed about 30,000 copies of its own newspaper for local distribution. It aided members in need and found employment especially for those who were former political prisoners or who had been expelled from Ireland for political reasons. Careful monitoring of security and revolutionary activities was maintained. At the meetings dynamite conspiracies against England were reviewed. The group included working men of all kinds, but also physicians, lawyers, and college professors. It is notable that the old minutes record that at each meeting patriotic songs and recitations were enjoyed. Drawing from the rich treasury of Irish folk songs and rebel songs, the members were always able to supplement the business of the day with rousing renditions of such songs as "The Rising of the Moon," "Ireland for the Irish," "The Government Spy," and "Dynamite." The Irish American Club represented the militancy that was never far from the surface of Irish organizational life in the nineteenth century.[5]

Even in the twentieth century the meeting places of Irish groups reflected strong differences of political outlook. The Ancient Order of Hibernians, for instance, was not especially militant about nationalist activities after the 1920s, but the Irish American Club was still militant indeed. The Ancient Order of Hibernians met for years at 1606 North Broad Street, while the Irish American Club was located at 1428 North Broad Street, a few hundred yards away, and in its hall members of the Irish Republican Army were welcome.

As Irish immigration diminished in the twentieth century and the character of the city's neighborhoods altered, these meeting halls became less popular. The coming of the automobile and large-scale commercial entertainment decreased the need for and interest in neighborhood-level activities. It even became possible for working people to take vacations, so the old organization picnics, which were once great attractions and great fund-raising occasions, also lost their excitement. As housing conditions improved and the crowding of large Irish families decreased, it became less necessary for the men to find a refuge free of squalling children and questioning relatives. All kinds of facilities became available for wedding receptions and other celebrations. Movie theaters and the diversity of city life increasingly diluted the associations in local areas and lessened interest in neighborhood-level activities. The automobile also made it possible for the Irish and other immigrant groups to move more readily to suburban areas. After World War II the huge increase in the black population of the city induced a great expansion of black residential areas. These areas of black housing spread in glacial fashion through the inner city, largely as a result of the forces supporting racial segregation in the housing market. The Irish, like most other white groups, exited from the old neighborhoods as the black residents increased. Their meeting halls and private clubs lagged behind the general outward movement, but eventually the clubs, too, either disappeared entirely or found new locations.

The need for some newer facility to serve as a focus of Irish organizational life in the city had been discussed for some years informally by various groups in the city's Irish community. The problem of unity in the Irish community was as elusive as would be expected in any large and diverse ethnic group. Philadelphia had representations of immigrants from various counties in the old country, with counties from the North of Ireland and the West very much predominating. This was a historic condition. Philadelphia had always had strong representation from Ulster, partly because the early ties with the linen-manufacturing and other textile trades. These county differences led to divergences of viewpoint among people who, although they lived in America, were still imprinted with the local loyalties and suspicions of the various Irish counties.

One of the most important organizations that would help to support an Irish center through leadership and social activities was the Donegal Society, incorporated in 1896. The bylaws adopted in 1908 stated the goal of the society to be "rendering mutual assistance to the members and their families in case of sickness, accident or death" and "furthering any good cause in the success of which their countrymen were interested." The society met first at 314 North Broad Street. The treasury was small as the organization sought to meet the sick benefits and death payments of members in a time when this was the only form of aid for workers who fell ill or died. Activities included meetings with such addresses as that in 1897 by Rev. P. H. O'Donnell, who talked to the society in Irish on the subject of the life of Saint Colmkille. Begging priests appeared before the group frequently. One in 1905 asked aid for a proposed college in Letterkenny. Others sought aid for hard-pressed parishes in the mountains of Donegal. In 1905 the treasury contained only $225. By 1928, however, there were 1300 members. The society conducted a building and loan assocation, which by 1935 had assets of $22,226. Year after year the society continued to pay benefits, hold its annual ball, and provide enjoyable gatherings for its members.[7]

Aside from the county organizations, such as the Donegal and Cavan societies, a number of contending factional elements existed whose views would affect any attempt to set up a common Irish social facility. There were several prominent tavern keepers whose businesses were sites for Irish social activities. Then there were the musicians who played at the Irish dances and balls. These men earned extra money through their musical performances, and they would be concerned about the changes affecting their activities that any new facility would bring. In addition to a number of different societies that needed meeting facilities, a federation of Irish societies had worked for some years to coordinate calendars of social events and to encourage common projects, but its functions were largely advisory and it could not bind the member organizations.

One organization that had been active for a number of years was the Commodore Barry Society, named in honor of the "Father of the American Navy," Commodore John Barry, a Wexford-born seaman whose services to the young American republic challenged England's might at sea during the Revolutionary War. A statue of Barry had been erected outside Independence Hall in Philadelphia, and an annual Mass and observance at Barry's grave in nearby Saint Mary's church had been held for some years. The ceremonies in Barry's honor drew people from all sections of Philadelphia and even from New York, where there was a society of Wexford men. Whether by design or by default, Commodore Barry's name became the rallying point for efforts to found a new center for the city's Irish.

Discussions of a new site and facility became earnest in 1957. Taking the lead in the quest for an appropriate property were Michael (Mickey) Cavanaugh and Michael Scullion, two tavern keepers widely known in the city. Cavanaugh owned several properties, and his Railroad Bar at Thirtieth and Market streets was a haunt for Irish railroaders, postal employees from the nearby central Post Office, and newspapermen from the nearby Philadelphia *Evening Bulletin* offices. Scullion, a Derry man, owned a small saloon in the Northeast section of the city. Hugh Breen; a widely respected Derry man and also a saloon keeper, was involved as well, as was Robert V. Clarke, born in County Mayo, an employee of the Philadelphia Navy Yard and a man who had helped to publish several short-lived Irish newspapers in the city.

A suitable property was found, and in 1958 a corporation was chartered as Commodore John Barry, Inc., and 1,000 shares of stock were issued for a capitalization of $100,000. The president was Mickey Cavanaugh; vice-president, Michael Scullion; treasurer, Hugh Breen, and secretary, Robert V. Clarke. The corporation was simple in its purpose. It was a holding company for real estate. Thus, many of the difficulties of endowing it with other objectives were avoided. The Board of Directors of the corporation included other well known Irish men, such as Frank Burke; Frank Algeo, a power in the Donegal Society; J. Patrick Brown; and John Mulligan. [8]

The site for the Commodore Barry Club was a large rambling building in the middle-class Mt. Airy section of the city. The property had formerly been known as the "Ross House" and had been a restaurant and social facility rented for family and fraternal functions. It contained several bars, restaurant facilities, meeting rooms, and an auditorium that seated about 800 people. The facilities were duly renovated, and a portrait of Patrick J. McNelis, a longtime leader in the city's Irish affairs who was recently deceased, was hung in the auditorium.

The Mt. Airy neighborhood was one of large Victorian single houses. After World War II it had begun to experience extensive racial change, but in the 1950s when the Barry Club was established there was little prospect that the neighborhood would lose its substantial white character. Although racial change had proceeded over the years, the tree-lined streets of the area still made it one of the most attractive in the city. The new Barry Club could be reached by the Chestnut Hill commuter train line, but by the 1950s the general ownership of cars made the availability of public transportation less important.

In the 1950s the Irish fraternal leaders were aware of the declining memberships of their organizations, but they were persistent men. The foundation of the Barry Club gave them an opportunity to centralize their activities. The dispersion of the Irish population, paradoxically, led to a concentration of its activities. The prestige of the club's founders was involved in the process of making a success of its facilities. Soon the Barry Club was humming with a fairly steady bar patronage, a calendar of meetings, and a cycle of Irish society balls and dances.

Irish political figures were still plentiful in Philadelphia's City Hall in the 1950s and 1960s. They could be relied on to launch their electoral drives by gleefully attending any and all Irish social functions. Fund-raising benefits for Irish missionaries, memorial services for veterans of the IRA, the crowning of "Miss Mayo," or just the opportunity to mingle with Barry Club patrons drew Irish people to the premises.

The Irish-born population in the Philadelphia area in 1970 was about 20,000. Many of these people were not affiliated in any way with Irish organizations. In 1970 only 47 of the 1,049 persons naturalized as citizens in the city were Irish. The Irish may have no longer represented huge numbers of bloc votes in the city, but their penetration power in local politics still could not be ignored. For this reason politicians often took complimentary advertisements in the programs of the groups sponsoring events at the Barry Club.[9]

Perhaps the most important service of the Irish Center was as a communications focus for the leaders of the various organizations. Many people relied on the weekly Irish radio shows beamed from two of the Delaware Valley's smaller stations for their information about local events. The Irish Center made available a joint mailing list that permitted direct mailings of newsletters and notices of gatherings. Most of all, the informal grapevine at the center transmitted news of leadership changes, families, local events in Ireland, and political and social gossip.

In 1965 Frank Algeo of the Donegal Society was elected president of the board of the center, and Sean Hughes was manager. The Irish organizations lobbied to have a regular flight established between Philadelphia and Shannon in Ireland. They did not prevail, so they arranged charter flights to Ireland for large groups every year. The flights were an important service to the Irish community, and several travel agents cooperated enthusiastically.

At the Clan na Gael Commemoration in 1969 John. J. Reilly gave a talk emphasizing the patriotic ties to Ireland, and these were never far in the background. Robert Clarke, editor of the *Donegal Bulletin*, a monthly newsletter, editorialized in August 1966 about the "gravity of the 'Ulster' situation." At that time few people in America were aware of the deep discontent in the six northern counties of Ireland still occupied by England. People from Donegal were concerned, however, and the *Donegal Bulletin* called for "an overhaul of the electoral system" in Northern Ireland to foster a democratic reform of the English-backed regime that openly discriminated against Catholics.[10]

With a renewal of ethnic interest among the public in the late 1960s, the Irish community also began to be enlivened. The Friday night dancing classes at the center were full. Gaelic lessons were started again. A television crew filmed an evening's activities at the center, and rallies were held for the Northern Ireland Civil Rights Association. The people who drank at the bar and came to the dances began to be more diversified. Younger immigrants and American-born people came around. By the 1970s the Irish Center had developed a new clientele.

A survey of Irish Center members and their friends and relatives who registered to fly to Ireland on one of the center's charter flights in July 1975 reveals some facts about the kind of people who supported and used the center and what attracted them to it. Of the sixty-four persons filling out questionnaires eighteen were residents of the city of Philadelphia, and almost all of the remainder lived in nearby suburbs. They ranged in age from fifteen to seventy, with thirty being between twenty and thirty years old. Twenty-four respondents had nine to twelve years of school completed, and twenty-two had thirteen to sixteen years of school.

Thus, the people related to the center were relatively young and well educated.

Only eight of the sixty-four were born in Ireland, but twenty-one had one or both parents born there. Their families identified predominantly with three counties—Donegal, Mayo, and Tyrone—but twelve other counties were listed by respondents as places from which their families emigrated. Forty-two had visited Ireland previously, and twenty-three had been associated with the Irish Center only one year previous to their charter flight.

Forty-two respondents had learned of the Irish Center from friends or relatives. Twenty-one people visited the center once a week. The thing that most people enjoyed at the center was the music and dancing, but twenty-one people listed those they met there as the most enjoyable feature. Thirty-nine had attended events of the Ceili Society. *(Ceili* is an Irish word for "a friendly gathering." These weekly events involved music, dancing, and occasional lectures. Concerts and organization meetings drew others. County society balls also were an attraction. The interesting factor in these responses is the high level of interest in music, dancing, and sociable gatherings.

Of the sixty-four respondents, thirty listed radio programs as their chief link to Irish affairs. Twenty-five read Irish newspapers, and a great majority purchased Irish books and records.[11]

These responses indicate that the center had by 1975 developed an interested, fairly well educated, American-born following. They were people tending their ethnic roots. Although all had joined the Barry Society, few were members of the Irish county societies whose stock holdings in the center gave them control of it. There was, therefore, a clear distinction between many of those who patronized the center and the Irish-born groups that controlled it.

In 1976, the year of the bicentennial of American independence, all kinds of groups were feting the birthdate of the nation's founding. A Bicentennial Commission had been set up in Philadelphia, and public monies were distributed to aid ethnic organizations with commemoration programs. Polish clubs, Italian societies, and black groups made their plans, and the Irish Center leaders were anxious to salute the occasion as well. An ad hoc group was formed at the center to obtain funds for a program of concerts and lectures. In the process certain tensions arose that were revealing.

There had always been a degree of closeness about the older leaders of the center that manifested their particular ethnic style. These were Irish country men. They competed among themselves for offices in the various organizations. They limited the role of women and outsiders. With the growth of interest in the center by younger people with college educations and a different style, the older leaders became wary. When the group was formed to seek bicentennial funds, there were articulate American and Irish-born people as part of it who did not have the same view of the center as the older leaders.

To those who had been on the board of the center, it had long been clear that the income from bar patrons was very important to keep the center going. Groups that talked a lot and drank moderately—such as the James Joyce Society, composed of college professors and literary types—were not as easily accepted as groups that worked up a great thirst dancing Irish set dances. When the Philadelphia Folk Song Society met at the center for an evening of wonderful singing, some blacks had been part of the gathering, and this caused some uneasiness. Then, too, those promoting what seemed to be highbrow cultural programs, although Irish, were less close-knit and more open than the long-standing leaders. They included women who were intelligently assertive and people who made the older leaders nervous. There was no formal confrontation on these differences, but agitation, verbal exchanges, and some hard feelings were experienced.[12]

There was another issue that caused mixed feelings at the center. This was the issue of support for the Provisional Irish Republican Army in Ireland. After the violence in Northern Ireland erupted in 1969, groups of Irish-born people in the United States took the lead in forming chapters of Irish Northern Aid. These groups stated that they sought to assist victims of the violence in Ulster by providing charitable funds for relief of suffering. Officials in Ireland and the United States alleged that Irish Northern Aid was a channel for support of the violence in Ulster. Opinions differed among people frequenting the Irish

Center. Most shared a detestation of England's role in Northern Ireland. Some supported the Provisional IRA. Others did not see that violence would produce any acceptable solution to the complex Northern Ireland problem. Again, no clear confrontation occurred between those holding these different views, but personality conflicts and factional differences fell along the line of divided opinion.[13]

There was as well a growing sense of the limitations and even the partial isolation of the Irish Center in the city.[14] Despite the revived interest in Irish subjects among younger American-born people, the Irish Center really did not stand out as a focus of that interest. International House, various colleges, and other facilities often sponsored Irish concerts and gatherings. The Irish-oriented population in the Philadelphia area was simply too large and diverse to be related effectively to one facility like the center. The Irish Center was primarily an immigrant social facility controlled by the county societies. Other kinds of Irish groups did not fit into the center. One was the prestigious Friendly Sons of Saint Patrick, founded in 1771, a group that included many professional and business men. Another was an organization called the Irish Society, which was begun in 1975 by a coalition of political and labor figures who wanted to have a downtown Irish club where they could lunch and discuss their affairs. Judges, lawyers, political-party officials, and others set up this club in a convenient downtown location, much in the same way as Jews had done with their Locust Club and the Anglo Protestants had done in the past with the Racquet Club and the Philadelphia Club. Rarely if ever were the Irish political and labor-union figures from the downtown club, the Irish Society, seen at the Irish Center, which one of them referred to as "the greenhorn club."

The leadership of the Irish Center continued to be composed of men and women born in Ireland. More important, they were men and women born in small-town and rural Ireland. Their attempts to maintain social ties in Philadelphia were conditioned by their Irish background, naturally enough. Their experience in such a community as Philadelphia required extensive reorientation even if some traditional values were to be preserved. The need for ties with similar people, the craving for familiar accents, character types, observances, and entertainment was pursued through the center, but the entry of people of different backgrounds and the competition of other groups accentuated the insecurity and factional strains that are always present in immigrant organizations. Whether the emotional stress and instability produced under these conditions was greater or less than might be expected is difficult to determine because there are not enough studies of similar facilities to make comparisons. What is evident is that the Irish Center set a very modest community role for itself and during the first thirty years of its operation maintained itself according to the formula originally set forth for it. Whether it can continue to sustain itself in the 1980s, when Irish immigration to the city is likely to be reduced to a trickle, is a question that can be answered only by conjecture about the future of immigrant and ethnic organizations in the life of the country as a whole.

NOTES

1. Edward M. Levine, *The Irish and Irish Politicians* (Notre Dame, Ind.: University of Notre Dame Press, 1966), pp. 53–68; Marjorie R. Fallows, *Irish-Americans: Identity and Assimilation* (Englewood Cliffs, N.J.: Prentice-Hall, 1979), p. 48.

2. U.S. Department of Commerce, Bureau of the Census, 1970 Census of Population, Subject Reports, National Origin and Language, Table 11, p. 74.

3. Dale Light, Jr., "Ethnicity and the Urban Ecology of a Nineteenth Century City: Philadelphia's Irish, 1840–1890," Doctoral thesis, University of Pennsylvania, 1979.

4. Dennis Clark, *The Irish in Philadelphia: Ten Generations of Urban Experience* (Philadelphia: Temple University Press, 1973), pp. 175–76.

5. Minute Book of the Cavan Men's Catholic Social and Beneficial Association (1907–20), Historical Society of Pennsylvania, Philadelphia.

6. Minute Books, Irish American Club (1889–1901), MacSwiney Club collection, Jenkintown, Pa.

7. Minute Books, Donegal Beneficial Social and Patriotic Association (1899–1920), The Irish Center collection, Philadelphia.

8. Interview with Robert V. Clarke, May 17, 1968, Philadelphia. (Tape in possession of author.)

9. *Donegal Bulletin*, Philadelphia 1958–69, property of James McGill.

10. Ibid., August 1966.

11. This survey was conducted by the writer. Questionnaires were distributed and interviews held with sixty-four persons.

12. Interviews with Owen B. Hunt, a longtime observer of the city's Irish community, were held in May 1976 in Philadelphia. (Tapes in possession of the author.)

13. Dennis Clark, *Irish Blood: Northern Ireland and the American Conscience* (Port Washington, N.Y.: Kennikat Press, 1977).

14. A feeling of inadequacy in relating to American institutions is common among immigrants. See Alexander Callow, ed., *American Urban History* (New York: Oxford University Press, 1969), p. 147. The complex process of social adaptation is summarized in L. M. Bristol, *Social Adaptation* (Cambridge, Mass.: Harvard University Press, 1915), and C. E. Black, *The Dynamics of Modernization* (New York: Harper and Row, 1966), p. 24.

15 Echo of the Gael

In his book *The Great Silence*, Seán de Fréine tells of the subversion of the Gaelic language in Ireland in the nineteenth century through repression, the growing cultural influence of English, and finally the disaster of the Great Famine. By the second half of the century this extraordinary language, which had resisted all manner of punishment and intimidation, was on the verge of extinction. A treasure house of literary forms and poetic achievements reaching back to the ages of the epic and saga was crumbling. As famine placed the national life of Ireland in eclipse, the ancient language along with its social and cultural molds shrank under the steady pressure of oppression, poverty, and emigration.[1]

In the great American cities such as Philadelphia, the incoming throngs of Irish immigrants were beset with grim problems of survival. Having fled Ireland, they faced a critical test in adjusting to urban life. Obtaining jobs, housing, and the education needed for an urban environment left them little time to recall or revive the use of the language that for many was their native tongue. Gaelic became for these immigrants an all but secret usage, retained by a few who were often poor and bereft of formal education. Frequently, they were ambiguous about using the old speech so deeply identified with suffering in the stricken rural districts of their homeland. The necessity of using English in their jobs and in schools further curtailed use of Irish. Here and there, however, there were occasional flickers of devotion to the language. Among the struggling working people of the industrializing city of Philadelphia, the Irish were accorded the least desirable jobs. Along the busy Schuylkill River and by the banks of the broad Delaware in the Port Richmond section, the Irish heaved coal off the barges that came down to Philadelphia from the upstate Pennsylvania mining regions.[2] In Port Richmond Irish was spoken among these workers.[3] In Southwark, now a portion of South Philadelphia, there were numerous Irish working on the docks and at other menial labor. Here also Irish was spoken; on the occasion of the death of Daniel O'Connell in 1847 there was a Mass celebrated at Saint Philip's Church at which the sermon was in Gaelic.[4] There were probably other instances of the public use of Gaelic, but documentary evidence of the fact is hard to find.

During the first half of the century, interest in Gaelic was sustained by some individuals who still had a connection with the living font of scholarship that stretched back through the centuries.[5] Such a man was Matthias O'Conway. Educated for a time in Spain, but a native speaker of Irish, O'Conway came to Philadelphia, sojourned for a while on the frontier where he learned some Indian dialects, and then settled in the Quaker city to pursue his skill as a translator of French and Spanish. O'Conway spent the later years of his life in the 1830s and 1840s working with enormous patience on his pet project, a Gaelic dictionary containing several thousand words with cognates in six other languages.[6] It is to such a man that the Catholic bishop John Neumann would have gone to learn Irish in order to better serve the famine immigrants who knew no other language. Bishop Neumann, who was of German background, studied Irish to help him in his ministry to the Irish in the city.[7]

There is evidence that some Gaelic scholars in the United States kept in touch with one another. Those interested in the language could pursue its study in America with a freedom made all the more sweet by the memory of repression in Ireland. However, the works of the mind were difficult to cultivate among an immigrant population struggling among poverty and discrimination. It was the singular men who persisted. One of these was John O'Mahony, who was, among other things, head of the Fenian Brotherhood in the United States. O'Mahony found time to translate the chronicles of the historian Geoffrey Keating into English. In the introduction to the edition published in 1857, he thanks James Slevin of Philadelphia for the use of his library. Slevin was a man who had become wealthy in business. He had collected a fine library, including a number of Gaelic books. Scholars like O'Mahony and Slevin apparently corresponded and aided one another.[8]

However thin the ranks of the Gaelic scholars, they were bound by ancient ties. Scattered by emigration, they found ways to further their interest in grammar, literature, and poetry. The *Catholic Standard and Times*, the Catholic newspaper in Philadelphia, in 1869 advertised an international essay competition for compositions in Gaelic.[9] In 1870 the annual meeting of a local Celtic Society was noted in the press. The president of the group was Dr. William Carroll, a doctor born in Donegal who later became a friend and personal physician of Charles Stewart Parnell. Carroll was a Fenian and tireless partisan of Irish causes.[10] This organization devoted to Celtic studies was later succeeded by the Philo-Celtic Society, which was still meeting in 1894, reporting its vitality, and inviting interested persons to Gaelic lessons given at its meetings.[11]

A flyer distributed by the society in the 1890s urged study of Gaelic:

Aibeoduiġ An Ġaedilge
REVIVE THE IRISH LANGUAGE
The Philo-Celtic Society of Philadelphia,

respectfully reminds all who wish to preserve and cultivate the Irish Language, that with the present patriotic movement there has also sprung up an increased desire for the revival of our National Language. "A nation," says Thomas Davis, "without a language is only half a nation." When the people of any country permit their National language to perish, it is in itself a proof that they are being denationalized. Thus, it has ever been the object of the conqueror to force his language on the conquered, that the work of denationalization might be the more easily accomplished. As a proof of this we may cite the anxiety of the Russian Czar to abolish the language of noble Poland and establish that of Russia, and also the efforts of the German government to crush the French language in Alsace and Lorraine and foster that of Germany. The Poles and Alsatians struggle bravely to maintain their mother tongue. We point out these facts for the purpose of reminding our fellow-countrymen of how nobly our ancestors laboured and suffered to keep alive the Irish tongue . . . .

To enlarge the English and extinguish the Irish has been the steady and consistent aim of the English Government for centuries. So long as the Irish people used the Irish language they were unable to Saxonize us. "When the language of the children shall be English," says Sir Wm. Petty, "the transmutation will be very easy, easy indeed." Sir John Perrot recommends to Queen Elizabeth that "orders should be immediately sent down for enlarging the English and extinguishing the Irish, in as short a time as conveniently may be." Elizabeth, who was never slow in adopting such advice, sent the orders accordingly. The Irish schools were closed. The teachers were banished to foreign parts, with the caution that execution would be their doom if ever again found in Ireland. Some did return and were executed. Notwithstanding this, the language continued in general use, not only among the "meere Irish," but many of the English planters, captivated by its sweetness, ceased to use the English and adopted Irish. To prevent this, we find a law enacted by the English Parliament "that if any Englishman shall use the Irish language, he shall forfeit his lands and tenements and give security in the Court of Chancery, that he will conform to the English tongue and custom in every respect." Contemporary writers tell us how rigourously these laws were executed. Every succeeding administration from then until the present time, has directly or indirectly continued to discourage the use of the Irish language. . . .

But it must be here acknowledged that previous to the formation of the Philo-Celtic Societies, the Irish language—that language that persecution could not crush—was slowly and surely perishing through the neglect and carelessness of the Irish people. . . .

The Philo-Celtic Societies of New York, Brooklyn and Boston have several classes meeting bi-weekly, and are doing good work. Philadelphia, with an Irish born population of over one hundred thousand, of whom at least ten thousand can converse in the Irish language, is behind in this movement. It is time for the Irish people of Philadelphia to arouse themselves in this matter. . . .

THE PHILO-CELTIC SOCIETY CLASSES MEET EVERY

SUNDAY NIGHT AT PHILOPATRIAN HALL, 211 S. 12th St.
INSTRUCTION   FREE.   PATRICK   McFADDEN,   Pres.
CHARLES McCANN, Rec. Sect'y.

The fact that the Philadelphia Philo-Celtic Society existed in the
1890s indicates that its members were probably animated by the
new wave of interest in Gaelic that spread through Ireland and the
Irish overseas at about this time. Headed by Douglas Hyde and
others, the Gaelic revival led to the formation of branches of the
Gaelic League in most of the larger American cities. In the
immigrant Irish communities the study and popularization of
Gaelic was more than an exercise in nostalgia. It enabled
Irish-Americans to gain a sense of the cultural ideals of those who
led in the establishment of Irish independence.

Under the influence of the scholarly revival in Ireland and the
nationalist impulse that achieved a free Irish state in the 1920s,
Gaelic studies in the city were for a time a fashionable pursuit. A
number of Irish organizations sponsored them. The difficulties of
maintaining interest against strong cultural countertrends soon
eroded the enthusiasm, however, and Gaelic study again receded
to the status of an exotic avocation. Nevertheless, a faithful cadre
held to the ideals of the language movement. Some were teachers,
some simply people who loved the old language.

The Gaelic coterie met for many years at the Irish American
Club on North Broad Street. There not only classes but sociable
conversation around the bar in the old tongue could be held.
Active then was Francis O'Kane, a chemist and friend of Douglas
Hyde's and Thomas O'Neill Russell's, both of whom visited
Philadelphia in their tours in America to promote the language.[12]
O'Kane had been one of those who championed the carrying of a
column in Gaelic in the Irish-American newspapers that were so
influential at the end of the last century. Frank O'Hagan and John
Maunsell were two other dedicated teachers of Irish who held
classes in their homes through the 1930s.[13]

By the 1940s Gaelic had been installed as a regular component
of the curriculum in schools in Ireland, and graduates of those
schools emigrating to America had usually studied and used the
language through the secondary level of their education. Some

were strongly proficient in the language, but most were not. Gaelic was then still taught in Ireland according to the rote methods inherited from the study of classical languages. Modern scholarship in linguistics and "immersion" methods of language teaching had not yet begun to affect classroom practices, although phonograph records for instruction did become available in the 1940s. The enormous cultural impact of the mass media, however, made it increasingly difficult to maintain an interest in any language except English because of the saturation power of the English-speaking culture. Still, the interest of both young and old people based on the use of the language in their families or thier curiosity about the language growing out of their reading about it in English spurred study of it.

Occasionally, teachers would set up small classes on their own. Patrick Darcy, a man who made his living as a translator of Slavic languages, was holding such classes into the 1950s. There was no chair of Celtic studies at a local university, and Gaelic books were a rarity, but students did gather intermittently as groups of friends to delve into the syntax, vocabulary, and niceties of the language.

In 1969 at a rally in Philadelphia addressed by Bernadette Devlin to raise funds for the civil-rights drive in Northern Ireland, Miss Devlin sang—and sang well—a Gaelic song for the audience. From a balcony amid the applause came a fitting salute, when a man thundered out, "Beg Altach Abu!"—the ancient war cry of the O'Devlins. Somebody had been at the books.

In the 1960s two trends developed that augmented the thin ranks of the diehard devotees of Irish in Philadelphia. Those who had studied Gaelic in modern Irish schools lost their shyness about using it and defending it in America. The Irish American Cultural Institute from its headquarters in St. Paul, Minn., sent touring speakers from Ireland on a broad American circuit. These speakers often began their lectures in Irish and extolled its riches. Such scholars as Thomas Kinsella, who became poet in residence at Temple University, were examples of extraordinary gifted people who revered the language.

A second trend was the growth in tourism that enabled literally millions of Irish Americans to visit Ireland. On these visits many strengthened their ties with families that still spoke Irish or whose children studied it in school. In addition, they were made aware of the prestige of the language among educated Irish people. They were informed also of the disillusion of many with the revival of Gaelic and the difficulties encountered by the revival movement. This did not deter at least some of these Irish-Americans from returning to the United States with a resolution to study Irish if the opportunity to do so arose. In Philadelphia such people were drawn to classes at the Irish Center conducted by a pert and charming woman named Nora Campbell, whose classes in the 1970s included people of all ages in both basic and advanced sessions. Other enthusiasts were drawn to the Celtic League headed by musician and piper Eoghan Ballard, who developed classes in Gaelic, Welsh, and Breton at his home in the old Irish community of Schuylkill in South Philadelphia. Problems existed in obtaining books, tape-recorded teaching aids, visual materials, and classroom space, but the will persisted.

Why did people come, often at great inconvenience, to these classes? Based on interviews with Nora Campbell's class members, the following reasons emerged. For some the motivation was simple sentiment, an emotional attraction to a language associated with a vast history and a treasury of myth, legend, and poetry. Others were language teachers, specialists who sought to add a Celtic tongue to the modern languages they knew or taught. Some, of course, had family ties with Gaelic, had heard or used it as children, and sought to expand their knowledge of it. For some the political heritage of Irish nationalism bade them know the language as part of the fulfillment of Irish identity and as a cultural compensation for the long period when study of the language was repressed in Ireland. Most saw Gaelic as a crucial key to the culture that was theirs by inheritance, and they worked to fashion that key by honing memory of verbs and polishing rules of grammar.[14]

For other Irish Philadelphians for whom the language was a native tongue or who were fairly or fully fluent in it, Gaelic represented a bittersweet element in their lives. Tape-recorded interviews in Gaelic with these people by this writer revealed them to be subject to mixed emotions about Gaelic and what it meant to them as immigrants or natives in an English-speaking society. As students in an independent Ireland, native speakers had been taught to hold the language in esteem but had also had to work at its study in school. Those from Gaelic-speaking households and communities in County Donegal, County Mayo, or County Kerry had a very strong affection for the language and were usually replete with extensive memorized poems, songs, and stories in it. They regretted not being more learned in it. Most used it to some extent in their homes among friends and relatives. Moreover, these Gaelic speakers were sad that the language was not more used. They were somewhat militant about this, and proud of their own competence in the language.

One woman interviewed asserted that it was "the way of the world to be ignorant of flowers, birdsong and Irish." Another man, who had perfected his family Gaelic by translating into English materials written in Irish about a relative who was a noted author, looked back on the study of the tongue as a tremendous delight for him when he was younger. For most native speakers, to have come to a society in which the language of their childhood, with its potent emotions and memories, was subtracted from their environment was a cultural wound. They spoke of this feelingly, and the recollection of family ties, the secret conversations of children, and the great legacy of an ancient tongue clouded their expression.

Those interviewed agreed that having English was a necessity. They did not resent any inconvenience of bilingualism. They did, however, miss the opportunity to use Gaelic more. One girl sent tape-recorded greetings and accounts in Gaelic of her activities in America to her family at home in Donegal.

Whether they were native speakers or those who had learned conversational Irish in America, these people advocated further study, use, and encouragement of Gaelic. They recognized that an enormous work of scholarship and pedagogy had been carried out in modern Ireland by the Gaelic League, the schools, and language teachers. The revival of Gaelic as a full medium for daily concourse in Ireland had failed, but the techniques and skills for the preservation of the language had been developed. They saw the future as making it easier to perpetuate their minority language because of broader education, organized action, and teaching aids, although they still resented and feared the acculturating power of English-dominated mass media and daily discourse.

There was a clear difference between those who had only primary- and secondary-level educations and those who had university educations. For those who had not gone on to higher education, Gaelic was still something about which to be somewhat shy. They could seldom be articulate about it, yet they were founts of lore and oral inheritance in it, full of stories, and able to delight in certain words and phrases. For university people, younger people, a higher education had given them a richly poetic view of the language. They knew of the vast literature of epics and exquisitely detailed metrical traditions in Old Irish, and they had memorized at school the poems of Daithi O'Brudair, Eoghan O'Rathaille, and the seventeenth- and eighteenth-century poets of Munster. While doing graduate work at the University of Pennsylvania, Maurice Bric, a graduate of University College, Cork, missed conversation in Irish so much that he would call his friend Michael O'Kennedy in New York and chat by telephone in Gaelic. Microbiologist Dervla Mellerick, doing her own graduate work in Philadelphia, was quick to take the chance to speak Irish and delighted to recall her school days studying it. These were the "new Gaels," proud of the language and assertive about its qualities and pleasures. They were confident about its use and committed to its future.

At a reading of his poetry at a lecture series presented by the Irish-American Cultural Institute at Chestnut Hill College, poet Michael Hartnett from County Limerick explained how he had resented the compulsory Irish he was made to study in school, and, after traveling to France, Italy, Spain, and Morocco for some years, he had returned to Ireland and become enthralled with the language. He has written radio plays and highly praised poetry in Gaelic, and although his poetry in English was successful, he has largely abandoned writing in English. His Gaelic poems are lyric. Many are devoted to nature themes, and some echo the ancient meters that were old when they reached a height of artistic grace during Elizabethan times. Hartnett is singular because the intellectual journey from English back to Irish runs counter to the enormous force of Anglicization. However, his work as a poet and translator is acclaimed, and he has been awarded coveted prizes with handsome monetary purses twice in recent years.

Gaelic speakers, scholars, and students in the audiences that hear the readings or lectures of Michael Hartnett, Thomas Kinsella, Maurice Bric, and others, or listen to the Gaelic songs recorded by Mick Moloney or Mary O'Hara, recognize the difficulty of furthering the language. They have studied other languages and see the differences and obstacles involved with Gaelic. Discussions with them reveal that they are encouraged by the great effort that has been made in Ireland in the last two generations, and the new technology of tape recordings and popular books tend to offset the blunders of the Irish government in its language policy. Interviews with such people immerse the interviewer in a startling atmosphere of ancient cultural reflections, modern pressures, and fascinating personal interests.

These interviews indicate the continued commitment of people of Irish background to the difficult nurture of their language heritage. It is encouraging that an interest in Irish today grows steadily out of the study of Irish literature in English courses in colleges and universities. Reading Lady Gregory, William Butler Yeats, and Liam O'Flaherty stimulates students to study further the Gaelic background from which the works of these writers emerge. The persistence of the interest in Gaelic in an American city, even on so minimal a basis as has been indicated here, should prompt more cultural activity dealing with the Gaelic heritage on the part of Irish embassies and consuls in the United States. The survival of Irish interests amid the turbulence of American cities is part of the ethnic richness running through the country's life. A language driven almost to extinction in its homeland, and nurtured so fitfully in an American city, merits support wherever it is found. Such support is part of our debt to the past and is a celebration of a long-delayed cultural liberty won after a profound struggle.

NOTES

1. Seán de Fréine, *The Great Silence* (Dublin: Foilseacháin Náisiúnta Teóranta, 1965), pp. 61–75.

2. Sam Bass Warner, *The Private City: Philadelphia* (Philadelphia: University of Pennsylvania Press, 1968), p. 71, gives details of the city's labor force.

3. George Morgan, *City of Firsts* (Philadelphia: Historical Publication Society, 1926), p. 246.

4. J. Thomas Scharf and Thompson Westcott, *History of Philadelphia: 1609–1884*, 3 vols. (Philadelphia: L. H. Evarts Company, 1884), 2: 1392.

5. Robin Flower, *The Irish Tradition* (Oxford, England: Clarendon Press, 1947), pp. 1–22.

6. Lawrence F. Flick, "Matthias James O'Conway," *Records of the American Catholic Historical Society* 10, no. 3 (September 1899): 257–99.

7. Michael Curley, *Venerable John Neumann* (Washington, D.C.: Catholic University of America Press, 1952), p. 459.

8. Geoffrey Keating, *The History of Ireland*, trans. by John O'Mahony (New York: P. N. Haverty, 1857), p. 17. For a biographical note on James Slevin, see John H. Campbell, *History of the Friendly Sons of St. Patrick* (Philadelphia: The Hibernian Society, 1892), p. 521.

9. *Catholic Standard and Times* (Philadelphia), March 20, 1869.

10. Philadelphia *Public Ledger*, March 14, 1870.

11. *Irish Echo* (Boston) 4, no. 10 (January 1894): 160.

12. Dominic Daly, *The Young Douglas Hyde: The Dawn of the Irish Revolution and Renaissance* (Totowa, N.J.: Rowman and Littlefield, 1974), pp. 32–33.

13. Interview with John O'Riordan, January 5, 1979.

14. These interviews were conducted in 1978 and 1979 with twenty-seven respondents in Irish or English. Topics covered where the respondents came from, when they came to the United States if they were immigrants, what jobs they held, what they thought of social changes in Ireland and the United States, and what they thought and felt about the study and use of Irish in their own lives.

A Note on Sources

In ancient Ireland the bardic historians who kept the genealogies and chronicles of their people were important figures, and when they joined in the formal feasts of clan leaders and high kings they had allotted to them a special place and a special portion of the meats at the feast. The special portion of the historian, we are told in the ancient tales, always contained a crooked bone. I have pondered why this should have been so and have concluded that the crooked bone signified the difficulty that characterized the scholar's effort to get at the truth, to get at the marrow of things. It is no different today. It is difficult to compose the story of one's people, and readers correctly require that whatever is asserted be supported by evidence, for imagination and presumption are always lurking to divert historians from accuracy and the truth. In the interest of confirming the evidence underlying the chapters in this book, I have thought it appropriate to discuss some of the sources of information used in its compilation.

To relate the lives and circumstances of well-to-do and prominent people who have preceded us is not difficult, for they were usually notable in their communities and left public and private records of themselves. To trace the lives of working people or minor figures in large communities, people significant in ethnic communities but largely unknown to the broader public, is a more tedious task. The conditions surrounding such people, however, can be reconstructed from various sources, and inferences can then be made about their lives. Thus, scanty direct evidence can be supplemented. No archive of evidence is more helpful in this process than the many documents kept as public records by governments, especially local governments. Americans may presume that government was insignificant before the twentieth-century advent of big government, but record keeping has been one of the social habits of officials everywhere and in all periods.

Data about Irish immigrants and their descendants are found in such public records as the U.S. Census, which have designations of the foreign-born, household size and composition, age, and occupation. In Philadelphia the Social History Project of Dr. Theodore Hershberg and his colleagues at the University of Pennsylvania has further refined census data by location, ethnic group, and income level, an incredible labor even with computer aid. Public records also show the misfortunes of the immigrant poor. Tax ledgers show their poverty, court dockets their crimes and misfortunes, vagrant registers their outcast status, and coroners' reports their final end. Reports of investigations and public hearings tell of working and living conditions. Lists of liquor licenses and voter registration books give some idea of their local activity, and the case records of social service agencies tell of their family problems. Thus, from the earliest certificates of indenture in the seventeenth century to the modern computerized tabulations of census data, official records convey social information about those too humble to have left other personal or public notice of themselves.

The opportunities that the city represented for the Irish are reflected in the school and parish records and graduation lists of local institutions. Family histories for the group are very rare, as are autobiographies, and it is a great good fortune to come across an actual set of papers and correspondence retained by some individual. The minutes and records of the fraternal and nationalist organizations tell of the long tradition of mutual aid and agitation for Irish liberty. The general-circulation newspapers are, of course, full of references to Irish personalities and affairs, but Irish and Catholic newspapers are even more significant. I was astonished to learn that there have been eighteen Irish-American newspapers published in Philadelphia since 1820, and only one-third of these are listed in any catalogs.

Business directories are especially helpful in tracing economic activity, but a familiarity with Irish names and residential areas is very necessary for their effective use. For contemporary materials that refer back to historical events and conditions, interview questionnaires gather valuable recollections, and tape-recorded oral interviews are extremely valuable.

All of the above sources are accessible enough thanks to the splendid and patient services of archivists and librarians, truly the unsung heroes and heroines of modern scholarship. However, there is more to the ferreting out of references and evidence than just knowing where the sources are. In order to indicate some of the human diversions of the quest for evidence, let me recount some of the historiographical impulses and bafflements that have accompanied the compilation of this book. At the outset I must confess that I am not a really dedicated researcher, nor a full-time academic scholar. I am a full-time executive whose rule of conscience has always been not to let his personal studies intrude on his daily job. As a result, my research is done in bits and pieces, on lunch hours, on Sunday afternoons, and in the gap between quitting time and those later evening meetings. I puzzle out things during commuter rides, while tramping in the city, or while working in the garden. This method is inefficient, but it is better than no research at all, and it is, in its way, a reflective procedure grounded in a rather plodding patience.

The chapter on Irish indentured children was inspired by references to indentures in the works of Richard Morris, a historian of American colonial life. That chapter took me almost four years to complete. Evidence of indentures was quite discontinuous, and I kept hunting for some firsthand personal accounts of Irish indentured people but after much searching found not one memoir of an indentured Irish person. Perhaps illiteracy, perhaps shame, or just the toll of time kept such a memoir from being retained.

The chapter on women workers was, of course, stimulated by all the good work now being done on women's history. It was a debt I owed. In my book *The Irish in Philadelphia*, largely researched in the 1960s, there are few references to women, and I wanted to correct such an omission. Also, I knew many women who had worked in the city's great mills. My own grandmother, Ellen Devlin, came from Cork to begin textile work in the Falls of the Schuylkill at the age of nine.

"Hazardous Pay," about the perils and accidents of Irish workers, was prompted by an exhibit that I hurriedly viewed after a conference at the wonderful Eleutherian Mills–Hagley Library near Wilmington, Del. In the exhibit were the names of some workers killed in an explosion at the Du Pont Powder Mills. It took me three years to get back to that library to dip into its records of explosions. The conditions of work at Midvale Steel Company were made difficult to trace because the company is now bankrupt, the great black mills empty, silent, and abandoned. Hospital records at the Pennsylvania Hospital were particularly helpful, but I was sad to see them stored in a badly ventilated attic. "Why can't physicians take better care of these great old books of records?" I asked. "They're busy caring for the living, not the records of the dead," I was told by the medical historian Maurice Vogel of Temple University.

The chapters on Irish businesses and businesspersons began with the problem of trying to explain political leadership. Everybody knows about political bosses, but few have looked at their business involvements. The whole subject of ethnic businesses is little studied and even taboo. Originally, my chapter on Irish contractors compared them with Jewish department-store founders and founders of Italian food businesses, but journal editors shied away from such a comparison, largely, I believe, because of sensitivity about describing Jews in a mercantile setting. As a result the chapter was shortened. The chapter on travel-agent businesses was developed to show the persistence and the crucial nature of the ties with the old country and the way these have changed over time.

Irish nationalism has been one of the chief components of Irish identity among Irish-Americans, and sources for its study range from the personal recollections of activists to newspapers founded and maintained specifically to advance the Irish cause in America. The Fenian Brotherhood was the fountainhead of modern Irish nationalism, and studies of it that I read largely omitted references to Philadelphia, yet the city was a vigorous nationalist center. While searching the archives of the American Catholic Historical Society, I had the good fortune to come across Fenian correspondence and papers never previously used in the study of Philadelphia's Irish revolutionaries. This interest in revolutionaries led me to search out information about Luke Dillon, whose name I had heard many times in Irish circles. One night the late Owen B. Hunt, himself a fiery Irish nationalist, sat with me in the Commodore Barry Club. He was eighty at the time, and he recited a ballad about Luke Dillon that he had heard sung after coming to the city from County Sligo. The powerful memories of such people as Owen Hunt have been invaluable sources for me. John J. Reilly was another man with a wonderful memory, but, even more important, he had kept his correspondence and organizational files for a forty-year period, and these enabled me to reconstruct the activities opposing the partition of Ireland that he carried out for decades. Thus, the three chapters on nationalist themes arose out of interest in "the old cause "

In addition to uncovering unused Fenian records, I had an even greater stroke of good fortune in finding the secret letter book of a British spy who reported to London on the underground work of such men as Luke Dillon. Major Henri LeCaron worked in the United States as a spy on Irish organizations in the 1870s and 1880s. His letter book of secret reports was brought to my notice by a former bank official who retrieved it as a curiosity from files about to be discarded. He did not know what it was except that it dealt with Irish topics. Reading of a lecture I gave, he contacted me and kindly let me examine it. It took me some months to identify, verify, and analyze, but eventually I realized that the document was indeed that of Luke Dillon's enemy, the English master spy.

The chapters on Irish relations with other ethnic groups were produced because of my interest in intergroup relations. Having worked in race relations and edited the *Interracial Review,* I have always been concerned about the problem of Irish-black relations. The chapter posing the Rittenhouse Square socialite area against the Irish Ramcat district began when I took part in a community history project of the Philadelphia Center City Residents Association in 1975 with Mrs. Bobbye Burke. Sharing a lecture platform with E. Digby Baltzell to discuss the two communities extended my study, which was at length published in a book *The Divided Metropolis,* edited by William W. Cutler and Howard Gillette (Westport, Conn.: Greenwood Press, 1980). For the research on the Irish and the Jews I am indebted to instructive, and almost always comical, discussions with Max Whiteman, librarian of the Philadelphia Union League; Milton Mustin of the Philadelphia City Archives; and the ever-thoughtful Murray Friedman and Judge Isador Kranzel of the American Jewish Committee.

To study this Irish community was to see that it obtruded in countless ways into the life of Philadelphia. It was there in its animation and organizations and concerts and celebrations. It was full of stories and memories and living ties to yesterday, and also to contemporary Ireland. As a result, the final three chapters were written to substantiate these ties. It is hard to believe, but in a nation full of immigrant social centers we have very few studies of them. Hence, the chapter on the Irish Center is an attempt to delineate one such facility. The Saint Patrick's Day Observance Association kindly made its files available to me to write a history of that group, and my chapter on it is based on that work. Finally, the record of scholarship and interest in Gaelic was an irresistible subject for me, and the oral interviews that are part of it were a thorough delight even for one whose spoken Gaelic is far from admirable.

Having fitted the information from all these sources together, having cited Gaelic manuscripts and recordings by storyteller Joe Heaney and secret letters and the indentures of long-forgotten children bound to years of labor, I can assure any historian that there is much, much more to be found and to be told about these Irish people of whom I have written. As such storytellers as Joe Heaney would say after an evening of three or four hours of tales, ". . . there's more to be known than by hearing and sight; there's more to our tales than we can sing, say or write."

Bibliography

BOOKS

Abbott, Grace. *The Child and the State*. Chicago: University of Chicago Press, 1938.

Adams, William Forbes. *Ireland and the Irish Emigration to America*. New Haven, Conn.: Yale University Press, 1932.

Anonymous. *An Alarming Portraiture of the Pernicious Effects of the Customary Use of Distilled Spirituous Liquors*. Philadelphia: Kimber and Conrad, 1813.

Baltzell, E. Digby. *The Protestant Establishment: Aristocracy and Caste in America*. New York: Random House, 1946.

Billington, Ray Allen. *The Protestant Crusade: A Study of the Origins of American Nativism*. Chicago: Quadrangle Books, 1964.

Bridenbaugh, Carl. *Cities in the Wilderness*. New York: Capricorn Books, 1968.

Briggs, Asa. *Victorian Cities*. New York: Harper and Row, 1970.

Bremner, Robert H., ed. *Children and Youth in America*. 3 vols. Cambridge, Mass.: Harvard University Press, 1970.

Brody, Hugh. *Inishkillane: Change and Decline in the West of Ireland*. London: Penguin Press, 1973.

Brooke, Robert C., ed. *Bryce's American Commonwealth*. New York: Macmillan Co., 1939.

Brown, Thomas N. *Irish-American Nationalism, 1870–1890*. Philadelphia: J. B. Lippincott Co., 1966.

Burt, Nathaniel. *The Perennial Philadelphians*. Boston: Little, Brown and Co., 1963.

Campbell, John M. *History of the Friendly Sons of St. Patrick, 1771–1892*. Philadelphia: The Hibernian Society, 1892.

Carleton, William. *The Works of William Carleton*. 3 vols. New York: P. F. Collier, 1881.

Cochran, Thomas C. *The Inner Revolution*. New York: Harper and Row, 1964.

Clark, Dennis. *Irish Blood: Northern Ireland and the American Conscience*. Port Washington, N.Y.: Kennikat Press, 1977.

Clark, Dennis. *The Irish in Philadelphia*. Philadelphia: Temple University Press, 1973.

Clark, Dennis. *Proud Past: Catholic Laypeople in Philadelphia*. Philadelphia: Catholic Philopatrian Literary Society, 1976.

Cohen, Charles J. *Rittenhouse Square: Past and Present*. Philadelphia: Privately Printed, 1922.

Commons, John R., et al. *Documentary History of American Industrial Society*. 11 vols. Cleveland: Arthur H. Clark Co., 1910.

Connell, Kenneth H. *Irish Peasant Society*. London: Oxford University Press, 1968.

Donnelly, James F., ed. *The History of the Archdiocese of Philadelphia*. Philadelphia: The Archdiocese of Philadelphia, 1976.

Cronin, Sean. *The McGarrity Papers*. Tralee, Ireland: The Anvil Press, 1972.

Cullen, Lawrence M. *Life in Ireland*. London: B. T. Batsford, 1968.

Custis, John Trevor. *The Public Schools of Philadelphia: Historical, Biographical, Statistical*. Philadelphia: Burk and McFettridge Co., 1897.

Dabney, Joseph Earl. *Mountain Spirits: A Chronicle of Corn Whiskey from King James Ulster Plantation to America's Appalachians*. New York: Charles Scribner's Sons, 1974.

Daly, Charles P. *The Settlement of the Jews in North America*. New York: Philip Cowen, 1893.

Daly, Dominic. *The Young Douglas Hyde: The Dawn of the Irish Revolution and Renaissance*. Totowa, N.J.: Rowman and Littlefield, 1974.

D'Arcy, William. *The Fenian Movement in the United States*. Washington, D.C.: The Catholic University of America Press, 1947.

Davis, Allen, and Haller, Mark., eds. *The Peoples of Philadelphia: A History of Ethnic Groups and Lower-Class Life, 1790–1940*. Philadelphia: Temple University Press, 1963.

DeBow, J. B. D. *A Statistical View of the United States: Being a Compendium of the Seventh Census*. Washington, D.C.: Government Printing Office, 1866.

Denieffe, Joseph. *A Personal Narrative of the Irish Revolutionary Brotherhood*. New York: Gael Publishing Co., 1906.

Donaghy, Thomas. *Philadelphia's Finest: A History of Education in the Archdiocese of Philadelphia*. Philadelphia: American Catholic Historical Society of Philadelphia, 1972.

Doyle, David. *The Irish-Americans: Native Rights and National Empires*. New York: Arno Press, 1976.

Doyle, David, and Owen Dudley Edwards, eds. *America and Ireland, 1776–1976: The American Identity and the Irish Connection*. Westport, Conn.: Greenwood Press, 1980.

Drummond, William H., ed. *The Autobiography of Archibald Hamilton Rowan*. Shannon, Ireland: Irish University Press, 1972.

Duffy, Charles Gavan. *Young Ireland: A Fragment of Irish History*. New York: D. Appleton Co., 1881.

DuBois, W. E. B. *The Philadelphia Negro*. Philadelphia: University of Pennsylvania Press, 1899.

Edwards, R. Dudley, and T. Desmond williams, eds. *The Great Famine*. Dublin: Browne and Nolan, 1956.

Ehrlich, Richard L. *Immigrants in Industrial America, 1850–1920*. Charlottesville, Va.: University Press of Virginia, 1977.

Elazar, Daniel, and Murray Friedman. *Moving Up: Ethnic Succession in America*. New York: Institute on Pluralism and Group Identity, 1976.

Fallows, Marjorie. *Irish-Americans: Identity and Assimilation*. Englewood Cliffs, N.J.: Prentice-Hall, 1979.

Farrell, Michael. *The Orange State*. London: Pluto Publishers, 1976.

Featherman, Sandra, and William Rosenberg. *Jews, Blacks and Ethnics*. New York: American Jewish Committee, 1979.

Feldberg, Michael. *The Philadelphia Riots of 1844: A Study in Ethnic Conflict*. Westport, Conn.: Greenwood Press, 1975.

Flower, Robin. *The Irish Tradition*. Oxford, England: Clarendon Press, 1947.

Folks, Homer. *Destitute, Neglected and Delinquent Children*. New York: The Macmillan Co., 1902.

Fréine, Seán de. *The Great Silence*. Dublin: Foilseacháin Náisiúnta Teóranta, 1965.

Fuchs, Lawrence. *American Ethnic Politics*. New York: Harper and Row, 1968.

Geiser, Karl Frederick. *Redemptioners and Indentured Servants in the Colony and Commonwealth of Pennsylvania*. New Haven, Conn.: The Tuttle, Morehouse and Taylor Co., 1901.

Gilbert, James B. *Work without Salvation: America's Intellectuals and Industrial Alienation, 1880–1910.* Baltimore: Johns Hopkins University Press, 1977.

Glazer, Nathan, and Daniel P. Moynihan. *Beyond the Melting Pot.* Cambridge, Mass.: MIT Press, 1970.

Golab, Caroline. *Immigrant Destinations.* Philadelphia: Temple University Press, 1977.

Griffith, Robert. *The Politics of Fear: Joseph R. McCarthy and the Senate.* Lexington, Ky.: University of Kentucky Press, 1970.

Handlin, Oscar, and John Burchard, eds. *The Historian and the City.* Cambridge, Mass.: MIT Press, 1963.

Handlin, Oscar, and Handlin, Mary. *Facing Life: Youth and the Family in American History.* Boston: Little, Brown and Co., 1971.

Hansen, Marcus Lee. *The Atlantic Migration.* Cambridge, Mass.: Harvard University Press, 1940.

Haraven, Tamara, ed. *Family and Kin in Urban Communities, 1700–1930.* New York: New Viewpoints, 1977.

Harley, Lewis R. "The Redemptioners: An Address to the Montgomery County Historial Society." Norristown, Pa.: Montgomery County Historical Society, 1893.

Herrick, Cheesman A. *White Servitude in Pennsylvania.* Philadelphia: John J. McVey, 1926.

Hershberg, Theodore, ed. *Philadelphia: Work, Space, Family and Group Experience in the Nineteenth Century.* New York: Oxford University Press, 1981.

Hutchinson, Edward P. *Immigrants and Their Children.* New York: John Wiley and Sons, 1956.

Jensen, Merrill, ed. *English Historical Documents.* London: Eyre and Spottiswoode, 1955.

Jones, Maldwyn Allen. *American Immigration.* Chicago: University of Chicago Press, 1960.

Joyce, J. St. George, ed. *The Story of Philadelphia.* Philadlephia: City of Philadelphia, 1919.

Kirkland, Edward C. *Industry Comes of Age.* Chicago: Quadrangle Press, 1961.

Lane, Roger. *Violent Death in the City.* Cambridge, Mass.: Harvard University Press, 1979.

Levine, Edward. *The Irish and Irish Politicians*. Notre Dame, Ind.: University of Notre Dame Press, 1966.

Lonn, Ella. *Foreigners in the Union Army and Navy*. Baton Rouge, La.: Louisiana State University Press, 1951.

Lyons, F. S. L. *Ireland since the Famine: 1850 to the Present*. London: Weidenfeld and Nicolson, 1971.

McAvoy, Thomas. *History of the Catholic Church in the United States*. Notre Dame, Ind.: University of Notre Dame Press, 1969.

MacGowan, Michael. *The Hard Road to the Klondike*. Translated by Valentin Iremonges. London: Routledge and Kegan Paul, 1962.

McMullen, William J. *An Appeal to the Taxpayers*. Philadelphia: Jared Craig, 1852.

Mahony, Daniel H. *Historical Sketches of Catholic Churches and Institutions in Philadelphia*. Philadelphia: D. H. Mahony, 1895.

Mandelbaum, Seymour. *Boss Tweed's New York*. New York: John Wiley and Sons, 1965.

Moody, Theo W. *The Fenian Movement*. Cork, Ireland: The Mercier Press, 1967.

Morais, Henry S. *The Jews of Philadelphia*. Philadelphia: The Levytype Co., 1894.

Morgan, George. *Philadelphia: City of Firsts*. Philadelphia: Historical Publication Society, 1926.

Morris, Richard B. *Government and Labor in Early America*. New York: Harper and Row, 1965.

Motley, James D. *Apprenticeship in American Trade Unions*. Baltimore: Johns Hopkins University Press, 1907.

Nelson, Daniel. *Managers and Workers: Origins of the New Factory System in the United States, 1880–1920*. Madison, Wis.: University of Wisconsin Press, 1975.

Newman, Stanley, ed. *The Politics of Utopia*. Philadelphia: Temple University, Political Science Department, 1975.

O'Crohan, Tomas. *The Islandman*. Translated by Robin Flower. New York: Charles Scribner's Sons, 1935.

O'Donnell, Daniel Kane. *The Song of the Iron and the Song of the Slaves and Other Poems*. Philadelphia: King and Baird, 1863.

O'Grady, Joseph. *How the Irish Became Americans*. New York: Twayne Publishers, 1973.

O'Brien, George. *A Hidden Phase of American History*. New York: Dodd-Mead Co., 1920.

O'Broin, Leon. *Revolutionary Underground: The Story of the Irish Republican Brotherhood: 1858–1924*. Totowa, N.J.: Rowman and Littlefield, 1976.

O'Cuiv, Brian. *Irish Dialects and Irish-Speaking Districts*. Dublin, Ireland: Institute for Advanced Studies, 1971.

Reichley, James. *The Art of Reform*. New York: The Fund for the Republic, 1959.

Rice, M. H. *American Catholic Opinion and the Anti-Slavery Controversy*. New York: Columbia University Press, 1944.

Ryan, Desmond. *The Fenian Chief*. Coral Gables, Fla.: University of Miami Press, 1967.

Scharf, J. Thomas and Thompson Westcott. *History of Philadelphia: 1609–1884*. 3 vols. Philadelphia: L. H. Evarts. Co., 1884.

Schlesinger, Arthur M., Jr. *The Age of Roosevelt: The Politics of Upheaval*. Boston: Houghton-Mifflin Co., 1960.

Shannon, William. *The American Irish*. New York: The Macmillan Co., 1963.

Shapley, Rufus E. *Solid for Mulhooly*. Philadelphia: Gebbie and Co., 1889.

Sinclair, Andrew. *The Era of Excess*. New York: Harper and Row, 1962.

Smith, Page. *Daughters of the Promised Land: Women in American History*. Boston: Little, Brown and Co., 1970.

Sowell, Thomas. ed. *American Ethnic Groups*. Washington, D.C.: The Urban Institute, 1978.

Stivers, Richard. *A Hair of the Dog: Irish Drinking and American Stereotypes*. University Park, Pa.: Pennsylvania State University Press, 1976.

Sullivan, William A. *The Industrial Worker in Pennsylvania, 1800–1840*. Harrisburg, Pa.: Pennsylvania Historical and Museum Commission, 1955.

Taylor, Philip. *The Distant Magnet*. New York: Harper and Row, 1971.

Tilly, Louise A., and Joan W. Scott. *Women, Work and Family*. New York: Holt, Rinehart and Winston, 1978.

Vaugh, W. E., and A. J. Fitzpatrick, eds. *Irish Historical Statistics* Dublin: Royal Irish Academy, 1978.

Wallace, Anthony F. C. *Rockdale: The Growth of an American Village in the Early Industrial Revolution*. New York: Alfred A. Knopf, 1978.

Ward, Alan J. *Ireland and Anglo-American Relations*. London: Weidenfeld and Nicolson, 1969.

Warner, Sam Bass. *The Private City: Philadelphia*. Philadelphia: University of Pennsylvania Press, 1968.

Watson, John F. *Annals of Philadelphia and Pennsylvania*. 3 vols. Philadelphia: Edwin S. Stuart, 1884.

Webster, Richard. *Philadelphia Preserved*. Philadelphia: Temple University Press, 1976.

Wishy, Bernard. *The Child and the Republic*. Philadelphia: University of Pennsylvania Press, 1968.

Wittke, Carl. *The Irish in America*. Baton Rouge, La.: Louisiana State University Press, 1956.

Woodham-Smith, Cecil. *The Great Hunger*. New York: The Macmillan Co., 1962.

Younger, Calton. *Ireland's Civil War*. New York: Taplinger Publishing Co., 1969.

JOURNAL ARTICLES

Baltzell, E. Digby. "The Protestant Establishment Revisited." *The American Scholar* 45:499–521.

Barron, Milton. "Intermediacy: Conceptualization of Irish Status in America." *Social Forces* 27:256–63.

Brannigan, Colm. "The Luke Dillon Case and the Welland Canal Explosion of 1900." *Niagara Frontier* 24:36–44.

Carter, Edward C. "A Wild Irishman under Every Federalist's Bed." *Pennsylvania Magazine of History and Biography* 94:331–46.

Flick, Lawrence F. "Matthias James O'Conway." *Records of the American Catholic Historical Society of Philadelphia* 10:257–99.

Foner, Philip. "Radicalism in the Gilded Age: The Land League and Irish-America." *Marxist Perspectives* 1:6–55.

Foster, George. "Philadelphia in Slices." *Pennsylvania Magazine of History and Biography* 43:23–72.

Glasco, Laurence. "The Lifecycles and Household Structure of American Ethnic Groups." *Journal of Urban History* 1:339–64.

Glassberg, Eudice. "Work, Wages and the Cost of Living: Ethnic Differences and the Poverty Line, Philadelphia, 1880." *Pennsylvania History* 46:17–58.

Hewitt, Warren F. "The Know-Nothing Controversy in Pennsylvania." *Pennsylvania History* 2:69–85.

Kett, Joseph F. "Adolescence and Youth in Nineteenth Century America." *Journal of Interdisciplinary History* 2:283–98.

Lampard, Eric. "Historical Contours of Contemporary Urban Society." *Journal of Contemporary History* 4:3–26.

Laurie, Bruce. "Nothing on Impulse: Lifestyles of Philadelphia Artisans, 1820–1850." *Labor History* 15:337–66.

Leary, Lewis. "Thomas Brannagan: An American Romantic." *Pennsylvania Magazine of History and Biography* 78:332–80.

Nelson, Daniel. "Taylorism and the Workers at Bethlehem Steel." *Pennsylvania Magazine of History and Biography* 101:487–505.

Shover, John L. "The Emergence of the Two Party System in Republican Philadelphia." *Journal of American History* 60:985–1002.

Shryock, R. H. "Historical Traditions in Philadelphia and in the Middle Atlantic Area." *Pennsylvania Magazine of History and Biography* 68:115–41.

DISSERTATIONS

Cale, Edgar B. "The Organization of Labor in Philadelphia." Ph.D. diss. University of Pennsylvania, 1940.

Dickinson, Joan Younger. "The Role of the Immigrant Woman in the U.S. Labor Force, 1890–1910." Ph.D. diss., University of Pennsylvania, 1975.

Greenberg, Irwin. "The Philadelphia Democratic Party: 1911–34." Ph.D. diss., Temple University, 1972.

Light, Dale. "Ethnicity and the Urban Ecology of a Nineteenth Century City, Philadelphia's Irish: 1840–90." Ph.D. diss., University of Pennsylvania, 1979.

Loughran, Miriam E. "The Historical Development of Child Labor Legislation in the United States." Ph.D. diss., Catholic University of America, Washington, D.C., 1921.

McKinley, Blaine Edward. "The Stranger at the Gates: Employer Reactions Towards Servants in America, 1825–75." Ph.D. diss., Michigan State University, 1969.

Quimby, Ian M. G. "Apprenticeship in Colonial Philadelphia." M.A. diss., University of Delaware, 1963.

Sears, Irwin. "Growth of Population in Philadelphia: 1860–1910." Ph.D. diss., New York University, 1960.

Sheridan, Peter B. "The Immigrant in Philadelphia, 1827–1860: The Contemporary Published Report." Ph.D. diss., Georgetown University, 1957.

NEWSPAPERS

Catholic Herald (Philadelphia)
The Catholic Standard and Times (Philadelphia)
The Evening Bulletin (Philadelphia)
The Irishman (Dublin)
The Irish-American (New York)
The Irish Echo (Boston)
The Irish World (New York)
The Jewish Exponent (Philadelphia)
The Mechanics Free Press (Philadelphia)
Philadelphia Daily News
New York Times
Philadelphia Hibernian
The Philadelphia Inquirer
Philadelphia North American
Philadelphia Press
Philadelphia Public Ledger
The Philadelphia Record
The Philadelphia Times

PUBLIC DOCUMENTS, ARCHIVES OF THE CITY OF PHILADELPHIA

Record Group 219.1, Board of Commissioners Minutes, Richmond District (1852–54).
Record Group 5.19, Deed Book Th. 100 (1853).
Record Group 21.7, Desertion Docket, 1865.
Record Group 215.2, *Digest of the Acts of Assembly Relating to the Kensington District of Northern Liberties*. Philadelphia: Isaac Ashmead, 1847.
Record Group 35,118, Female Vagrant Register, 1874–76.

Record Group 35.23, Guardians of the Poor, Minutes of the Committee on the Children's Asylum.

Record Group 214.2, Indenture Book, Moyamensing Board of Commissioners.

Record Group 35.134, Indentures Made to Girard College, 1847–1853.

Record Group 21.13, Liquor Seizure Docket 19 (1924–25).

Record Group 27.3, Magistrate's Court Number 5, Criminal Docket, 1909–12.

Record Group 60.1, Records of the Coroner of the City of Philadelphia, 1878–80.

Record Group 21.12, Records of Liquor Licenses (1888).

Record Group 21.2, Records of the Quarter Sessions Court of Philadelphia (1820).

Record Group 65.6, Register of Nurses, Attendants and Petty Office, Department of Charities, 1888–91.

Record Group 76.30, Register, Training School for Nurses, 1897–1901.

Record Group 60.1, Report of Mayor Samuel G. King, 1882.

Record Group 1.9, Passyunk Township, County, State and Personal Tax Assessment Ledger (1850).

Record Group 40.2, Sixty-second Annual Report of the Board of Education of Philadelphia. Philadelphia: E. C. Merkley, 1881.

PUBLIC DOCUMENTS, U.S. GOVERNMENT

Reports of the U.S. Immigration Commission: Immigration in Cities. Sixty-first Congress, Second Session, Committee on Immigration (1910). Washington, D.C.: Government Printing Office, 1911.

United States Census of Population, 1850, 1880, 1890.

United States Census of Manufacturing, 1870, 1880.

REFERENCE WORKS

Atlas of Philadelphia. Philadelphia: G. M. Bromley and Co., 1889, 1896.

Biographical Encyclopoedia of Pennsylvania in the Nineteenth Century. Philadelphia: Galaxy Publishing Co., 1874.

Biographies of Philadelphia Merchants. Philadelphia: James K. Simon, 1864.

Boyd's Co-Partnership and Residence Directory of Philadelphia City, 1859–60.

Boyd's Philadelphia Business Directory (1877).

McElroy's Philadelphia Directory (1859).

INSTITUTIONAL PUBLICATIONS

DuPont: The Autobiography of an American Enterprise. New York: Charles Scribner's Sons, 1952.

The Midvale Steel Company Fiftieth Anniversary, 1867–1917. Philadelphia: The Midvale Steel Company, 1917.

Saint Mary's Hospital, *Third Annual Report*. Philadelphia: Hardy and Mahony, 1871.

ORGANIZATION RECORDS

Cavan Men's Catholic Social and Beneficial Association, Minute Book (1907–1920).

Child Labor Association of Philadelphia. Urban Archives, Temple University.

Donegal Beneficial Social and Patriotic Association, Minute Books (1899–1920). The Irish Center, Philadelphia, Pa.

Irish American Club, Minute Books (1889–1901). MacSwiney Club, Jenkintown, Pa.

Pennsylvania Hospital, Casualty Book (1885–87).

Pennsylvania Hospital, Fractures Book (1854–56).

Pennsylvania Hospital, Patients' Records of Accidents (1866–70).

Philadelphia Society to Protect Children. Case Records (1877–78). Urban Archives, Temple University.

Saint Patrick's Day Observance Association of Philadelphia. Minute books. Historical Society of Pennsylvania.

Western Soup Society, Register of Recipients (1878–79).

Western Soup Society, Subscription Book (1850).

ORGANIZATION BULLETINS

The Donegal Bulletin (Philadelphia).
Irish Catholic Benevolent Union Journal (Philadelphia).
Our Union (Philadelphia).

PAPERS AND COLLECTIONS

Fenian Papers, American Catholic Historical Society of Philadelphia.
Lammot DuPont Papers. Eleutherian Mills Historical Library.
Midvale Steel Company Papers, 1876–87. The Franklin Institute.
Martin I. J. Griffin Papers. American Catholic Historical Society of Philadelphia.
Letterbook of Major Henri Le Caron. Property of the author.
John J. Reilly Papers. Historical Society of Pennsylvania.
Trainer, Francis. "History of the Trainer Family," Mimeographed. Unpublished manuscript.

INTERVIEWS

Frank Boyle
William Brennan
Charles Campbell
Nora Campbell
Robert V. Clarke
Honora Conn
Patrick Darcy
Margaret Dougherty
James Duffin
Joe Heaney
Owen B. Hunt
John Kelly
Patricia Lynch
John A. McDermott
Norbert McGettigan

John McMonagle
John O'Riordan
James Patterson
May Quinlan
Thomas Regan, Sr.

RECORD JACKET NOTE

Moloney, Mick. "John McGettigan and His Irish Minstrels" 12T367.
   London: Topic Records, 1978.

Index